681656

D4 80 1

INTRODUCTION TO
URBAN ECONOMICS

INTRODUCTION TO
URBAN
ECONOMICS

Douglas M. Brown

GEORGETOWN UNIVERSITY

A C A D E M I C   P R E S S   New York and London

A Subsidiary of Harcourt Brace Jovanovich, Publishers

ACADEMIC PRESS, INC.
111 Fifth Avenue, New York, New York 10003

947,284

United Kingdom Edition published by
ACADEMIC PRESS, INC. (LONDON) LTD.
24/28 Oval Road, London NW1

Library of Congress Cataloging in Publication Data

Brown, Douglas M.
    Introduction to urban economics.

    Bibliography: p.
    1.   Urban economics.   2.   United States—Economic
conditions.   3.   Cities and towns—United States.
I.   Title.
HT321.B76   330.9′73′092   73-9418
ISBN 0−12−136650−2

To Sally

CONTENTS

3 The Economics of Urban Growth

4 The Economics of Intraurban Location Decisions

5 Land Use

6 Housing

7 Urban Transportation

Contents

PREFACE

The purpose of this book is to introduce urban economics to the student who has only a background in economic principles. Unlike other urban economics texts at this level, this book offers a complete and self-contained coverage of the field. Coupled with an up-to-date discussion of problems and policies, the expansive coverage should mean an end to the purchasing of numerous paperbacks and the long hours of going over library reading lists that have been the norm of most undergraduate urban economics courses to date.

In a sentence, the nature of this book involves a detailed analysis of: (1) the economic rationale of cities, (2) the growth and development of cities, (3) the theory and empirical analysis of urban markets, and (4) the problems and policies of urban economies. The book is divided into inter- and intraurban analysis, with the latter comprising 70 percent of the volume (Chapters 4–10). The basic rationale of the intraurban chapters is to cover (1) the theories of urban markets, (2) empirical tests of the theories, and (3) the implications of the empirical findings for policy decisions. In general, the thrust of the discussion is toward an understanding of problems and their alternative solutions.

Although a basic knowledge of economic principles is the only prerequisite for this book, many advanced undergraduate economics majors
and some graduate students in economics and related social sciences will
find useful analyses and information here not presented in a single source
elsewhere. A minimal knowledge of elementary statistics will prove to
be useful for one's study of urban economics, and I have taken the liberty
of describing the findings of a number of statistical studies that seemed
important for assessing the efficacy of policy. Finally, I have minimized
the use of mathematics to the point where anyone with an average
knowledge of high-school algebra should feel comfortable with the tools
of analysis.

The contemporary city is beridden by many social and economic problems. Yet we have the resources and know-how to solve most of these
problems. My experience has been that students enter their urban
economics course with a great deal of interest and anticipation. This is
fine, because the challenge of urban economics is clear: to learn enough
urban economic analysis so that one can identify the nature of and
alternative solutions to problems *well enough* to take an active and
effective role in solving these problems.

The reader will soon note that I have a great intellectual debt to such
eminent regional economists as August Losch, Edgar Hoover, Charles
Tiebout, and Melvin Greenhut, and also to contemporary urban economists such as William Alonso, John Meyer, Edwin Mills, Richard Muth,
Dick Netzer, John Kain, and Jerome Rothenberg. Many others could be
added to this list. Personally, I would like to acknowledge a great debt of
gratitude to the following former teachers and colleagues: William Baird,
Robert Schultz, Robert Cauthorn, Anthony Stocks, William Miernyk,
Frederick Zeller, David Kidder, and Harvey Lapan. In addition, my
former students at Northeastern University and Georgetown University
aided the book in many ways. Warren Shows of the University of South
Florida and Robert Saunders of Kent State University reviewed the entire
manuscript and made many valuable suggestions. I alone, of course, am
responsible for any remaining errors. Georgetown University helped
finance the typing, which was ably performed by Cynthia Steele and
Dave Nerkle. It was a pleasure writing under the staff at Academic Press.
Finally, my most important acknowledgment is to my wife and daughter,
who gave up a great deal so that I could meet a demanding writing
schedule.

1

INTRODUCTION

I. THE NATURE AND FUNCTION OF CITIES

The city is a permanent concentration of people in space. Why do people concentrate in space? To attain a higher standard of living. This is possible for two reasons: (1) cencentration enhances the productivity of man, and (2) concentration allows a greater variety of goods and services (and personalities). In terms of production, the concentration of persons and firms means that more specialized modes of production can occur; thus more output can be produced with a given level of resources. On the consumption side, a densely settled area provides a large enough market to ensure that a wide variety of products will be accessible to all. The key characteristic of a city, then, is access. Workers are accessible to firms, and firms to each other. And buyers are accessible to retailers. Accessibility means high living standards.

Our definition of a city does not call for any specific minimum size in terms of population. In general, we could easily accept the U.S. Census Bureau's definition of urban, which refers to any town of 2500 or more persons. Given this definition, over 70 percent of the people in the United States live in urban areas. In this book, however, much of our discussion will be concerned with the typical metropolitan area (a central city with surrounding suburbs).

Cities have many economic and noneconomic functions. We have already noted that cities provide a mechanism (accessibility) that brings consumers and producers together. Historically, the clustering of people in space occurred for protective as well as economic purposes. In the modern world of guided missiles, this protective function has not only been outmoded, but in fact has been reversed. Indeed, decentralization would be preferable in case of nuclear attack.

Cities facilitate the exchange and distribution functions that are basic to any economy. Again, accessibility is the key here: resources and goods and services can be exchanged and distributed more quickly and efficiently if buyers and sellers are easily accessible.

Cities, then, are concentrations of economic agents in space. The benefits of population concentration essentially add up to a higher standard of living than could be obtained if people and firms were evenly distributed across space. But there are costs to concentrating in space. And these costs have become so important in recent years that many cities have not been able to perform their functions efficiently.

What are some of the costs of concentrating in space? A simple example may be useful here. Regardless of city size, almost everyone goes to work around 8 or 9 A.M. and returns at 4 to 6 P.M. Our transport capacity is fixed and cannot handle everyone at the same time, so the result is congestion. Backed-up cars, trucks, buses, and trollies are the norm during these peak demand periods. After World War II the U.S. believed this ever-present congestion problem could be resolved by building expressways around and through our cities. This solution has not helped much in most cities. Why? Because to enable everyone to go to work or home at the same time without congestion, we would have to use nearly all of the land in cities for expressways. And there would still be problems of entering and leaving the expressways. To an individual, then, one of the costs of living or working in a city is that he has far less control over his destiny; for example, if everyone else decides to use the roads when he does, his travel time will be increased considerably. And there is nothing he can do about it.

Clearly, although accessibility is the key to the benefits of city life, being too close to each other is the basis of many of the costs. Certainly if people and firms were evenly scattered over space, there could be a much smaller congestion problem. Suburbanization has been the reaction of high-income persons to the costs of city life for centuries. Pockets of poverty, crime, and slums in our large cities have always been with us. Maybe this is one of the inherent costs that some must pay in order for most to enjoy the fruits of a higher standard of living via concentration. It is hoped that the student will be able to gain enough knowledge from this book to shed some light on this question.

II. What Is Urban Economics

As we have noted, the problems of cities—slums, crime, poverty, congestion, pollution, and many others—have been a part of society for centuries. All of these problems have economic aspects. In fact, most can be minimized if not solved by means of economic tools. Given all of this, it is somewhat surprising that economists began a systematic study of the economics of the city only in the past decade. Before the early 1960's, urban studies were primarily the bailiwick of geographers, city planners, and other social scientists.

As a discipline, urban economics attempts to explain and predict the allocation of resources and the distribution of real income (goods and services) within and among urban areas. In other words, we are interested in how goods and services are produced and distributed, not only inside a given city but also across cities. We shall find that concentrating in space can alter the efficiency of resource allocation and also the distribution of income. The task of the student of urban economics is to determine whether the impact of concentrating in space is, in a net sense, beneficial. This is a large order, but we can make a solid beginning in filling it.

The nature of urban economic analysis involves the identification and analysis of inter- and intraurban economic relationships and problems. In the former area, we are interested in the following questions: Why do cities grow and develop? Do cities compete with each other? Why do firms and people migrate to certain cities? Is there an optimal size of cities? In the area of intraurban analysis, we are concerned with the following questions: How are location and land-use decisions made? Do residents choose locations on a rational basis? How can efficient transportation systems be developed within urban areas? What is the most efficient structure of government? How are poverty and pollution affected by heavy concentrations of people in space? Although urban economists do not have final answers to many of these questions, an important first step is to identify properly the economic aspects of each question and its related problem.

III. ABOUT THIS BOOK

The purpose of this book is to provide the student with a basic understanding of urban economic analysis and problems. We assume that the reader has had an introductory course in economics, along with an elementary course in statistics. The latter is important because, given the early developmental stage of urban economics at present, one must have a basic understanding of statistical research in order to assess intelligently the relevance of research studies. Indeed if one's basic interest in studying urban economics is to identify urban problems and alternative solutions, a basic knowledge of elementary statistics is indispensable.

The chapters of the book follow a logical sequence. We begin with a detailed history of urban areas and their economies in Chapter 2. Some students may prefer to skip this chapter, but they will do so at the cost of not learning why cities began and developed in the world as well as the U.S. and, more important, that we have been unable to solve the same urban problems (pollution, crime, slums, poverty, congestion, and so on) for centuries. Next we consider the determinants of urban growth in Chapter 3. Whereas Chapter 2 is a descriptive historical account of the development of cities, Chapter 3 provides an analytical basis for answering why cities grow, die, or stagnate. Chapters 2 and 3 are our coverage of interurban relationships.

The heart of this book is the coverage of intraurban analysis and problems. Beginning with Chapter 4 on intraurban location decisions of firms and people, we progress through the topics of land use, housing, transportation, the public sector, poverty, and the environment in the remaining six chapters. Each chapter contains tools of analysis and a discussion of policy issues. Often the tools are accompanied by empirical tests and their findings, which are presented to give the student information with which to come to grips with real policy issues. For example, we go into a fair amount of detail on studies of demand and supply (price) elasticities of urban housing in Chapter 6. We make this effort because the efficacy of measures to solve housing problems hangs in the balance. If we find, for instance, that the price elasticity of supply of ghetto housing is near zero, it may not pay us to subsidize the housing expenditures of ghetto dwellers, assuming that we desire to help them consume more housing. With a nearly vertical supply curve, increased housing expenditures will merely drive up the price of housing. Under these conditions, taxpayers would be merely making landlords rich without helping the ghetto dweller.

The topics covered under intraurban analysis—location, land use, transportation, and so on—are presented on a piecemeal basis. However, we should continually remind ourselves that these areas are highly interdependent. For example, if a firm decides to locate in a specific area of a given city, it may have the economic power to outbid residents for land and thus possibly alter land uses. This will cause changes in housing decisions and commuting patterns, which may call forth possible changes in the transport system. Many of these changes are decided, of course, by the public sector. And if this hypothetical firm relocates from the central city to suburbia, it may have an immediate impact on the level of poverty and environmental quality in the central city. In short, any given change in the spatial structure of a city has important interaction effects with most other sectors in the city. This fact is very useful to keep in mind when we consider policies, for what may be a solution in one sector can be a new problem in another.

SUGGESTED READINGS

Dorfman, Robert. "The Function of the City." In *Thinking About Cities*, edited by Anthony Pascal, pp. 32–40. Belmont, California: Dickerson (for the Rand Corporation), 1970.

Hirsch, Werner, ed. *Urban Life and Form*. New York: Holt, 1962.

Lampard, Eric. "The History of Cities in Economically Advanced Areas." *Economic Development and Cultural Change* 3 (1955): 81–102.

Leven, Charles. "Determinants of the Size and Spatial Form of Urban Areas." *Papers, Regional Science Association* 22 (1969): 7–28.

Mills, Edwin. *Urban Economics*, Chapter 1. Glenview, Illinois: Scott, Foresman, 1972.

2

AN ECONOMIC
HISTORY OF
URBAN AREAS

I. INTRODUCTION

The purpose of this chapter is to provide the student with a sound background in the economic development of urban places over time. Our historical discussion will begin with the birth of urban places (in Mesopotamia and the Nile Valley) and continue on a catholic scale through the post Middle Ages. At that point we shall turn our attention to the Colonial cities of the U.S. and proceed with a discussion of urbanization in the U.S. through the contemporary scene. The discussion will show that most present-day urban problems are centuries old. For example, pollution was a pervasive problem in Hellenic and Roman cities. Congestion also hampered Rome. We shall particularly emphasize the "solutions" that did not seem to work out as we cover the urban problems over time. This chapter will help the student obtain a firmer grasp of why cities exist and the inherent problems of cities. Equally important, a historical perspective allows one to see how contemporary urban society fits into the long-run urbanization process of man. Such a perspective can be quite useful in evaluating whether continued urbanization by man has positive net benefits.

Before we begin our historical journey into urban development, it may pay to stop a moment and ask ourselves what we might look for.

II. MODELS OF URBAN DEVELOPMENT

Economists have developed numerous approaches for describing urbanization. In this section we shall consider three of these methods: (1) ad hoc explanations, (2) broad, culture-based approaches, and (3) a stages model. Ad hoc explanations of the origin and development of cities are very simple, yet quite useful hypotheses. The cultural approach to the explanation of city development emphasizes social–psychological, technological, and other factors as the keys to urban development. Stages models break down the development of cities into periods or stages, with each stage describing a further step in the maturing of the city's economic structure. Each of these approaches offers an alternative way of viewing the origin and development of cities; when taken together they provide a useful framework for identifying significant determinants of the development of cities over time.

Ad Hoc Models

Ad hoc explanations of urbanization are by definition special cases that for the most part defy generalization. However, many of the ad hoc explanations provide valuable insights into the overall urbanization process. What might we include under this category? Certainly the initial-advantage argument is a candidate. Cities are said to develop because of initial advantages such as being near a needed resources. Readily available water for household and transportation usage would be an example of an initial advantage. Edgar Hoover [1] cites many cases in which cities have developed at transshipment points. Many of the early seaports in the U.S. were places where foreign goods were unloaded from ships and placed on wagons for shipment inland to agrarians (who were the majority of the population until 1860).

Another ad hoc explanation is the threshold effect. Many small villages grow into cities because there is a viable demand for their products from the surrounding population. When this demand reaches a strong enough level to induce citification, the threshold is reached. Another ad hoc principle is external or agglomeration economies [1, pp. 78–80; 2]. Firms are attracted to cities that produce inputs for their products, and also if buyers are nearby. Much more will be said about this later, but external economies allow a greater scale of output, and thus lower per-unit costs of production, along with a greater market.* Finally Myrdal's circular and cumulative causation hypothesis [3] can be used to explain the development of urban areas.† This principle states that any social (or economic) change calls forth supporting changes that move the system in the same direction, but farther. For example, if a city builds a new airport on the edge of town, a new highway is built and the surrounding area will become dotted with restaurants, motels, and service stations.

Each of these ad hoc principles may explain the (1) birth, (2) early development stages, or (3) later development stages of cities; but with the possible exception of the last two principles (agglomeration econo- mies and the principle of cumulative causation), none describes or ex- plains the general development of urbanization over time.

The Lampard Culture-Based Approach

A more general and integrated analysis of urbanization is made by Eric Lampard in a study called "The history of cities in economically advanced areas" [5]. Lampard develops what may be termed the spa- tial–technical–cultural approach to urbanization. Urbanization has its be- ginning in specialization and the division of labor, which are as much cultural phenomena as they are economic, according to Lampard. Spe- cialization and the division of labor are extended by technical innova- tions in a dynamic and cumulative process. The spatial ordering of eco- nomic activities is a direct result of this process; production and distribu- tion are now mainly concentrated in cities. The economic parts of the community now become more interdependent, and begin to be a cen- tripetal force on resources in the hinterland. Since not all urban areas grow, however, one must turn to the law of comparative advantage to explain relative city growth.

Although very broad in nature, the spatial–technical–cultural approach points up a number of characteristics of a society we might look for

---

* As scale economies rise, that is, average costs decline with increasing output, firms can now ship to more distant buyers, thereby increasing the size of their market.

† Allan Pred uses this principle, supplemented by economic analysis, to explain urban and industrial growth in the U.S. between 1800 and 1914 [4].

in tracing the history of urban areas: (1) levels and patterns of special-ization, (2) technical changes and innovations, (3) the concentration of population, and (4) comparative advantages of cities in the produc-tion of certain goods and services.

Stages of Urban Development: A Modified Rostow Model

The ad hoc and spatial–technical–cultural approaches both lack an important ingredient—a consideration of urbanization as a *process*. To solve this problem we might consider a few models that describe urban development as a series of stages over time. It is important to keep in mind that none of these stages models implies that *all* cities must go through *every* stage as they mature.* Stages models are oversimplified but potentially useful descriptions of processes.

Robert Lopez [7] and Eugene Smolensky [8] have both built interest-ing and useful stages models of city development, but neither takes us much beyond the early 1900's in the U.S. What about the contempo-rary urban scene and beyond in this country? Are stages models of any value here? It is possible to alter slightly the stages model of (ad-vanced) nations built by W. W. Rostow [9] and apply it to urban devel-opment. This modified stages model goes beyond the development point of most, if not all, urban areas in the U.S. today.

Rostow divides the economic development of nations into five stages: (1) the traditional society, (2) the preconditions for takeoff, (3) the takeoff, (4) the drive to maturity, and (5) the age of high mass con-sumption. Stage 1 is the traditional society, where people may be concen-trated in space, but few, if any, internal or external economies of scale are involved. Everyone is primarily a farmer or craftsman, and little manufacturing occurs. The major constraint of this stage is that a ceiling exists on productivity. Rostow classes the Chinese dynasties and the Aztec and Inca societies in this stage.

The stage of preconditions for takeoff is a transitional period when people not only concentrate in space but also learn that specialization can reap rewards. With the steady flow of innovations accompanying this stage, markets will expand. Risk-takers appear, and excess profits may arise. Thus either a free market system or an efficient centralized government is a necessary condition for this stage. During the precondi-tions stage, the structure of the economy either is or becomes export oriented. Examples would be European trading cities in the fourteenth century (and onward), the U.S. Colonial cities, and the coal, gold, and

---

* For a critical review of stage models see *Leading Issues in Development Eco-nomics* [6].

silver mining towns that grew up across the frontier during the eighteenth and nineteenth centuries in this country.

The takeoff stage is characterized by growth, with continual shifts in capacity and its utilization. New industries appear, linked to existing export sectors. Local service sectors expand rapidly, even though exports may still remain the more important sector. New techniques in the export sectors are induced by the new suppliers. Thus production becomes horizontally integrated, with internal and external economies of scale being consumed. The city is clearly an attractive force; thus urban agglomerates appear.

The fourth stage is the drive to maturity. Rostow describes this stage (for nations) as one of sustained but fluctuating progress, during which modern technology is extended to the whole of economic activity. It is my judgment that most U.S. cities are still in this stage. Whereas nations supposedly "find" themselves in the international economy (goods formerly imported are produced at home, new import requirements arise, and new exports are developed) in this stage, cities begin to be self-sufficient and to service the surrounding region. By self-sufficiency we mean that the majority of employment in a city is used in the production of goods and services for that city. Rostow argues that it takes about sixty years for a nation to complete its drive to maturity.

We can get an idea of the incidence of the drive-to-maturity stage by comparing ratios of manufacturing employment to total employment, a proxy for total export activity.* Once the share of total employment in export activity is less than 50 percent, the city is probably beginning its drive to maturity. This datum has been developed by Eric Lampard [10] for selected cities in the U.S. between 1870 and 1950. Table 2-1 shows the manufacturing-to-total employment ratio for two satellite cities (Paterson and Worcester are satellites of New York City and Boston, respectively), two major urban areas (Philadelphia and Pittsburgh), and a regional node (Albany). Note that the two satellite cities had not begun the drive to maturity by 1870, and even by 1950 these two cities were still relatively export oriented. The information in Table 2–1 is not a test of the Rostow 60-year thesis; the thesis cannot be tested unless we know under what conditions a city reaches maturity. Nevertheless, the information is interesting, in that many view Pittsburgh as a steel town and Worcester as an insurance town; thus the a priori argument would be that Pittsburgh should have the higher ratio. A quick check [11] of the 224 standard metropolitan statistical areas

---

* All manufacturing activity is assumed to be producing for customers outside the city. This is an oversimplification, which is discussed in more detail in Chapter 3.

TABLE 2–1

Ratios of Manufacturing Employment to Total
Labor Force for Selected Cities, 1870–1950

	1870 (%)	1950 (%)
Paterson, New Jersey	64.2	47.3
Worcester, Massachusetts	55.2	42.4
Philadelphia	48.8	35.5
Pittsburgh	41.5	28.2
Albany	43.9	16.3

(SMSA's)* for 1960 shows that only 38 have 40 percent or more of their total employment in manufacturing. Three SMSA's had a ratio of 50 percent or more; thus the vast majority of our metropolitan areas have been in this stage for at least ten years, and (as shown in Table 2-1) some urbanized areas began this stage over 100 years ago.

The final stage in Rostow's repertoire is the age of high mass consumption. This is a period when per-capita income is high enough for many to purchase durables and services beyond their basic needs. Society also begins to show cares for something besides extending technology and growth per se; social welfare and security find their way into the forefront of the social utility function. Although Rostow believes this stage has been pressed to its logical conclusion for the U.S. during the postwar period [9, p. 11], I think many of our cities are just beginning this stage. We are only beginning to understand the real roots of our urban problems, and few if any cities have taken the bold steps needed to solve them. For example, the public sector of our cities, it is fair to say, redistributes income in the wrong direction (from the have-nots to the haves) through its taxation and spending policies, but we see little evidence that this trend is being reversed. The age of high mass consumption for cities involves not only a redirection toward social welfare but also the development and utilization of new technologies for meeting the massive service needs of an urban society. Productivity growth in our service sectors is said to lag badly behind manufacturing [12]. Possibly this finding is reflective of productivity measurement problems (for example, what is the "output" of a cellist?). Or it may be

---

* The definition of a SMSA is rather lengthy, but in general, an urban area qualifies as a SMSA when its central city has at least 50,000 persons, and together with its surrounding area the population is at least 100,000. For a detailed definition see the *City and County Data Book* [11].

that by the nature of the product, service productivity cannot be increased quickly. Whatever the case, when we are able to produce and deliver desired services efficiently in our cities (where the test of efficiency is growth in the rate of productivity), then cities will be in the stage of high mass consumption. Clearly, concentrated populations need more and more services as specialization and interdependence continue.

Summary

Cities grew and developed because of (1) having initial advantages, (2) being at transshipment points, (3) reaching threshold effects, (4) offering agglomeration economies, and (5) circular and cumulative processes. Not only does the urban development process have economic and spatial characteristics that are significant, but technical and cultural factors are probably of equal importance. It is possible to describe urban development as a stages process, although it is important to remember that in general, stages models do not explain *why* growth has occurred. This question will be taken up in the next chapter. We are now ready to consider the history of urbanization.

III. URBANIZATION FROM THE BEGINNING TO THE AMERICAN COLONIAL PERIOD

Before beginning our discussion of the origin of villages, it may be appropriate to point out that the consensus of urban historians is that our knowledge of the structure and ways of cities in the neolithic era and possibly up to the Hellenic period is only partially factual [13, 14]. Man's ingenuity plays a large role in attempting to describe the beginning of cities, even though archeological evidence is increasing.

Origin of Villages and Cities

In his book *The City in History*, which is the basic source used in the writing of this section, Lewis Mumford notes that like animals, man no doubt chose special places for breeding and feeding. Thus temporary aggregates of people probably occurred near places of natural beauty or bounty, such as a spring or estuary. In its earliest form, man's economy probably consisted of feast or famine on a day-to-day basis, at least until he learned to salt fish. The first reliable food supply occurred as many as 15,000 years ago. Archeological evidence from India to the Baltic Sea shows a culture based on shellfish and fish, hamlets with clearings for agriculture, and domesticated animals such as pigs, fowl, and dogs.* The major innovations of these initial villages, according to Mumford, were not weapons and tools, but containers. Stove and pottery utensils, jars, cisterns, vases, bins, and so on increased the efficiency of the household by allowing permanent storage. Thus man did not have to spend nearly all of his time in agriculture, fishing, and hunting. The possibility of specializing in other tasks—the preconditions for concentration—were at hand.

The early villages dotted Mesopotamia and the Nile Valley at least from 9000 to 4000 B.C. Before water transport was developed, each village was no doubt a world in and of itself. The emergence of cities came after significant technological breakthroughs in agriculture:† (1) the domestication of grains, (2) the introduction of plows, and (3) the extensive use of irrigation. When one compares the hoe to the plow, and ditches to organized canals, it is easy to see that the productivity differences could mean that a greater population could be cared for.

As man began to citify, the human composition of settlements changed from hunters, farmers, and fishermen to include the miner, woodman, engineer, boatman, and sailor. According to Mumford, the primary catalyst in this birth of the urbanization process was the ruler. Hunters often became rulers. From their hunting experiences, they had wider horizons than others, and were risk-takers. They gave leadership during crises, and thus emerged as leaders. In time, rulers built citadels for repressive as well as protective purposes. Violence from within as well as from external sources was the logical and actual result; thus Plato declared in "The Laws" that "every city is in a natural state of war with every other."

We have not gone beyond the "traditional society" stage of urban development discussed in the previous section, and evidence of urban socioeconomic problems is already clear. Contemporary urban violence in the U.S. is certainly not a unique happening.

Early Cities of the Ancient World

One piece of strong evidence we have on the village–city transformation is the size of built-up areas. In the third millineum, a capital of the Indus civilization covered 600 acres. Nineveh in 600 B.C. covered

---

* These animals, besides being pets, provided useful sanitation functions.
† For an opposing view, see Jane Jacobs, *The Economy of Cities* [15].

almost 1800 acres. Babylon was large enough to be surrounded by 11 miles of walls. The archeologist Frankfort estimates the density of Ur, an ancient Sumerian city on the Euphrates River, to have been about 120 to 200 persons per acre, similar to that of the workmen's quarters in Amsterdam during the seventeenth century [13, pp. 62–63]. Ur's population is estimated between 24,000 and 36,000. The spatial size of cities was not limited solely by the availability of food and water; intracity transportation and communication also played a role. Early cities did not expand beyond walking or hearing (via bells) distance. Although streets existed, most of the traveling was done in small alleyways. All of the major early cities were located in river valleys or beside some body of water. Boats with sails and oars were used, allowing an extension of markets and an increase in the scale of overall production.

What were the basic functions of these early cities? We have already noted the increased specialization in production and the initial advantages of nearby water; thus early cities performed as significant production and consumption centers. They were also permanent meeting places for religious and family gatherings, and markets for exchanging goods and services. No less important, cities were a storehouse of knowledge, for with the advent of the permanent record, people could learn how problems had been attacked in the past. Finally, many early cities were places of royal monopolies, where rulers lived in luxury (in fireproof buildings, with paved areas, drains, running water, bathtubs, and open spaces) off the surpluses of their lords and slaves.

The division of labor was extended greatly in these cities. In the course of time, the occupation of the typical worker changed from farmer to craftsman. In the latter occupation, one might work for the temple or himself (in the market place). In Egypt around 2000 B.C., there is evidence of over 18 trades, ranging from barbers to embalmers. The professions included printers, physicians, and architects. It was now possible to spend a lifetime in one (nonagricultural) occupation.

As explained in the previous section of this chapter, specialization, division of labor, and technical innovations are all interrelated factors in the urbanization process. Early cities were not without a myriad of technical innovations. The alphabet was introduced between 800 and 600 B.C. Money was coined in 650 B.C., which certainly helped to extend markets and facilitate trade. In Cretan cities hydraulic and sanitary appliances were developed. Metal tools were perfected.

In summary, a small part of the earth's population began to urbanize before the Greek–Roman era. Although little factual evidence is available on the beginnings, it is clear that the urbanization movement was real by about 500 B.C.

Greek Cities

Agricultural and other pressures during the sixth through fourth centuries B.C. led to colonization by certain segments of the early cities; thus Greece, Marseilles, and Sicily were founded. Athens, of course, became the center of activity, although Miletus and Corinth were probably its equal in population.* Few Greek cities had more than 10,000 persons. No walls were built until after the first Persian invasion during the fifth century.

Traders and bankers were the organizers and catalysts behind the economy of Greek cities. In the agora (commercial meeting place), trade was facilitated by the stamping of gold and silver coins by the seventh century. Tradesmen came from all over the world, although native Grecians did not take to the new business of exchange. Greek cities were certainly market type cities, and they began their takeoff by 400 B.C.

Although Athens was the cultural center of the world, it was not without its socioeconomic problems. The major share of housing was built of unbaked bricks and tile roofs, or mud and wattle with thatched roofs, a rather crude setup. Interestingly, the quarters of rich and poor were side by side, and indistinguishable except for size and inner furnishings. Street systems were incoherent, and the streets were unpaved. Sanitary facilities were abominable, and quite backward when compared to those of Ur of 2000 years earlier. Refuse piled up, and (unwanted) babies were left to die. Often, when a city reached a few thousand, it would search for colonies.

In the midst of these urban problems, persons arose who questioned the goals of society. Urban philosophers and planners developed models of utopian cities. Hippodamoses' utopian city held no more than 10,000 persons. Plato traced urbanization from a basis of a desire for luxuries not attainable in the countryside. Plato noted [16] that the inequality of native abilities and skills gave a logical basis for specialization and interdependence. However, Plato also felt that once a person chose a skill he should keep and practice *that* skill *only* for the remainder of his life. Aristotle's discussions of the ideal city went much further than those of his predecessors. He argued that the growth of cities must be controlled, because after a city becomes too large it cannot be governed efficiently.

Land-use planners also made their mark on cities of the Hellenistic era. Following Miletus, some cities had straight streets of uniform width

* Mumford [13, p. 130] argues that all three cities had around 100,000 people.

and length crossing at right angles. Such a layout became known as the gridiron plan.* Cities thus became divided into definite neighborhoods. The city of Thuriun in 443 B.C. had a new gridiron plan that included the division of blocks into ten neighborhood units based on social segregation. Tribes were assigned to neighborhoods. As cities grew larger, two- and three-story buildings arose. Heavy concentration and segregation had set in on the Greek cities.

Roman Cities

Rome was founded in 751 B.C., according to Cicero. Rome began as an enclosed rectangle, but developed into a whole society that built thousands of new towns. Rome itself expanded in area and population throughout the third century A.D. In 274 A.D. it covered 3323 acres, and it is estimated that by 312 A.D. the population was about one million, with over 46,000 tenements. Since the economic structure of Roman cities was very similar to that of cities in Greece, we shall turn our attention directly to the urban problems with which Rome grappled.

A major problem in the city of Rome was congestion. Although streets were paved and sidewalks elevated, traffic became so heavy that Caesar banned wheeled traffic from the center of Rome during the day.† Of course the result was the creation of such noise at night that people could not sleep. Claudius extended this rule to municipalities, and later Marcus Aurelius applied the ban to every town in the empire. It was not until the second century A.D. that the banning rule was partially lifted, allowing Romans a better chance to get their proper rest at night.

A second major problem area was housing. Overcrowded tenements formed most of the housing stock. The wealthy, of course, had mansions. And many persons became wealthy by acting exactly like contemporary profiteering landlords. Quarters were continually subdivided to yield a higher rate of return per unit. A single quotation from Mumford tells the story:

> Crassus, who made a fabulous fortune in tenement house properties, boasted that he never spent money in building: it was more profitable to buy partly damaged old properties at fire sales and rent them with meager repairs. [13, p. 220]

---

* Most people have probably heard football fields referred to as the gridiron.

† Many contemporary transportation specialists have argued for this policy as a reasonable solution to our present-day core-city traffic problems. New York City and Boston have periodically banned traffic from certain shopping areas downtown for short periods, such as an afternoon or day.

Mumford describes many other Roman housing problems, such as systematic slum clearance, and compares them to contemporary urban situations in a very interesting manner.

A third major problem of Rome was the sewerage and sanitation practices. The water supply was very adequate, and some of the public sewerage facilities built then are still being used today. The masses did not have running water for their toilets, however, since they still used cisterns. Many of the great plagues have been tied to Rome's dumps, which were often nothing more than open pits at the ends of streets.

In retrospect, Roman cities provide firm evidence that the contemporary urban problems of slums, congestion, and pollution have been known to man for many, many centuries. The "solution" of expanding the empire and moving people out of the city to smaller towns did not seem to solve these problems, however.

Cities of the Middle Ages

From the fall of Rome until the Middle Ages, cities and societies were at war with barbarians. Walls were built everywhere around cities, and storefronts of brick were built in old market places. People flocked to these encased areas out of fear; thus urbanization was in a sense forced upon people. Kings now had captive slaves.

By the eleventh century, trade had revived and urbanization took on its more traditional form. According to Mumford [13, p. 253], the monastic orders are largely responsible for the economic expansion, since they built bridges among groups in society and helped extend markets. Luxuries began to flow in from the outside world, and the merchant population steadily increased in cities. Lords migrated to the larger cities, attracted by available luxury goods and the large rents to be earned in the housing markets. In general, the protectionist era was transformed into an almost capitalist economic structure during the Middle Ages.

What changes in technology helped spur the growth of urban areas during this era? One was the application of manure from cities to the farmlands. Increased supplies of food and power were generated by windmills, water mills, horse breeding, and use of the harness. Barter was steadily replaced by the use of money as a medium of exchange. Almost every worker belonged to a guild, which provided many more services than today's unions; however, the guilds often (inefficiently) regulated methods of production, distribution, and exchange.

What did medieval cities look like? Unlike their predecessors, many towns had open spaces used for orchards and athletics. In time, of course, these open spaces fell to expansion. Streets per se were nonexistent in some towns instead, clusters of structures were grouped and connected by paths. Vehicle traffic was light in such areas. Each cluster had its own churches, water supply, and political institutions; thus the first trace of political fragmentation is noticed. Many of the clusters were segregated by vocation or other interests; thus university, clerical, royal, and merchant precincts were founded. With this era, we find the end of walls and gates surrounding cities. However, with access being a significant factor, most cities did not extend beyond a half-mile radius. The Western European cities were not large. London had only 40,000 persons by the fifteenth century, although Paris had achieved 100,000 by then.

Houses in the medieval cities were usually two or three stories high, with materials used for construction varying by region. Many row houses were erected, and glass windows appeared in the late fifteenth century. Public health became a major concern during the Middle Ages, which brought forth public hospitals and other institutions. The German city of Breslau, with 30,000 persons during the fifteenth century, had 15 hospitals! Quarantines were practiced on outsiders, and isolation wards became common in hospitals. In 1388, English parliament passed an act forbidding the dumping of garbage in ditches, rivers, and water. Finally, for the first time since the ancient cities such as Ur, we see evidence that wastes were dealt with in a sanitary manner. This is obviously an important concern for any large concentration of persons, regardless of the time period under study.

At the close of the Middle Ages, Venice may have been the model city. It dumped its waste products into the sea, where salt and sunlight reduced the debris to relatively harmless states. A more significant economic characteristic of Venice was the location of its industry. The city has many islands, and each island was generally zoned for a single function. On separate islands one would find shipyards, munitions works, arsenals, glass factories, and churches. A major difference between Venice and other industrial cities was that Venice did not have street congestion.

From the fifteenth through eighteenth centuries, new urban complexes arose in Western Europe, mostly through the expansion of older cities. Inside the cities, streets were straightened and widened, and vehicular traffic was popular. Markets were spread out along the streets, rather than in the old clusters that had been traditional for ages. The birth of the modern city was occurring.

At this point we leave the European scene and turn our attention to the urbanization process of America.

IV. U.S. URBAN GROWTH AND DEVELOPMENT: 1625–1940†

1625–1743

Colonial urban America developed along the Atlantic Seaboard, the centers of activity being Philadelphia, New York, and Boston. Boston was the largest of the three until about 1760, when it was surpassed by both Philadelphia and New York (see Table 2-2). These colonial seaports were trading towns, with business generated from the hinterlands and Europe. Boston and Massachusetts were the leaders in trade as well as shipbuilding. Merchants performed many tasks, but by the end of the sixteenth century specialization set in; thus the exporter, importer, and wholesaler came onto the scene. Trade activity was generally enhanced by the use of paper currency, except when there were extreme upward or downward spirals in prices, which did occur. Insurance and credit facilities also helped trading, and as excess profits occurred, private investors who were risk-takers began to invest in land and manufacturing. As profits increased, cities expanded.

During the last part of the seventeenth century and the early part of the eighteenth, the seaports grew steadily, as shown in Table 2-2. An expansion of trade (accompanied by inflation) occurred between 1690 and 1709, but a depression set in afterward through 1715. By this time, traders had learned to specialize in the selling and buying of certain types of goods. Merchandising soon became important, and with

† The basic sources of information used in this chapter on the economics of urban Colonial America are by Carl Bridenbaugh [17, 18].

TABLE 2–2

Population of Philadelphia, New York, and Boston for Selected Years, 1650–1776[a]

	1650	1690	1720	1743	1760	1775	1776
Philadelphia	—	7,000	10,000	13,000	23,750	40,000	21,767
New York	1,000	3,900	7,000	11,000	18,000	25,000	5,000
Boston	2,000	7,000	12,000	16,382	15,631	16,000	3,500

[a] Source: Carl Bridenbaugh, *Cities in the Wilderness—The First Century of Urban Life in America, 1625–1742*, 2nd ed. (New York: Knopf, 1964); *Cities in Revolt, Urban Life in America, 1743–1776* (New York: Knopf, 1955).

the appearance of newspapers, advertising came into vogue as a means of expanding one's market.

From 1720 to 1743, the three seaports continued to expand, but the percentage of population living in towns declined from 8 to 5.4 percent [17, p. 303]. Is there any way of explaining this ruralization trend? Possibly cities were a repelling force on people. Housing construction did not keep pace with increases in demand, so that the price of housing increased greatly during this period. Properties were subdivided, and life in the tenements probably was not inviting. Steadily increased congestion hurt overall living conditions, and deadly fires became commonplace. Crime increased in all three of the cities, and prisons soon became overcrowded and in deplorable condition. Poverty and health problems were quite prevalent. Possibly urbanization declined because the cities were not a relatively attractive place to live.

1743–1760

The expansion of the seaports between 1743 and 1760 was greatly aided by immigrants from Europe. Urban construction flourished during this period, and geographical areas in cities became specialized; for example, warehouses on waterfronts, market centers, and retreats for the wealthy appeared. In Philadelphia, the housing stock nearly doubled from 1500 dwellings in 1743 to 2969 in 1760; yet excess demand still prevailed, and rents rose. In New York, British soldiers filled the town and drove up the housing prices. Fires also helped create severe housing shortages, especially in Boston. A suburban trend began during this period, supposedly for the same reasons people suburbanize today—to get away from congestion and noise, and to obtain more land per unit of housing. Boston had commuters entering the city daily from Roxbury, Medford, Dorchester, and Cambridge.

A major problem in our early cities was their streets. Taxes were levied for paving (stone was used), and people always seemed to complain of how dirty the streets were. New York and Boston passed cleaning laws in 1744 and 1746, respectively. Stray animals roamed the streets, making it dangerous to be out after dark. By 1751 Philadelphia had street lamps (oil). The horse and cart were a real threat to pedestrians. According to Bridenbaugh, many children were killed by oxcarts, and the majority of accidents resulted from speeding (which sounds familiar). As in early Rome, traffic was very noisy.* In addition to streets,

---

* In Boston, traffic was so noisy that the Great and General Court of Massachusetts in 1747 forbade traffic to go by the State House while the Court was in session; however, petty traffic laws went unobeyed until the Court chained the area off.

each seaport town used ferries extensively for the shipping of raw materials, final products, animals, and persons. Docks were well built and in some cases financed by the city.

Although wars often hampered economic activity, trading nevertheless carried on and even expanded greatly in Philadelphia. Philadelphia carried on a very profitable trading relationship with the Caribbean islands, which returned not only goods but cash or bills of exchange with London for the Quaker City's goods. Philadelphia did not need to import as much as the other U.S. cities because of the comparative advantage of its skilled artisans. New York lagged behind in trade, even though the British soldiers required a good deal of supplies. Boston's trade picture was weakened by wars, depression, and the almost total failure to have a comparative advantage in the production of any goods.

The seaport cities served as collection and distribution points. As agricultural and other surpluses arose in the hinterland, they were brought to the cities to be exchanged or traded for desirable foreign or other commodities. Since Philadelphia had developed extensive relations with the hinterland, she became the leader in economic activity. Satellite towns such as Easton, Brunswick, Trenton, Camden, Wilmington, and Lancaster regularly traded their production in Philadelphia. Boat service and/or highways were heavily utilized between the major city and its satellite towns. The road from Philadelphia to Lancaster had travelers year round.

Not only was trade hampered by wars, but fraud became a major problem. Cheating was common in the use of weights and measures and in describing the quality of goods. City regulations were difficult to enforce, and in some cases were merely dropped. Money shortages often arose, which gave rise to long-term credit. Because of these and other risks in doing business, the insurance sector expanded tremendously.

Some of the major socioeconomic problems of this era included fires, crime, poverty, and public health. Fires often resulted from wars, the failure to clean sooty chimneys, or other chance factors. Since fires in a high-density urban area can do so much damage so quickly, regulations were passed to require all housing to be built out of stone or brick. As cities grew, fire threats were even more potentially damaging because of inefficient water systems.

Large immigrations of sailors, soldiers, and runaways, among others, increased the supply of potential criminals. Since policemen were difficult to hire and keep, the private "price" of committing a crime declined; thus law and order was a real problem. Philadelphia was the first city to organize a police force and pay its policemen. According to Bridenbaugh, robbery and violent crimes were numerous, but did not attain the proportions incurred by urban Englanders. Counterfeiting appeared during this period. Prison conditions were deplorable, and escapes before trial were commonplace. This problem does not seem to have changed much in the past few centuries.

Many of the immigrants were unskilled and, to compound problems, did not speak English. War refugees also swarmed to cities, the overall result being a massive increase in the demand for public assistance. Relief was often provided in the form of cash grants, as well as basic staples (wood, provisions, and medical aid). Almshouses grew rapidly, as did orphan homes. After reaching the age of eight to ten, orphans were sent out to work.

Public-health measures worked better than those in England, but yellow fever and smallpox were major killers. More people seemed to die of dysentery, respiratory (or heart) ailments, and malaria than of the epidemics of plagues so common in Europe. Insanity was handled as a problem of poverty, rather than as a medical problem.

Overall, urban problems were attacked vigorously. Without strong traditions, the mostly middle-class urbanites were willing to tax themselves for the common good. The press helped a great deal in exposing the problems; thus some of the first citizens of the age were printers (such as Ben Franklin).

1760–1776

The decade and a half before the War of Independence was marked by continued urban expansion, but the mother country began to constrain trade. Since Boston was most hurt by these British actions, it is little wonder that the American Revolution began there.

Philadelphia enjoyed the greatest expansion in this period* (see Table 2-2). To meet its population boom, over 200 houses were built annually until 1770, at which time annual production was doubled. Still, real-estate values rose throughout the period and landlords became rich quickly. Continued influxes of British troops into New York caused the same situation to continue there. We all know who suffered during this stage of expansion—the poor. High rents and congestion drove many to the suburbs, and access being important, nearby suburban property values rose the highest.

Currency problems continued to constrain the flow of trade within

---

* Technically, Charleston, South Carolina had a slightly larger percentage increase in population.

and among cities. The result was the Currency Act of 1764, which forbade further printing of currency. It is a well-known principle of economics that if "good money" is scarce, people will ultimately prefer goods rather than currency in exchange. The logical result is a barter economy and severe depression, which is exactly what happened. Neither debts nor taxes could be collected. Tradesmen bore heavy losses. To get out of the depression, merchants introduced new goods to old markets and opened up new markets (Quebec and Montreal). Duties on traded goods became a popular method of raising public revenues.

Innovations also helped the trade picture with the hinterland settlements. Bred horses and Conestoga wagons greatly reduced overland travel time. Baltimore grew from 200 persons in 1752 to nearly 6000 in 1776 (making it the ninth largest city in the colonies) primarily by wresting away business in the hinterlands from Philadelphia. Baltimore built better roads to the common satellites.

Specialization in crafts flourished. General carpenters were replaced by joiners, turners, cabinet makers, chair makers, and others. Blacksmiths were replaced in the city by anchor forgers, ornamental ironworkers, coppersmiths, triplaters, and braziers. Women entered the crafts, and were excellent milliners, mantua workers, and dyers.

The problems of this period were similar to those between 1743 and 1760. Solutions were forthcoming in all areas except crime. Professional criminals appeared in every city, and prisons were always overfilled. After Parliament closed Boston's ports in 1774, the poor of that area began to suffer tremendously. Public-works programs were set up. The final seed of revolution had been served with Boston's quarantine; according to Arthur Schlesinger,

> Boston's primacy as the "Cradle of Liberty" may well have sprung from her lagging progress in relation to other ports, inciting her at any cost to remove the obstacles that Parliament was thrusting in her way [19].

Antebellum Urban Expansion: 1790–1860

The pre-Civil War period, or what historians refer to as the antebellum period, was one of great urban expansion. Of special significance for our purposes, the Federal Government began collecting decennial census data in 1790; thus for the first time we can not only get a more accurate view of the urbanization trends but also attempt to explain why urbanization occurred. First, though, let us continue with the time narrative left off in the previous section, and take a look at the overall urban economic dimension of this great expansion era.

*An Overview of the Economic Development of Cities**

The Revolutionary War brought many problems to the seaport trading cities. Currency was greatly depreciated, and trade with Britain and its allies was heavily restricted (unless one was willing to pay heavy duties). Colonial states exacerbated the trading problem by imposing customs barriers of their own, but this problem was solved in 1789 with the implementation of the U.S. Constitution. With the signing of the Jay Treaty in 1816, trade reopened with the British West Indies. But the significant trade story of this era is that U.S. cities no longer looked to foreign markets for primary customers; instead, cities right here at home became new markets.

Baltimore became a major trading city because of its relation to inland cities and its fine seaport. With Whitney's cotton gin, cotton made Charleston a major seaport. Cooperatives were formed in Cincinnati between homesteaders and merchants in 1803, and its population tripled in a decade. Many of Cincinnati's products were sent to New Orleans, a major center of trade activity.

Innovations in transportation and manufacturing helped strengthen the trading relationship between eastern seaboard and inland cities. In 1806 Oliver Evans developed the steam engine in Philadelphia, and by the next year Fulton's steamboat was chugging up the Hudson. This invention is of major importance in explaining the development of river towns such as Pittsburgh, Cincinnati, Louisville, New Orleans, St. Louis, and also Chicago. In fact, trade so developed on the Ohio and Mississippi Rivers that by 1835 New Orleans had a larger volume of (foreign) exports than New York City.

Canals became a popular means of linking up with inland cities, and the Erie Canal helped make New York the national leader in trading activity over Philadelphia. The Quaker city tried to regain western markets by building a canal to Pittsburgh, but this venture was a failure. Railroads were another form of transport that cities used to strengthen existing markets and open new ones. The railroad probably was the deciding factor in Chicago's victory over St. Louis by 1860 as the number one center of economic activity in the Midwest.

With the increased production of steamboats, locomotives, and rail tracks, the demand for iron increased. Cities in Pennsylvania (Scranton, Pittsburgh, and Harrisburg) met most of the demands, since ore deposits were nearby. As the iron-making process changed (the use of coke was introduced), and new, richer ore deposits were found in Michigan's

---

* The material presented in this section relies heavily on Constance M. Green, *The Rise of Urban America* [20].

upper peninsula, the Great Lakes and the railroads kept Pittsburgh in a very competitive position.

In the wake of this expansion, how were the cities doing with the traditional problem areas of housing, transportation, public health, poverty, and crime?* Naturally the housing shortages described in the earlier periods continued. New York City, where many of the immigrants first landed, had an acute shortage. By 1850, warehouses were being used, with up to five or six families housed in a 12- by 14-foot room.

As expected, the high rents and congestion continued to drive people into the suburbs. But the poor of New York City could not afford the $12\frac{1}{2}$ cent one-way fare on horsedrawn rail cars in 1837. Surprisingly, 25,000 persons per day could. Streets were paved only in the business districts and wealthy residential areas.

Health was still a major problem, as one might expect with such living conditions. Public water and sewerage systems were often faulty. Epidemics of dysentery and typhoid were common. In its worst yellow fever episode of the 1850's, New Orleans lost 25,000 persons out of its total population of 116,000.

Poverty and crime continued also. Many of the immigrants were discriminated against, and fled inland to work on canals and railroads. The anti-Catholic Know-Nothing or American party set fire to a convent in Boston, and threw a marble block sent by the Pope into a river in Washington. Shortages of uniformed police and an unwillingness to light streetlights except on cloudy nights kept the private cost of committing a crime rather low.

Urbanization Trends of the Population

In 1790 there were only 24 cities with at least 2500 persons, and these cities comprised 5.1 percent of the U.S. population. By 1860, 392 cities existed, and made up nearly 20 percent of the national population (see Table 2-3 for these and other urbanization trends). On a regional basis, by 1860 the Northeast had 35.7 percent of its population in urban places, while the South, North Central, and Western areas were at 9.6, 13.9, and 16.0 percent, respectively [10, p. 108]. New York grew from 60,515 to 312,710 between 1800 and 1840 [4, p. 146]. Baltimore nearly quadrupled its population during the same time period, while New Orleans exploded from 17,242 in 1800 to 102,193 by 1840.

Urbanization hits its peak in our nation's history during this era. Between 1840 and 1850, the number of persons living in places of 2500

* For a detailed and interesting account of the development and problems of particular cities, see Constance M. Green, *American Cities in the Growth of the Nation* [21].

TABLE 2–3

Urbanization Trends in the U.S., 1790–1860[a]

	1790	1800	1810	1820	1830	1840	1850	1860
Number of cities	24	23	46	61	90	131	236	392
Percent of total population that was urban	5.1	6.1	7.3	7.2	8.8	10.8	15.3	19.8
Growth of urbanization		59.9	63.0	31.9	62.6	63.7	92.1	75.4
Ratio of nonagricultural labor force to total labor force		17.4	16.2	21.2	29.4	36.9	45.2	47.1

[a] Source: Eric Lampard, "The Evolving System of Cities in the United States," in *Issues in Urban Economics*, H. Perloff and L. Wingo, eds. Tables 1, 3, and 7 (Baltimore, Maryland: Johns Hopkins Press, for Resources for the Future, Inc., 1968).

or more increased by 92.1 percent (see Table 2-3). During the same time period, the nonagricultural labor force as a share of the total labor force in the country made its greatest percentage gain up to that time.

How can these impressive trends of urbanization be explained? We have already given a historical description in the previous section, which showed that seaport cities were using innovations in water and land transportation to compete for external markets in the rising cities of the Midwest.* But what about the role of internal and external economies of scale?† Should they not be able to explain the faster growth of cities in the Northeast? Let us consider the urbanization process and the agglomeration economies question in turn.

Jeffrey Williamson [23] hypothesizes that changes in the urbanization rate for any region will follow a logistic curve over time (see Figure 2.1). The initial increase is supposedly due to the attractive power of

* An interesting discussion of these imperialistic practices is given by Richard C. Wade [20].

† Many illustrations of external economies and agglomerations exist during this period; for example, see Sam B. Warner, Jr. [7, pp. 63–69].

Figure 2.1   *Changes in the urbanization rate over time.*

TABLE 2–4

Percent of Growth in the Urban Share of Population by Region, 1790–1860[a]

	1790–1800	1800–1810	1810–1820	1820–1830	1830–1840	1840–1850	1850–1860	1860–1870
Northeast[b]	1.17	1.62	0.11	3.15	4.37	8.00	9.22	8.55
Middle Atlantic[c]	1.51	1.27	−0.18	2.95	3.85	7.41	9.88	8.87
New England[d]	0.68	1.87	0.44	3.47	5.40	9.34	8.77	7.79
South[e]	0.82	1.16	4.77	6.59	1.39	1.62	1.30	2.60
East North Central[f]	—	—	2.84	1.28	1.37	5.18	5.01	7.56
Northeast[g]	2.05	2.32	1.47	4.36	5.65	8.76	8.68	6.02
Middle Atlantic[g]	3.61	2.67	2.52	4.99	5.56	7.84	9.56	4.52

[a] Source: Jeffrey Williamson, "Antebellum Urbanization in the American Northeast," *Journal of Economic History* 25 (1965): 600.

[b] Includes Maine, New Hampshire, Vermont, Massachusetts, Rhode Island, Connecticut, New York, New Jersey, and Pennsylvania.

[c] Includes New York, New Jersey, and Pennsylvania.

[d] Includes Maine, New Hampshire, Vermont, Massachusetts, Rhode Island, and Connecticut.

[e] Includes Delaware, Maryland, the District of Columbia, Virginia, West Virginia, Kentucky, Tennessee, North Carolina, South Carolina, Georgia, Florida, Mississippi, Alabama, Arkansas, Louisiana, Oklahoma, and Texas.

[f] Includes Illinois, Indiana, Ohio, Michigan, and Wisconsin.

[g] Excludes western New York and western Pennsylvania.

agglomerative forces and relatively elastic labor supplies.* The downturn comes, according to Williamson, when labor supplies become price inelastic. As the data show in Table 2-4, Williamson's hypothesis of an abrupt acceleration and then (relative) decline is borne out by the data. Each acceleration takes three or four decades, on the average. Note the peak of urban growth as a share of the total population in the East was reached around 1860.

Although the data of Table 2-4 would trace out the logistic curve generally, this does not necessarily mean that agglomerative and supply elasticity forces were at work. In fact, no test of this impact of these forces was attempted by Williamson with these data. In a later study with Joseph Swanson [24], Williamson hypothesized that the north-

* Recalling the definition of elasticity, the percentage change in quantity supplied divided by the percentage change in the price of labor, firms could buy all they wanted at a given price under these conditions.

eastern cities should have grown the fastest in the U.S. during the antebellum period because they already had scale economies by 1800 and
1810; thus they could produce more cheaply than the frontier cities
that were just getting started by the middle of the nineteenth century.
However, the authors found that except for 1790–1810 and 1840–1850,
scale economies were not necessarily favorable to city growth unless
the city relied primarily on foreign trade.* Instead, they found the most
significant growth factor to be population growth in the city's hinterland.

Urbanization, Industrialization, and Suburbanization: 1860–1940

The period from 1860 to 1940 saw the U.S. become the industrial
giant of the world. Much of the industrial expansion took place in or
near cities. Many writers in the past have attempted to prove that indus-
trialization caused urbanization. Others have tried to prove the converse.
We shall leave these arguments to historians, and concentrate on the
trends of this period and a casual analysis of why these trends occurred.
Besides the great expansion in manufacturing, this period saw a continuation of the suburbanization move that began shortly after cities became
congested. In addition to suburbanization, we shall also cover the state
of urban problems.

Urbanization and Industrialization Trends

Although urbanization continued during this period, the pace was
much slower than that of the 1790–1860 period. The average decadal
percentage increase in the urban population was 33.1 percent, whereas
in the previous period it had been 64.1 percent. Between 1910 and
1920, over half the national population was urbanized. By 1940, 56.5
percent of the population lived in 3464 urban areas. The Northeast
was the first region to reach a majority of urban residents (50.8 percent
urban by 1880), and both the North Central and Western regions followed suit by 1920. In 1940, only 36.7 percent of Southerners lived
in urban areas.

The 1860–1870 decade marked the first time that the absolute increase
in urban population outstripped the absolute increase in rural population. In Philadelphia alone, over 60 factories were built annually between 1862 and 1864. By 1865, New York, Boston, and other seaport
cities had the vast majority of their economic activity directed toward
manufacturing and the distribution of their production to domestic
markets.

---

* This rationalization is based on the large-scale port facilities in the Northeast.

The expansion of railroads played a major role in the urbanization of the West during the late 1800's. According to Constance Green,

> Whereas Eastern cities built railroads, in the West railroads built cities. [20, p. 42].

The Union Pacific was primarily responsible for the rise of Omaha and Salt Lake City. Similarly, Kansas City and San Francisco showed solid growth after the railroads began to carry heavy traffic. Of course, the stimulus of the railroads did not benefit every railroad town to the same extent: for example, Cheyenne lost out to Denver by the turn of the century as the leader of the mountain states.

Innovations could often be identified as the major source of growth of specific cities. For example, after Minnesota farmers found a hard-kernel wheat that would withstand the cool weather, and roller grinders were introduced to grind wheat into high-quality flour, Minneapolis captured the Eastern flour markets and was on its way to becoming a major city. The perfection of the internal combustion engine in 1901 led to the rapid expansion of auto production in Detroit in 1910.

An indicator of inventions and innovation is the number of patents issued. In 1860, 27,000 patents were granted, while in 1910, over one million patents were granted—mostly of urban origin [4, p. 35]. Although it is difficult to explain (theoretically) the determinants of the number of patents, by 1890 the supply of good agricultural land had dried up. People were forced into the cities, and just by sheer numbers one would have expected an increase in patents.

Besides the expansion of railroads and innovations in manufacturing, many other factors determined the urban expansion during the period. Pred notes that almost every study omits the obviously important factor that the natural increase of urban natives certainly helped population increases [4, p. 41]. As mortality rates fell in the twentieth century, this factor became more significant. Another important urbanization determinant was the increase in real wages in the manufacturing sector. As people's incomes increased, they demanded more services and income-elastic goods, which had a multiplying effect throughout the urban economy.

Manufacturing did not provide the major impetus for urban economic expansion during the whole period [4, 19–24]. By 1910, commerce had replaced industry as the major source of employment. U.S. cities had taken some giant steps in their drive to maturity. Not all cities participated in this expansion to the same degree, however. New Orleans, Cincinnati, Louisville, and Albany were among the eleven largest cities in 1860, but they did not hold these positions by 1940. In fact, by

1910 these cities were ranked fourteenth, thirteenth, twenty-second, and forty-fourth in population. Other cities, such as Mobile, Charleston (South Carolina), and Portland (Maine) did much worse. Why is it that some cities grew rapidly while other cities grew only slightly?

We have already noted that railroad extensions and improvements were not equally dispersed among cities and regions. Where railroads built up, however, freight charges dropped drastically. Thus even firms having fixed budgets could increase their scale of output (by substituting other inputs for transportation). If firms were operating on the downward side of their average cost curves, this effect was even strengthened. As this cost-reducing and scale-increasing process continued, the minimum size of the plant required for new entrants into the industry increased. Thus old established firms in big cities had an edge, and it showed up in the population figures by the early twentieth century.

Many other factors besides reduction in freight charges favored the large firms in bigger cities. Large-scale economies attracted suppliers and buyers, who took advantage of the classical agglomeration forces. Chicago is an excellent example of the integrative effects across firms in an industry, with its great expansion in machinery and foundries, slaughtering and meatpacking, and the iron and steel industries.

Since most of the innovations led to the use of more capital, which required the large minimum-sized operations, larger firms were better off. Industrial concentration in corporate giants was a product of this era, and there is little (economic) doubt as to why such a change in structure occurred.

In summary, this period saw the greatest urban expansion (in absolute numbers) on record, helped immensely by the growth in manufacturing with its assembly-line techniques. By the early part of the twentieth century, cities had become more commerce and service oriented, with much of the business and financial activity in the hands of corporate giants.

Suburbanization

We have already discussed earlier trends in suburbanization, which were explained by increased congestion, noise, and property values in the big cities. With the growth of cities during this period, people had to go somewhere. Innovations in transportation—especially the electric trolley,* and, by the end of the period, the auto—helped continue the suburbanization trend. Unfortunately, we have no data on suburban

---

* For an interesting account of how Boston's suburbs developed from transportation sources, see Sam B. Warner, Jr., *Streetcar Suburbs* [25].

TABLE 2–5

Percent of Growth of U.S. Population, 1900–1960[a]

	1900–1910	1910–1920	1920–1930	1930–1940	1940–1950	1950–1960
U.S.	21.0	14.9	16.1	7.2	14.1	18.8
Urban	39.3	29.0	27.3	7.9	20.6	22.6
SMSA	32.0	24.9	27.1	8.8	22.6	26.3
Central City	37.1	27.7	24.3	5.6	14.7	10.7
Outside	23.7	19.9	32.3	14.6	35.9	48.5

[a] Source: U.S. Census of Population.

growth until 1910; but as Table 2-5 shows, population growth outside central cities but inside SMSA's had already outstripped the U.S. growth rate by 1910. During the 1920's, suburban growth surpassed central-city growth. This process is still going on.

At the turn of the century, many of the middle class who lived in the outer rings and suburbs became upset by the inability of city government to solve problems. According to Wade [22, p. 71–75], progressivism began as an intraurban conflict between the wealthy suburban class and the representatives of the relatively poor inhabitants of the city's core. A major weapon used by the former group was zoning. It kept the "undesirables" not only in the core, but also where the businessmen wanted them inside the core. New York's first zoning law, according to Wade,

> . . . stemmed from a crisis on Fifth Avenue where merchants feared the encroachments of the garment workers into buildings close to the fashionable shops on the great street. [22, p. 74]

From an efficiency standpoint, the auto probably became more of a major problem than zoning or other laws, at least by the end of the period. Whereas electric trolleys and interurbans had shaped suburban development before, by the 1920's the auto allowed people to settle anywhere within driving distance of their jobs. Sprawl began to occur rapidly, and the age of concrete and asphalt had begun.

*Urban Problems**

The traditional urban problems of housing, transportation, pollution, poverty, and crime did not "run away" between 1860 and 1940 but

* This section relies heavily on Green [20, pp. 101–118].

instead of remaining basically economic problems, they became institutional problems as well. As real incomes increased in urban areas, a greater share of the population was able to buy the necessary housing, transportation, and other services needed to exist comfortably. However, there were always seemingly sizable groups that found it difficult to do so, for many reasons.

Although transit improved and suburbanization increased, which certainly had a dampening effect on the demand for housing in the core, rents continued to rise and slums were expanding. In the 1880's, two and even three families were placed in single units of large tenement houses in New York—a step up from the previous years when warehouses were used. Black families were using overcrowded shacks in the alleys of Washington, D.C. at the turn of the century.

Where were the solutions to this housing problem? New York City began to regulate rented housing in 1867 by imposing limits on the number of persons allowed per building. By 1887, the regulations extended to plumbing and fire escapes. Stricter laws were written in New York and cities at the turn of the century, but enforcement always seemed to be impossible for some reason or other. Congress even got into the picture by holding inquiries into slum housing conditions in 1892, but the slums still grew.

There were few if any major intraurban transportation problems during this period. Almost all cities had street railways, and by 1887 electric trolleys appeared. To relieve congestion and move people faster downtown, Boston opened the first subway in 1897. Philadelphia followed suit in 1904, as did New York on a much larger scale. Paved streets became common within the total city limits. In short, people were able to travel faster (and farther) within urban areas than ever before. The auto had not yet taken charge.

In the public-health and pollution areas, sewage disposal was still a major problem. Baltimore had 90,000 backyard privies in 1900, and Washington still had several thousand in the 1930's. It was not until epidemiologists in Boston and elsewhere proved the causal relationship between contaminated water and the deadly typhoid and dysentery that city officials laid sewer lines separate from the water lines. Of course the sewage flowed untreated into the nearest river, lake, or ocean, where sunlight was thought to kill the germs.

Poverty was always a problem for the big cities during this period. Former slaves began to migrate north after the Civil War and did not enter the mainstream of the economy without serious adjustment problems. The same was true for many of the immigrants, who swarmed through Ellis Island in New York. Anti-foreign immigrant groups fostered many prejudices that made the adjustment problem longer and more difficult. The depressions of the 1890's and 1930's compounded the problem of poverty.

Although traditional crimes in the slum areas of cities continued and professional gangsters flourished, the problem of maintaining law and order added a new dimension during this period. Labor unions fought so bitterly to be recognized that strikes and minor disturbances often turned into riots. The upheavals in black areas of U.S. cities during the 1960's did not mark the first time savagery has overtaken the socio-economic development process.

V. SUMMARY

In this chapter we have covered a lot of ground, at least from a time perspective. Before beginning our historical journey of urban development, we considered three approaches to describing the origin and development of cities over time. Each of these three approaches—ad hoc principles, the cultural approach, and the stages model—gave us ideas and patterns to look for in tracing the urbanization process of man.

From a global standpoint, urban economic history shows quite clearly that the social and economic problems of contemporary urban society are literally centuries old. Man's reaction to the pollution, congestion, poverty, financial, and crime problems of the inner city has seemingly always been to run away to the outskirts of town or to suburbs, depending on the era under study. In the U.S., we found that continued urban economic growth and expansion always seemed to be at the fore, rather than any quest for solving our basic socioeconomic problems as we developed. In short, urban development to date is best described as the concentration of people, accompanied by a perpetual inability to solve many of the basic problems that have always been associated with (if not caused by) urbanization itself.

SUGGESTED READINGS

Bridenbaugh, Carl. *Cities in the Wilderness,* 2d ed. New York: Knopf, 1964.
Bridenbaugh, Carl. *Cities in Revolt.* New York: Knopf, 1955.
Green, Constance. *The Rise of Urban America.* New York: Harper, 1965.
Handlin, O., and J. Burchard. *The Historian and the City.* Cambridge, Massachusetts: MIT and Harvard Univ. Press, 1963.
Hirsch, Werner. *Urban Life and Form.* New York: Holt, 1963.

Hoover, Edgar. *The Location of Economic Activity*. New York: McGraw-Hill, 1948.

Lampard, Eric. "The History of Cities in Economically Advanced Areas." *Economic Development and Cultural Change* 3 (1954–1955): 81–136.

Mumford, Lewis. *The City in History*. New York: Harcourt, 1961.

Pred, Allan. *The Spatial Dynamics of U.S. Urban Industrial Growth, 1800–1914*. Cambridge, Massachusetts: MIT Press, 1966.

Rostow, Walter. *The Stages of Economic Growth*, 2nd. ed. New York: Cambridge Univ. Press, 1971.

REFERENCES

1. Edgar Hoover, *The Location of Economic Activity* (New York: McGraw-Hill, 1948).
2. Walter Isard, *Methods of Regional Analysis*, pp. 338–342 (Cambridge, Massachusetts: MIT Press, 1960).
3. Gunner Myrdal, *Rich Lands and Poor*, Vol. 16, p. 13 (New York: Harper, 1957).
4. Allen Pred, *The Spatial Dynamics of U.S. Urban Industrial Growth, 1800–1914* (Cambridge, Massachusetts: MIT Press, 1966).
5. Eric Lampard, "The History of Cities in Economically Advanced Areas," *Economic Development and Cultiral Change* 3 (1954–1955): 81–136.
6. Gerald Meir, ed., *Leading Issues in Development Economics*, 2nd ed., pp. 92–102 (New York and London: Oxford Univ. Press, 1970).
7. Robert Lopez, "The Crossroads within the Wall," in *The Historian and the City*, Oscar Handlin and John Burchard, eds., pp. 27–43 (Cambridge, Massachusetts: MIT Press and Harvard Univ. Press, 1963).
8. Eugene Smolensky, "The Conception of Cities," *Explorations in Entrepreneural History* 2, 2nd Ser. (1965): 90–131.
9. W. W. Rostow, *The Stages of Economic Growth* (London and New York: Cambridge Univ. Press, 1964).
10. Eric Lampard, "The Evolving System of Cities in the United States," in *Issues in Urban Economics*, H. Perloff and L. Wings, eds., p. 132 (Baltimore, Maryland: Johns Hopkins Press, for Resources for the Future, Inc., 1968).
11. U.S. Bureau of Census, *City and County Data Book*, 1967.
12. Victor Fuchs, "The Growing Importance of Service Industries," National Bureau of Economic Research, Occasional Paper 96, 1965.
13. Lewis Mumford, *The City in History* (New York: Harcourt, 1961).
14. Robert McC. Adams, *The Evolution of Urban Society* (Chicago, Illinois: Aldine, 1966).
15. Jane Jacobs, *The Economy of Cities*, Chapter 1 (New York: Random House, 1969).
16. Aristotle's 'Politics.'
17. Carl Bridenbaugh, *Cities in the Wilderness: The First Century of Urban Life in America 1625–1742*, 2nd ed. (New York, Knopf, 1964).
18. Carl Bridenbaugh, *Cities in Revolt, Urban Life in America 1743–1776* (New York: Knopf, 1955).
19. A. M. Schlesinger, *Prelude to Independence: The Newspaper War on Britain, 1764–1776*, p. 6 (New York: Knopf, 1958).
20. Constance M. Green, *The Rise of Urban America*, Chapters II and III (New York: Harper 1965).

21. Constance M. Green, *American Cities in the Growth of the Nation* (London: Athlone Press, 1957).
22. Richard C. Wade, "The City in History—Some American Perspectives," in *Urban Life and Form,* Werner Z. Hirsch, ed., pp. 63–65 (New York, Holt, 1963).
23. Jeffrey Williamson, "Antebellum Urbanization in the American Northeast," *Journal of Economic History* 25 (1965): 592–611.
24. Jeffrey Williamson and Joseph Swanson, "The Growth of Cities in the American Northeast, 1820–1870," *Explorations in Entrepreneural History, Supplement* 4, 2nd Ser. (1966).
25. Sam B. Warner, Jr., *Streetcar Suburbs* (Cambridge, Massachusetts: MIT Press and Harvard Univ. Press, 1962).

3

THE ECONOMICS OF URBAN GROWTH

I. INTRODUCTION

If the earth were a homogeneous plain (that is, if resources were evenly scattered) and constant returns to scale existed in the production of all goods and services,* no spatial location for production (or consumption) would have any economic advantage; therefore the population would be evenly scattered, This gross oversimplification of reality, first discussed by Losch [1–3], is a valuable beginning point in our discussion of urban growth. Why? Because it points up the reasons behind (1) the concentration of people and (2) increasing real output per unit of resource. In other words, if resources were not evenly scat-

* Under constant returns to scale, average costs are constant over all levels of output.

tered over space, we would find concentrations of persons and production units near those resources whose demands are most price inelastic, *ceteris paribus.* Even if one kept the homogeneous-plain assumption, it is possible that through continued specialization over time, some areas would become more proficient in the production of certain goods and services; thus firms and persons would be attracted to those sites where increasing returns to scale existed. In other words, cities or regions would develop comparative advantages, and by each region doing what it does best the sum of all regions would have more goods and services to consume. Growth would have occurred.

Variations in resource types and production techniques, then, are sufficient conditions to cause concentrations of people and production in space, allowing the agglomeration economies discussed in earlier chapters to go to work. But the concentration of people by itself is neither a necessary nor a sufficient condition for growth. A standard principle of economics is that increases in the quantity or quality of resources will shift outward the production possibility curve of an economy. However, there are two significant factors that determine whether or not the economy can reach the new frontier:

(1) Is there a demand for the additional output that can now be produced?
(2) Is there an allocative mechanism for getting the demanded types and amounts of goods and services produced and consumed?

We shall assume that the first condition is met in urban areas, since the concentration of people provides a readily accessible market for goods and services. The second condition often breaks down *within* urban areas, as we shall see in the problem chapters in this book. On the other hand, when one is concerned with interurban problems, the price system seems to be a fairly efficient tool.

Clearly, then (1) the distribution of resources, (2) relative modes of production, (3) levels of demand, and (4) the efficiency of the price system are all important determinants of the growth process. It is important for the student to understand that these four factors are simultaneously determined. Given the spatial distribution of resources, firms choose the optimal site and mode of production in reaction to demand or market considerations. The latter, of course, are expressed via the price system. Because of the importance of the interrelations of these primary determinants of urban growth, the basic theme of this chapter will be the interdependencies behind urban growth.

We begin our study of urban growth with a discussion of the distribution of firms and persons across cities. We shall see that firms prefer to locate near markets and where resources (labor) are readily available.

People, of course, locate in cities where jobs are available. Thus, over time, the location decisions of firms and people are determined simultaneously. Next, we consider four models of urban growth. The first model covered is the simple Keynesian income-determination or multiplier model, which emphasizes the ramifications of changes in spending on the final change in urban income. Second, we consider urban economic-base models, which highlight the importance of trading relationships with the external world. Third, central-place models are covered, which tie the city's trade and service sectors to its hinterland. Finally, we consider input–output models, which simultaneously explain the production and distribution interrelationships of all industries in the urban economy. We complete the chapter with a discussion of some of the issues at the frontiers of urban growth analysis. Again, the student will find that in each of the issues discussed—income distribution, long-range urban growth prospects, and optimal city size—interdependence is basic to the overall discussion.

II. THE RUDIMENTS OF LOCATION ANALYSIS*

By explaining the locational factors of firms and people, we have a basis for identifying the distribution of resources across space. It is then only a simple logical step, given the existing techniques of production, to explain the absolute and relative production potentials of cities.

In general, people want to locate where they can maximize their satisfaction over time. Similarly, producers desire to locate where their profits are expected to be maximized over time. We may assert, however, that producers' motives are more important than workers' motives in determining the location of economic activity. Why might this assertion be true? Hoover cites at least two reasons:

(1) Because the businessman ordinarily has more to lose, intercity differences in wage rates and profit prospects are probably better known than differentials in living costs and conditions.
(2) There seems to be more change in the patterns that determine firm preferences than in the patterns that determine consumer's preferences.

If the first reason is true, more knowledge on the part of the producer, *ceteris paribus*, will allow him not only to make a move but do so when it seems most rational. An example of the second reason is technical change, which will change the firm's but not the worker's preferences.

---

* Much of this section is based on Edgar M. Hoover, *The Location of Economic Activity* [4].

Whatever one concludes on the importance of the relative motives of firms versus workers, we shall begin our discussion with the producer. We can break down the production process of any good or service into three stages:

(1) *procurement*—the purchasing and transferral of necessary supplies and materials to the production site;
(2) *processing*—the transformation of supplies and materials, via the employment of resources in an organized way, into (potentially) more valuable forms such as goods and services;
(3) *distribution*—the selling and delivery of these goods and services.

In regard to choosing a site for location, from a distribution standpoint the producer would like to know the spatial location of the demand for his product. For procuring his supplies and materials, cost data are needed, and in general costs increase with distance. It is rather clear, then, that both procurement and distribution costs have a common determinant: transportation or transfer costs. Thus procurement and distribution advantages very according to the distance from supplies and customers, respectively. Because of the powerful effect of transfer costs on the location decisions of firms, we shall consider this factor in more detail.

Transfer Costs and Firm Location

In this section we shall discuss the impact of transfer costs on the location decision of the firm, holding all other factors constant. To simplify the analysis, we shall assume that (1) transportation rates are given, and (2) both suppliers and buyers cannot completely absorb freight charges. If we allowed the price of transportation services to vary, we know that for any given price change there would be an "income" and "substitution" effect; thus, without any a priori way of knowing which effect would win out, we could not predict the impact of the price change on the firm's location. If both buyers and suppliers could absorb all transfer costs, which is highly unlikely, then transfer costs would have little if any effect on location decisions. Thus, although these assumptions simplify our analysis, we can still explain a good deal of location behavior.

Conceptually, the reduction of transfer costs is a rather strong incentive to concentrate the three stages of production at a single point in space. Except for the production of a few goods and services in cities, such concentration is nearly impossible. Thus transfer costs must be considered, especially in relation to distance. For given modes of trans-

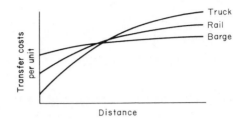

Figure 3.1   *Transfer cost–distance relationships.*

portation, transfer costs per unit of product generally increase with distance; but at longer distances, the increases begin to tail off. In other words, as distance increases, the marginal cost of shipping a good another mile declines. This pattern is illustrated in Figure 3.1 for trucks, barges, and railroads. Note that to go short distances the truck is cheapest, and barge most expensive. The decreasing marginal cost of each mode is primarily due to the spreading of terminal and other fixed costs over more and more output.

How do transfer costs affect the individual producer? Consider a producer in a single, linear market, where neither the volume of business nor his processing cost varies with his location—as long as he locates on the line. William Alonso illustrates this case with a bakery selling to customers situated along a road [5]. The bakery hires a boy for deliveries, and the boy can carry only one customer's order at a time. Where does the firm locate to minimize the boy's trips? One might quickly argue for the mean or average distance traveled, but this is wrong.* The *median* is the proper solution, for it minimizes the sum of the distances traveled. To the extent that the median point of customers is in cities, based on this principle alone, we might expect cities to increase their number of firms over time, or at least not lose existing firms.

What if we complicate our example somewhat by assuming that the firm buys a single material but still sells in a single market, and that all other assumptions hold? Again the problem reduces to minimizing transfer costs. If total procurement and total distribution costs are linearly related to distance, we have a simple problem. In this case, if the marginal procurement cost exceeds the marginal distribution costs, it will pay to locate at the materials site, as shown in Figure 3.2a. In the figure, distance is on the horizontal axis, and the vertical axis represents costs. The marginal cost of procurement is measured by angle *a*, while the marginal cost of distribution is represented by angle *b*.

* The mean would minimize the sum of the squared distances.

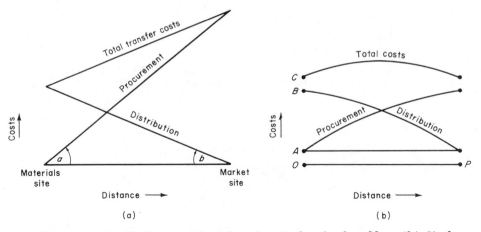

Figure 3.2 (a) *Single materials and market site locational problem.* (b) *Single materials and market site with terminal costs and transfer economies.*

The (vertical) sum of procurement and distribution costs equals total transfer costs. Obviously, if angle *b* exceeded angle *a*, tranfer costs would be minimized by locating at the market site. Thus, when firm's markets are cities and the marginal procurement costs are relatively low, we would expect firms to locate in cities, if our assumptions are met.

Where would the firm locate if angle *a* equaled angle *b* in Figure 3.2a? The answer, of course, is that the firm could locate at the material site or the market site, or anywhere in between. If we respecify our definition of transfer costs by including terminal costs, or if we allow economies of long-haul movement to occur, which will cause the marginal procurement or distribution costs to decline with distance, a unique locational choice will exist. This case is shown in Figure 3.2b. Terminal costs are depicted by *OA* (= *BC*); the rest of the figure resembles Figure 3.2a, except that the costs are curvilinear. Even if the lines were straight, it would still pay producers to locate at the material site *O* or the market site *P*, for at these points the firm could save terminal costs on materials or the final product, respectively. It is obvious that declining marginal costs will also lead to an endpoint solution.

In general, producers will be oriented toward markets when the product:

(1) is weight-gaining during manufacture, as is beer;
(2) has higher transfer costs on distribution than on procurement;
(3) is perishable, as are ice, baked goods, and fresh agricultural produce.

An alternative to locating production facilities at the material or market site is to locate them at a transshipment point. Often rail meets water, and if both transport media are used, the most favorable production location will be at the transshipment point, because the producer saves the terminal costs of transferring the good from rail car to ship or vice versa. Seaports are often transshipment sites, and many cities owe their existence to this principle. (Buffalo and San Francisco are examples.)

It has been argued by many persons that in the real world an increasing number of manufacturing plants are becoming footloose; that is, they do not locate at the materials, market, or transshipment sites. Although there are now many footloose firms in existence, this does not mean that one site is just as good as any other; rather, it means that transfer costs are becoming relatively less important in the firm's location decision.

Processing Costs and Firm Location

The processing needs of the producer are labor, capital, land, and governmental services. Firms usually try to minimize their costs of these services—wages, interest, rent, and taxes—for a given level of output. Factor price differentials arise primarily because of immobility, especially for capital and labor. If a factor is mobile, we would argue that it moves toward its highest reward, other things being equal. The more immobile the factors, the greater the price differential we might expect. Because of these factor price differentials over space, firms have a locational decision to make, given that (1) markets are not at a single point and (2) transfer costs to that single market are not infinitely high.

What will the decision-maker look for in a prospective site? He will attempt to choose a site where his production process can be set up to attain the maximum utilization of all resources employed. This often involves producing at a level at which scale economies can be obtained. Hoover discussed three principles that help reduce costs in a plant at the scale of production increases:

(1) Certain types of highly specialized labor and capital are indivisible, and after the minimum scale of output is reached to employ such factors, per-unit costs will be much lower.
(2) The larger the plant, the smaller the percentage of its resources it must tie up in reserves of materials, equipment, and supplies.
(3) As the scale increases, the per-unit price of materials, services, and utilities will usually decline, because suppliers often give reductions in rates for bulk purchasers.

Thus, on the basis of (3), a sufficient (although not necessary) condition for obtaining certain external economies is the attainment of a large scale of output.

Empirical Studies of Plant Locations

Now that we have made a conceptual argument for the factors that determine plant-location decisions, it might be useful to see whether these arguments hold up under empirical testing. Traditionally, researchers have gone out and interviewed new plants, new branches, or new relocatees with a checklist of economic and personal reasons, and then recorded the responses in an array.* This type of research is very misleading, because all factors are working simultaneously, and it is difficult to identify the true importance of each factor. One way out of this methodological quicksand is to use a multiple regression equation to compute the relative importance of factors in explaining the location decision. This approach was used by M. I. Logan in a study of location decisions of Wisconsin plants between 1962 and 1967 [7]. Logan found that market potential and factors that have a depressive effect on the price of labor were significant determinants of locational choices. A confirmation of the learning-by-doing hypothesis was uncovered, since relocatees reacted more strongly to economic factors than branch or new plants, given that all desired to make an economically rational decision.

One of the more interesting issues not yet resolved by researchers is the impact of state and/or local tax breaks or subsidies on the location of firms. Supposedly, such incentives lower the price of governmental services, and, other things being equal, a firm would be attracted to a city or area offering such a plan. In a 1961 review article [8] of previous studies, John Due concluded that taxes were not driving firms out of states, except possibly in border areas. W. V. Williams [9] found that the interstate differences in the average costs of establishments for selected manufacturing industries were not significantly affected by the inclusion of state and local taxes. Taxes then, have not been proven to be a major factor in the location of firms.

What about negative taxes, or subsidies? In 1963 there were more than 3100 local development corporations, primarily in cities having less than 50,000 persons [10]. Do these and similar institutions affect the location decisions of plants? Questionnaire studies show subsidies to be of secondary importance, but we all know about the vagaries

---

* For example, see Eva Mueller and James N. Morgan [6].

of questionnaires. One of the few studies done on the impact of subsidies on costs showed that revenue bond financing could eliminate a 3–5 percent cost differential in labor-intensive sectors, while in capital-intensive industries as much as 56 percent of the cost differences across space could be eliminated [11]. Clearly, for firms with high capital–output ratios, certain financial schemes provided by local development groups can be significant in attracting plants.

Thus far we have primarily considered (factor) cost differences across space as the empirically relevant explanatory variables of the location decision. A more general and realistic approach would be to ask firms whether they moved to or began at a given site because *profits* were expected to be higher there. Melvin Greenhut, a pioneer in this field, did such a study for 752 plants that located in Florida during 1956 and 1957 [12]. Greenhut divided location factors into three types: (1) demand, as exemplified by access to existing or potential markets; (2) costs, such as wages, transfer costs, and so on; and (3) purely personal reasons, which were noneconomic. To check the respondents' answers, if the decision-maker said his reasons for locating in Florida were purely personal, then the answer was unacceptable unless it could be verified that he could earn higher profits in his next best non-Florida site. Demand responses were accepted only in light of the opportunity set of the plant; that is, only if costs in Florida were greater than or equal to the next best alternative area could one say the profit-maximizing plant was located in Florida because of access reasons. Cost data are easy to gather and interpret unambiguously; thus no checks were required. Using this framework, Greenhut found that the majority of firms located in Florida for market-access reasons. Moreover, the most significant factor behind choosing a specific city in Florida was access to markets.

The Location Decision of Persons

Let us turn briefly to a discussion of the location decisions of persons. Recall that we asserted earlier that a firm's motives are more important in determining the location of economic activity than a person's motives. It follows, then, that people will tend to be "pulled" to the centers or areas of rising economic activity.

Rising economic activity can be represented by increases in output per capita or wage rates, or by reductions in unemployment rates. People will be "pushed" away from areas having low levels of income per capita or wage rates, and high unemployment levels. When considering the movement of persons between two given cities, these "pull" and "push" factors diminish as the distance between the two cities increases, partly because increased distance often means that people have less information about job opportunities.

These ideas can be expressed in a simple gravity model,* in which the movement of a family from city A to city B is positively related to (1) the pull forces in B, and (2) the push forces in A, and negatively related to the distance from A to B. Ira Lowry [14] tested a model of this type for migration between 90 SMSA's during the 1955–1960 period. He found that the model did not explain the movement of people particularly well unless one standardized for a number of socioeconomic characteristics of the movers (such as age, income, and education) and other factors.

Obviously the gravity model is oversimplified. People migrate from city A to city B because they *expect* their net earnings over their remaining lifetime in B to exceed that in A. Thus we cannot merely look at today's labor-market signals (wages or unemployment rates) if we want to get behind the real determinants of migration. When one takes this longer-run view of the migration decision, factors such as moving costs become less important, because they are fixed costs. On the cost side, the psychic and economic costs of readjustment have been found to be far more important than distance or moving costs [15]. And when one considers his expected earnings over his remaining lifetime, he must discount this stream of earnings to its present value. That is, the value of these earnings must be put into present-day terms so one can compare the net earnings of moving to city B versus staying in city A. This expected net earnings approach to explaining migration has yielded encouraging results [16].

Summary

Firms and persons respond to price differences by relocating across space. Firms attempt to choose a place where expected profits will be maximized over time. Under highly simplified conditions, we found this could often be at the materials or market sites. Empirical studies on locational choices have not consistently shown any specific factors to be most significant, although economic factors in general are useful for explaining locational choices. People respond to income differentials across space, especially if they can get the proper information. Theories of movements of persons are strongly corroborated by empirical studies.

* See Walter Isard, *Methods of Regional Analysis* [13]. For a more detailed view of migration and gravity models see Chapters 2 and 11.

III. MODELS OF URBAN GROWTH

Now that we have a basic understanding of the determinants of location decisions, it is possible to consider some more general models of urban growth. In this section we shall cover four models that attempt to explain the growth process of urban areas. The first two models—income determination and urban base—are highly aggregative and emphasize the importance of exogenous changes on the urban economy. The next two models discussed—central place and input–output—are more disaggregative and attempt to highlight the interdependence of the urban economy with its hinterland or itself, respectively.

A Short-Run Model of Income Determination

The traditional approach to measuring income determination in the short run in any economy is that of the Keynesian multiplier. Most readers will recall from earlier studies that the multiplier is equal to the reciprocal of the quantity (1 minus the marginal propensity to consume). Thus, if people spend three-fourths of any given change in their income, the multiplier will have a value of $1/(1 - \frac{3}{4}) = 4$. In addition, you will also doubt recall that when any given change in spending is multiplied by the multiplier, one gets the final change in income. This type of model can be applied to any urban area, if we make our assumptions explicit and keep in mind that urban areas are more open* than the nation.

Assume we are viewing a city in the short run, which, for purposes of this model, means that wages, prices, technology, the level of resources, and the distribution of income are fixed. We know that net aggregate income or production in the city Y will equal the sum of consumption C, investment I, and government expenditures G, along with net exports X. We also know from basic economics that demand is determined by price, income, and tastes. Thus, for a given level of tastes, recalling that we have already assumed prices to be constant, demand will be determined by income alone. The demand or spending parts of the city are C, I, and imports M. Government spending and exports are determined exogenously. It may be easily shown [17] than under these conditions, the multiplier equals the reciprocal of

---

* An open economy has a large share of its total economic activity determined externally, whereas a closed economy has very little of its production determined exogenously. The U.S. has only about 10% of its GNP in exports; thus we have a closed economy.

[1 — (marginal propensity to consume + marginal propensity to invest — marginal propensity to import)]. We shall refer to the term inside the curved parentheses as the marginal propensity to spend locally. Thus, assuming excess capacity exists in the city, the final impact of any autonomous change in consumer or investment spending, or any exogenous change in government or export activity, can be measured by use of this "urban" multiplier.

The urban multiplier concept is illustrated in Figure 3.3. Local spending in the given city is measured on the vertical axis, while the income of the city is measured on the horizontal axis. The 45° line represents supply. If we begin at an income level of Y_1, and the local spending increases from S_1 to S_2, we can see that the increase in income (Y_2Y_1) is greater than the change in local spending. This is due to the multiplier.

It is important to remember that the urban multiplier derived from this income determination model has relevance only if resources are not being fully utilized. If no excess capacity existed, real income could not increase in the wake of an increase in spending. Only prices could increase, but we have held them constant. Another point to note about the urban multiplier is that because of leakages (M), it is probably much smaller than multipliers for the nation. The urban multiplier could be understated, however, since as Y increases, M rises, which causes the income of other areas to increase. To the extent that the city under study exports to these areas, we have underestimated the final change in Y.

The short-run income-determination model is useful because it highlights the factors that cause changes in the income of a city. However, it is probably an oversimplified model, because many of our assumptions do not square with the real world. Because of data difficulties, this model has not been empirically tested for a city. One of the major

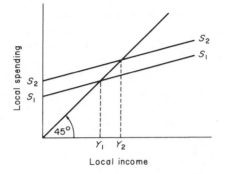

Figure 3.3 *The income multiplier.*

blocks has been the scarcity of export and import data. No secondary data on exports or imports of cities exist, and primary data are difficult and expensive to gather. The urban-base model, to which we shall turn next, does provide an indirect means of estimating exports, and from these indirect data one can obtain an estimate of the urban multiplier.

Urban Economic-Base Models

The rationale behind economic-base models is very simple when compared to the income-determination model just covered. The rationale is that the economy of a city may be divided into two sectors: (1) the exporting or basic sectors, which bring income into the city by selling goods and services outside the city, and (2) the service or non-basic sector, whose output is sold within the city. The basic sector is said to be the key to the growth process because it does not force the city to continue merely to take care of its own needs. Certainly mining towns are corroborations of the explanatory power of export-base theory. The strength of basic activity as the key to urban growth is certainly borne out in history. For example, our major eastern seaports (New York, Boston, Philadelphia) and some of our major inland urban centers (Chicago, Pittsburgh, St. Louis, Detroit, Cleveland) were primarily exporters during their developing stage.

To be sure, export-base theory is founded on a somewhat simple notion,* but until recently it received a great deal of attention from urban planners and economists. Base studies were done by *estimating* the amount of employment that was used to produce goods and services sold outside the city. Many ingenious methods have been developed to estimate "export employment." Two of these are location quotients and the minimum-requirement technique.

The location quotient for any sector is found by comparing that sector's share of the total employment in the city with the share of employment for that sector in a benchmark area—usually the U.S. Thus if the chemical sector in a given city has 20 percent of the city's total employment, while chemicals' share of total employment in the U.S. is only 10 percent, this method would allocate half of the chemicals employment in the city to export, because only half of the employment is needed to service local demands on the average.

Besides assuming similar production and consumption patterns between the city and the benchmark area, location quotients have a more

---

* See the exchange by Charles Tiebout and Douglas North in Friedman and Alonso [5, pp. 240–265] and Charles L. Leven [18].

basic shortcoming. They understate the real level of exports because they actually estimate *net* rather than gross exports.* Nevertheless, location quotients are easy to calculate, and they account for indirect exports. Indirect exports occur when firm A ships all of its output to firm B, and B sends, say, 80 percent of its output to export. In this case, we would argue that A indirectly exports 80 percent of its output.

A second approach to calculating the urban economic base is the minimum-requirements technique [20], which involves arraying the percentage of total employment by industry for a number of cities. Usually cities are grouped according to population size class. The percentages are arrayed from smallest to largest, and after any anomalous values at the lower end of the range are removed, the remaining lowest percentage is considered that share of employment required to service local needs. Any remaining employment is said to be basic. One of the major benefits of this technique is that one can sum the minimum requirements for all sectors, and then compare the totals by city size class. Ullman and Dacey found that the sum of the minimum requirements increases with city size, which corroborates the argument that cities become more self-contained as they get larger. Possibly, base theory is more applicable to smaller towns.

The criticisms leveled against location quotients are equally applicable to minimum requirements. In addition, one of the major problems of the minimum-requirements method is that there is no foolproof method for choosing the cutoff or minimum-requirements level of employment for any given sector. However, we should let the final decision on the efficacy of this technique rest on how well it explains or predicts. Greytak has found that the error between actual exports and exports calculated by the minimum-requirements technique is much smaller, in terms of percentages, than the error between real exports and those calculated by location quotients [21]. Thus we would probably choose the minimum-requirements approach over location quotients.

Uses and Extensions of Urban Base Studies

Once data on exports are obtained, either through a survey or the indirect techniques just discussed, it is then possible to approximate the urban multiplier discussed in the previous section by assuming that the marginal propensity to spend on local goods is equal to the ratio of nonbasic to total employment in the city. Then, if we can further accept all of the assumptions of the short-run model of income determi-

---

* Roger Leigh compared estimates of exports using location quotients with actual export data for Vancouver; the former were always less than the actual data [19].

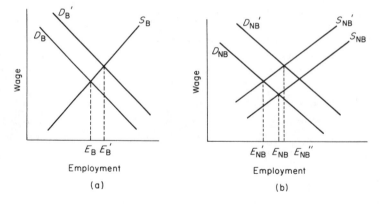

Figure 3.4 *Wage rollout hypothesis:* (a) *basic sector;* (b) *nonbasic sector.*

nation, the economic-base multiplier can be used to forecast the growth of the city attributable to increases in exports.

Many urban and regional planners have used the base multiplier for forecasting the future growth of cities and regions. Any change in spending by government, consumers, or investors—in addition to exports—has an impact on the local economy that can be measured by the base multiplier using the same procedure we discussed earlier with the income-determination model. Yet critics have argued that base models are too simple.

Wilbur Thompson [22] has attempted to answer the critics and extend the export-base logic by specifying more clearly the impact of changes in exports on the urban economy. Thompson asserts that not only are wages in cities determined by the industry mix and types of occupations, but also the relationship between exporting and local sectors is important. These relationships are illustrated in Figure 3.4. Assume that the city labor market is closed* and that workers are easily substitutable between the basic and nonbasic sectors. Beginning from a point of equilibrium, if there is an increase in the demand for basic output from D_B to D_B', wages in the basic sector will rise. The increase in wages will attract workers from the nonbasic sector in the amount of $E_B E_B'$. Thus the supply of labor in the nonbasic sector shifts from S_{NB} to S_{NB}', causing an increase in the wage rates of those left in the nonbasic sector. As wage rates rise in both sectors, total income in the city will increase; thus the demand for local services will rise from D_{NB} to D_{NB}'. To meet the increase in demand, new workers will have to be attracted into the labor force by an amount $E_{NB}' E_{NB}''$.

---

* Thus we find no changes in the labor force either from in- or out-migration or from changes in participation rates.

Thus the Thompson model shows that wages "roll out" from the basic to nonbasic sector. It illustrates the details behind the multiplier. Unfortunately, no empirical work has been completed that tests this rollout hypothesis. Moody and Puffer [23], however, have noted that the poor forecasts of earlier base studies may be due to the time delays in the reaction of nonbasic employees to changes in basic employment. Using data for San Diego, Moody and Puffer found that when a lagged adjustment process was accounted for between the basic and nonbasic sectors, the urban multiplier was much larger than usual. In addition, the reaction of the nonbasic sector was found to be quite long.

In retrospect, we have seen that the urban-base model emphasizes the exporting sector as the key to economic growth in a city. Many alternatives exist for indirectly measuring the base, but most empirical tests of these indirect measures show that the results are subject to a great degree of error. This does not mean that the ideas behind base models are necessarily wrong, even though we know cities do not have to export or die. Rather, in their present form, base models are too simple. More refined explanations of the base and its impact, such as Thompson's wage rollout argument, will have to be generated and tested.

Central-Place Models

The income-determination and economic-base models emphasize the demand side of the urban economy. However, in their simplest forms, they fail to explain (1) how the demand is generated, and (2) the spatial and economic interrelationships between cities and their rivals and hinterlands. The central-place model answers these criticisms.

Walter Christaller laid the foundations of central-place theory to explain the size, number, and distribution of towns across space [24]. The basic premise of the theory is that the primary function of a city is to provide goods and services to its surrounding hinterland. The word central comes from the relatively efficient location of the city with respect to its hinterland; that is, if the city is indeed centrally located, both consumers and producers will be better off.

The degree of centrality of any city is measured by its order. High-order cities offer high-order goods, have many establishments, large populations, and a vast hinterland. In general, higher-order goods are shopping goods the consumer would travel a sizable distance to purchase (mink coats, diamonds, alligator shoes, professional sports). Relatively few establishments provide higher-order goods; thus entry conditions are tight, and the trading areas are relatively large. Lower-order places, on the other hand, provide lower-order goods to small surrounding areas,

Lower-order goods are primarily necessities, such as groceries and gasoline, which require frequent purchase with minimal travel. In general, it is not difficult to enter the lower-order goods sectors. It is important to recognize that high-order places also offer low-order goods. Bostonians, for example, must eat and gas their cars.

The origin and size of central places are explained by two concepts: threshold and range [25]. The *threshold* is the minimum level of demand required to support the production of a good or service by (at least) a single establishment. That level of output associated with the tangency between demand and per-unit costs would be the threshold level of output. In general, the determinants of the threshold level of output are the unique factors of any central urban area: (1) a nearby, large market, allowing the realization of scale economies, and (2) agglomeration advantages.

Once production is originated for any good or service, how far does the market extend? This is determined by the *range* of a good, which delineates the zone around any central place from which persons would travel to obtain the good. Since the price of any good rises with distance, the range is limited by the relevant transportation costs. In addition, if consumers can get to a competing center more cheaply, the range will be shortened. Technically, the boundary of the range is that point in space where a person is indifferent in choosing between two central places that offer the same good. Clearly, any change that can reduce economic distance will increase the size of the range, other things being equal.

Because only a few cities produce very high-ordered goods and services, while many cities and towns produce lower-ordered goods and services, it should be intuitively clear that a hierarchical system of central places exists in space. And since high-order centers also produce lower-order goods, there is a "nesting" of lower-order trade areas within the higher-order trade areas. Economists have developed elaborate models to explain the hierarchical distribution of cities or central places across space, using location theory and simple mathematics. However, one needs only the threshold and range concepts to establish that a hierarchy exists.

How well does the central-place model as a theory of urban growth withstand scrutiny? Conceptually, central-place theory has many shortcomings. It has been argued that the model should include criteria to identify just what goods and services are central. This, however, is an empirical question for any system of cities. Another criticism of the central-place model is that as cities grow there are increased service demands within the city, whereas the central-place theory says that growth is determined by relationships with the hinterland. Although the criticism may be valid when one considers the emphasis of the model, it is clear that the origin and size of new service activities within cities are explained by the threshold and range concepts.

Two further criticisms of central-place models seem to have more validity. First, the theory is said to be more applicable to rural areas than to large urban complexes such as the northeast corridor of the U.S. Certainly the empirical studies for which central-place theory has been validated are more or less restricted to areas with broad spaces between towns. These areas include regions in the Midwest of the U.S. However, it may be that the test procedures used on large urban complexes are invalid. A second shortcoming of the central-place theory as an explanation of growth is that the growth of some cities depends on the export of manufactured goods to national and world markets. This is no doubt true, but as city size increases, the share of employment in local service sectors rises; thus the consequences of this criticism are probably of little empirical importance.

The value of the central-place theory in explaining urban growth lies in its emphasis of the spatial and economic aspects of interdependence. Location theory and price theory are integral parts of the threshold and range of any good, and thus of the hierarchical ordering of central places.

Input–Output Models*

Input–output models describe the interrelationships among industries and final users of products for any economy, be it a city, region, or nation. Industries are defined on a product basis, each industry being assumed to produce a single homogeneous product. Final users are the spending categories discussed earlier in connection with the income-determination model. The input–output model shows how the output of each industry or sector is *distributed* to all of its users, including other sectors and the final users. The latter is referred to as final demand, and includes sales to households (consumption), investment, governments, and exports. In addition to the distribution pattern of each sector in the economy, the input–output model simultaneously shows the *production* function or recipe of each sector. That is, the purchases of inputs from all other sectors and factors of production are carefully described by the input–output table.

A hypothetical input–output table for a city having two sectors is

* The basic source of this section is W. H. Miernyk, *The Elements of Input-Output Analysis* [26].

TABLE 3–1

Hypothetical Input–Output Table[a]

Sales to / Purchases from	(1) Sector 1	(2) Sector 2	(3) Final demand	(4) TGO
(1) Sector 1	$20	$40	$40	$100
(2) Sector 2	30	80	90	200
(3) Value added	50	80		
(4) TGO	100	200		300

[a] W. H. Miernyk, *Economics* (New York: Random House, 1971).

shown in Table 3-1. Although this table is obviously oversimplified, it still shows all of the rudiments of more detailed input–output models. The rows of an input–output model show the distribution pattern of a sector. Row (1) of the table shows that sector 1 sells $20 of total gross output (TGO) to itself, $40 to sector 2, and $40 to final demand. Sector 2 sells $30 of its output to sector 1, $80 to itself, and $90 to final demand. Row (3) is called value added, since it represents that portion of TGO that is not paid for intermediate goods from other sectors. Value added is essentially payments to the factors of production and imports. Since the major portion of value added is usually payments to households (wages and salaries), we shall refer to row (3) as services provided by households.

If we look down columns (1) and (2) of Table 3-1, we can see the production recipe of our two sectors. Sector 1 buys $20 from itself, $30 from sector 2, and $50 from households to produce its $100 of TGO. Looking down column (2), we see that sector 2 purchases $40 from sector 1, $80 from itself, and $80 of household services to produce its $200 output level.

In order to use our hypothetical input–output model for more than descriptive purposes, we shall make a number of simplifying assumptions:

(1) the inputs of each sector are a unique function of that sector's output only;
(2) the production recipes (per dollar of output) for each sector are fixed;
(3) what is produced in a given year is consumed, that is, no inventories are carried over;
(4) the economy is in equilibrium in all markets.

The first step in using an input–output model for analytical purposes is to obtain a table of direct or technical coefficients. These coefficients show the purchases of inputs per dollar of output for each sector; thus they are found by dividing the TGO for each sector into its purchases. Table 3–2 shows the direct coefficients for sectors 1 and 2. Given our assumptions, sector 1 must buy 20¢ worth of inputs from itself and 30¢ worth of inputs from sector 2 to produce a dollar's worth of output. The remainder of the dollar's worth of inputs (50¢) comes from households, but in the direct-coefficients table we are concerned only with purchases from other industries.

The table of direct coefficients is useful because it tells us the *direct* effects of any change in dollar sales to final demand. That is, if sector 1 sold $100 more to final demand, the direct effect on its own production (in addition to the $100) is an increase of $20, and sector 2's output directly increases by $30. However, the unique aspect of input–output analysis is that it can also show the *indirect* effects of any given change in sales to final demand. And in cities where industries are integrated (steel in Pittsburgh, autos in Detroit, printing and publishing in New York are examples), these indirect impacts are often more significant than the direct effects on the city's economy.

The direct coefficients are the basis of deriving the indirect effects of a given change of one dollar's sales to final demand. In our example of direct effects where sector 1's sales to final demand increased by $100, we noted that sector 2's output increased by $30. To produce an additional $30 of output, however, sector 2 must buy $6 of inputs from sector 1, and $12 from itself. This is the first round of the indirect effects of the $100 increase in sector 1's sales to final demand on sector 2. Of course there are indirect effects on sector 1 also, originating not only in sector 2 but also from within. And the indirect effects go through many rounds. If we continue this process of computing the indirect effects until they become very small numbers (tend toward zero), we obtain what is called the table of direct and indirect requirements per dollar of delivery to final demand. This table is shown in Table 3-3.

TABLE 3–2

Direct Coefficients per Dollar of Output

	(1) Sector 1	(2) Sector 2
(1) Sector 1	0.2	0.2
(2) Sector 2	0.3	0.4
(3) Value added	0.5	0.4

TABLE 3–3

Direct and Indirect Requirements per Dollar of Delivery to Final Demand

	Sector 1	Sector 2
Sector 1	1.43	0.48
Sector 2	0.71	1.90

The direct and indirect requirements table shows the effect of economic interdependence of any economy on overall economic activity levels. To see the quantitative magnitude of the effect of interdependence among industries, one can compare the sizes of the entries in Table 3-2 and Table 3-3. First note that the intraindustry entries in 3–3 exceed unity. This is because the direct and indirect requirements table is based on an additional *dollar's* sales to final demand; thus the direct impact on sector 1 of another dollar's sales of 1's output to final demand is the one dollar (plus 20¢ of intraindustry purchases). So besides the given dollar change in spending that starts the ball rolling, the direct effect on sector 1 is 20¢. Since the entry in row (1) and column (1) of Table 3-3 is 1.43, the indirect effect must be 0.23, which is slightly larger than the simple (intraindustry) direct effect (0.20). If we compare the direct and indirect effects on sector 2 of another dollar's worth of 1's output to final demand (0.71 versus 0.30), again we see that the indirect effects are significant.

Given that cities grow because of agglomeration economies and the locational advantages of horizontally integrated industries, the input–output model is a very useful tool for explaining and predicting this growth process.

Uses of Input–Output Models

To use the input–output model for explaining or predicting urban growth, one needs a table of direct and indirect requirements and final demand. Then for any assumed change in final-demand spending, we could determine the impact on each sector in the urban economy just as we explained with our hypothetical example. To simplify the procedure, one may merely sum the appropriate column of the direct and indirect requirements table, which gives the *total* direct and indirect effects of a dollar's delivery to final demand. This sum is often referred to as an impact multiplier. If our hypothetical model in Tables 3-1 through 3-3 were for the Greater Boston area, and sector 1 represented shipbuilding, a decrease of $100 million in government contracts to the Boston naval shipyards would decrease overall economic activity in Greater Boston by $100 million $\times$ 2.14 = $214 million. The total impact on the local economy is found by multiplying the sum of column (1) by the change in spending. Impact studies are the most popular use of input–output models, at least for local areas.

The input–output model has also been a popular forecasting tool. If we want to know the output level of each industry in 1985, we merely need an estimated level of final demand spending in 1985 and a table of direct and indirect requirements that describe the structure of our economy in 1985. The advantage of using an input–output model for forecasting the output of any given sector in the city or the TGO for all sectors is that one obtains a consistent forecast; all interindustry impacts are included in the forecast.

One of the major constraints facing those interested in using an in-put–output model for any city or region is that no secondary data exist for developing the table of direct coefficients. Thus one usually has to start from scratch, which is a long and costly procedure. Moreover, the best evidence we have to date is that one cannot approximate the direct coefficients of a given city by using those of another city or of the nation, because the industrial structures of cities and the nation vary so much. Whether or not the construction of an input–output model for any city is worth the cost is an empirical question. Nevertheless, the model has a number of strong points, the major one being that it depicts in explicit detail the direct and indirect effects of any given change in spending on the urban economy. Thus it brings out the effects of interdependence. Changes in spending are not restricted to exports, as the base model argues. Manufacturing is not left out, as in the cen-tral-place model. And a detailed account of the behind-the-scenes action is given, which is not the case when the simple urban multiplier is calculated from the short-run model of income determination.

Although forecasting and impact studies have been the traditional use of input–output models to date, there are many ways an input–output model can be used to explain and predict urban growth. For example, if one had a table of direct coefficients for a given city representing the interindustry relations for, say, 1950, 1960, and 1970, it would be possible to gather a great deal of interesting and useful information. First, one could determine not only what industries are growing or de-clining but how the sectoral growth or decline has affected the rest of the urban economy. Second, one could see how direct or roundabout the city's production patterns are by considering how many interindustry transactions it takes to meet a dollar's expenditure of final demand over time.* As specialization is extended, we would expect a more roundabout production pattern to result. A third use of the model would be to measure the degree of self-containment of a city over time, by computing the share of total output accounted for by imports. As a city becomes more self-contained, import substitution will occur. Finally, if we had input–output models for a number of cities, we could compare the degree of interdependence in each city's economy by comparing the value of total intermediate inputs per dollar of output for each sector.† As city size increased, we would expect a higher degree of self-containment and interdependence.

Can the input–output approach account for the trading (importing and exporting) relationships between cities and their hinterlands (or other cities)? It certainly can, although again the computational and data problems are somewhat formidable. As early as 1955 economists began to build interregional input–output models to show the trading relationships among regions in the U.S. Metropolitan areas no doubt provide a relatively large share of the intermediate goods markets of most sectors, and certainly of the markets for the final goods and services. To date no intermetro or intercity models have been constructed in which the intermediate sales are linked, although Karen Polenske‡ has recently completed an interregional model of the U.S. that divides the national economy into 44 regions. There have been a number of models of small urban areas that are tied to their surrounding areas. For example, W. H. Miernyk and co-workers [30] have developed a model for Boulder, Colorado in 1963 that explicitly shows the trading relationships between Boulder and Denver, Boulder and the rest of Colorado, and Boulder with the rest of the nation. A similar study has been done for Bucks County, Pennsylvania, a suburban area of Philadelphia [31]. In the Bucks County study, the manufacturing sectors are ranked according to their ties with the Philadelphia SMSA, which gives an interesting view of spatial interdependence.

We should not close our discussion of input–output models without pointing out some of their major shortcomings. When the model is used for an impact study or projecting any variable(s) over time, the question of the stability of the direct coefficients always arises. Whether or not the direct coefficients are stable over time in an urban area is an empiri-

---

* This has been done for the U.S. by Anne Carter [27].

† Charles Richter uses a much simpler approach to attain the same end for 57 SMSA's. He found that linkages were significant attractions for luring industry into SMSA's [28].

‡ A brief description of Polenske's study is found in Economic Development Administration [29].

cal question; however, it should be intuitively clear that as city size declines and the structure of the economy becomes less balanced, the coefficients will become less stable.* A more fundamental criticism of the input–output model is its assumption of no substitutability among inputs. In microeconomic terms, input–output models assume a right-angle isoquant among inputs. Although this is admittedly a very simple production function, it is again an empirical question as to whether this assumption squares with reality. Charles Tiebout considered these and other criticisms, and the reader is referred to his classic article, "Regional and interregional input–output models: an appraisal" [32], for further and more detailed criticisms.

IV. THE FRONTIERS OF URBAN GROWTH†

Thus far we have covered some of the more traditional models and principles of location and urban growth. However, there are many questions about growth that we have failed to ask or answer. For example, we have implicitly argued thus far that increases in real output per person are a reasonable measure of growth, yet it is quite possible that many city dwellers are not sharing in this growth. How can we measure the distributional impacts of urban growth? Even if we could, through some magic wave of the wand, get everyone sharing in the growth process, the question of how long cities can continue to grow will arise. Are there any characteristics of urban areas that may signal a decline in the future? Finally, many persons seem to think that some cities have grown too much, and are thus net costs rather than benefits. New York is the usual example given. This leads to a third question: When are cities too big; or more specifically, is there an optimum size for a city? Let us consider each of these three questions.

Distributional Impacts of Urban Growth

Almost every urban or regional growth model developed has been concerned with the factors that determine the "size of the pie," or increases in income. Not until the past few decades have economists begun to study seriously the determinants of how the pie is distributed empiri-

---

* With smaller areas, trade-pattern changes—the movement of new firms into or old firms out of the area—are especially damaging to the stability of the direct coefficients.

† This section presents some advanced material. Though it can be skipped without loss of continuity, the student is urged to read it at least once.

cally. The importance of this issue to contemporary urban poverty and other problems should be self-evident. Thus we should not conclude any study of income determination per se in urban areas without considering how changes in the distribution of income are measured and how they might affect the overall growth of income.

In general, the distribution of income is determined by how things are produced and the tastes of consumers. As models of production vary, the use of factors will also vary, thus changing the incomes of factors. Even if everyone had the same productivity as a worker—that is, if we were all robots—there would still be differences in the incomes of robots. Why? Because as tastes change, the demand for certain products increases, while demand for other products must decrease in proportion if income is fixed and the same for all robots. Now since the demand for labor is derived from the demand for products, an increase in income will occur for those working in the sector having the increased demand.*

Arthur Silvers [33] has laid the groundwork for measuring impacts on the distribution of income in local areas, the basic emphasis being on consumer patterns rather than production techniques. As net urban income grows, the share of consumption will also increase proportionally. Since consumption is such a large share of income, it would be a huge step in explaining changes in the local income distribution if one could explain the effect of local consumption expenditures on local income groups.

We can begin our analysis of the affect of local consumption patterns on the distribution of local income with a simple assumption similar to the one we made with the input–output model. We assume that any given income group or class will allocate its consumption expenditures over all other income groups in a given fashion. That is, the direct coefficients of local consumption—the income received by income group 1 from local consumer expenditures by income group 2—are a unique function of the level of income of group 2. Our table of direct coefficients then would tell us the probability that a dollar spent locally by group 2 would be earned by group 1.

Computationally, the direct coefficients of local consumption would be derived from information on consumer patterns, import patterns, and earnings patterns in each local goods and services producing sector for each income group. We can assume that these patterns are given and fixed. Once the table of direct coefficients of local consumption is obtained, we can proceed to derive the direct and indirect effects as we did with the input–output model. Knowing the direct and indirect

---

* Note that we have assumed that the supply of labor is not perfectly elastic. If it were, changes in demand would not affect the price of labor.

changes in the income recieved by group 1 from a given dollars change in the income in group 2, we are now ready to determine the distributional impact of any given exogenous change in spending.

Silvers, for example, used this approach to compute the impact of the Economic Development Administration's Business Loan Program on the distribution of income in the U.S. between 1962 and 1967. He divided income earners into three groups—low, middle, and high.* Employees in 41 affected firms earned $2.53 million more than they would have without the program. This is the direct impact of the program, and is the type of information often cited to justify programs. But how was this effect distributed? Low-income workers received 31 percent, middle-income workers got 57 percent, and the remainder (12 percent) went to high-income workers.

Now once this income was received, spending began; thus further changes in the distribution of income occurred through the *indirect* effects. The direct and indirect increase in income for all counties with firms receiving loans was $4.14 million, which was distributed to low-, middle-, and high-income classes in amounts of $1.0, 2.31, and 0.8 million, respectively. Thus, when the *total* spending process is accounted for, the share of the low-income group falls to 21 percent, while those having high incomes receive almost 20 percent, a substantial increase from the first round (direct effect). In short, the loan program helped high-income earners, in a final dollar sense, just about as much as low-income workers. To the extent that antipoverty programs are supposed to redistribute income from high- to low-income earners, this loan program has failed.

In summary, we have considered a model of the structure of income circulation within a community. Given the consumption, import, and earnings patterns in a city, we found that it was possible to derive the direct and indirect impacts of any given exogenous change in spending on the distribution of income within that city. With this model, one can determine what share of any "increase in the pie" is being received by any income class.

Is Urban Growth Immutable?

Although many of the larger cities in the U.S. have experienced population declines, overall metropolitan areas continue to grow. This growth occurs not only in the form of increases in population levels, but also as increases in incomes. Wilbur Thompson has argued that once a metropolitan area reaches a minimum critical size, which he argues may be

---

* Defined as follows: low—under $4000; middle—$4000–9999; high—$10,000 and over.

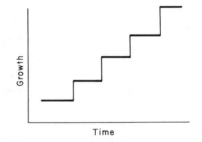

Figure 3.5   *The urban size ratchet.*

250,000 persons, growth will probably be ensured [22, pp. 21–24]. He argues that absolute decline is out of the question, and real-world data tend to bear out this argument. Thompson's thesis may be termed "the urban size ratchet," for as shown in Figure 3.5, the rate of growth never falls below zero, and the trend is a ratchetlike, upward function. Thompson argues that the ratchet holds because of a number of simultaneously operating factors:

(1) industrial diversifications exists;
(2) power politics gives larger cities more strength at state and national levels than smaller cities;
(3) large amounts of social overhead capital (streets, sewers, schools, and so on) make public service costs cheap enough to keep basic firms (and thus people) in the area;
(4) as cities grow larger, a greater share of (human) resources is used in the production of services, and there is a built-in demand for services due to the growth of the population or income;
(5) larger cities have a greater chance of spawning new industries, on the basis of size alone.

Although the ratchet hypothesis has not been tested empirically, it seems to be a fairly reasonable explanation of why big cities continue to grow. However, some economists might disagree with at least the fourth reason stated by Thompson. As the service sector grows in an urban economy, the sources of productivity growth decline.* William Baumol [34] has shown that under given assumptions, a city having two sectors, where one sector provides services and does not enjoy steady increases in productivity, whereas the other sector shows continuous increases in productivity, may become stagnant or even decline in real growth terms. By real growth terms, we mean the quantity of goods and services. Let us take a close look at this Baumol model.

---

* Recall from the preceding chapter that productivity growth in service sectors lags badly behind manufacturing productivity growth.

In the two-sector city, we can simplify our analysis by (1) ignoring all outlays other than labor costs, (2) assuming that wages rise and fall together in the two sectors, and (3) assuming that money wages increase as fast as productivity does in the progressive sector. Now if sector 1 is the service sector, and sector 2 is the progressive sector, where productivity grows cumulatively at a constant rate r, then output during any time period t is given by the following production functions:

$$Y_{1t} = aL_{1t} \tag{3-1}$$

$$Y_{2t} = bL_{2t}e^{rt} \tag{3-2}$$

where L is labor, a and b are constants, and e^{rt} denotes an exponential function with a natural log base (e) growing over time t at rate r. Equation (3–1) says that the output of sector 2 is directly related to the amount of labor used in sector 1. Equation (3–2) says that 2's output depends upon the amount of labor used in 2 *and* the productivity growth of 2's labor. Since labor productivity grows cumulatively in sector 2, it could keep the same *level* of labor and continue to grow. Sector 1, on the other hand, must increase its level of labor input in order to grow.

Recalling assumptions (2) and (3), we know that

$$W_t = We^{rt} \tag{3-3}$$

where W is a constant wage rate. That is, Equation (3-3) merely says that wages in the city will be set according to the productivity growth in sector 2.

Two properties of this model can yield some interesting information on the long-run growth prospects of cities that more or less fit our assumptions. First, costs per unit of output C will rise indefinitely in sector 1, while in sector 2 they will remain constant. Costs per unit of output of course are the wage rates times the amount of labor used in each sector. To show the path of per-unit costs over time for each sector, we merely substitute our given assumptions into C and algebraically cancel terms where possible:

$$C_1 = \frac{W_t L_{1t}}{Y_{1t}} = \frac{We^{rt}L_{1t}}{aL_{1t}} = \frac{We^{rt}}{a} \tag{3-4}$$

$$C_2 = \frac{W_t L_{2t}}{Y_{2t}} = \frac{We^{rt}L_{2t}}{bL_{2t}e^{rt}} = \frac{W}{b} \tag{3-5}$$

Clearly the numerator of Equation (3-4) (We^{rt}) tends to become very large over time, because we have a constant product (We) growing at an exponential rate (rt). Thus C_1 will rise indefinitely. On the other hand, C_2 remains constant over time, since W and b are constants. Thus it follows that relative costs (C_1/C_2) will increase without limit over time.

Going one step further, if we assume that both sectors are in perfectly competitive markets so that prices are proportional to costs, and that the price elasticity of demand is equal to unity, then the relative outlays on the two products would remain constant:

$$\frac{C_1 Y_1}{C_2 Y_2} = \frac{W e^{rt} L_{1t}}{W e^{rt} L_{2t}} = \frac{L_1}{L_2} = \text{constant } (A) \qquad (3\text{-}6)$$

Now the ratio of Y_1 to Y_2 shows that the output of sector 1 remains constant, while Y_2 rises indefinitely!

$$\frac{Y_1}{Y_2} = \frac{a L_{1t}}{b L_{2t} e^{rt}} = \frac{aA}{be^{rt}} \qquad (3\text{-}7)$$

What are the implications of Equations (3-4) and (3-7)? Clearly, if the real costs of producing services such as education, police and fire protection, and other services continue to rise, more and more of our resources will have to be transferred into these relatively nonproductive sectors. As this transferral process continues, the sources of growth in the urban area will decrease. Urban decay could set in. It may be argued, however, that as resources are transferred into service production and costs (prices) continue to rise, people may opt for fewer services. Could this happen in a large city? Is specialization such that people cannot get along without many services? I think the answers to these two questions are "not likely" and "yes," respectively. For urban areas to be assured of the growth patterns inherent in the Thompson size-ratchet hypothesis, resources will have to be allocated into the service sector at a rate faster than costs increase in this sector.

Obviously, this two-sector model has a number of simplifying parts that do not square with reality; nevertheless, it points up a possible future direction for some cities.

Is There an Optimum-Sized City?

The existence of a (theoretically) optimum-sized city has yet to be established in economic analysis. Many economists have said a lot about optimum-sized cities, but only in very specialized ways. It is hoped by most that some of our cities have already passed the optimum size, for if they have not, the optimum-sized city may be impossible to reach under existing technology and institutional constraints.* Clearly, demand

---

* William Alonso has shown that our largest cities may not have reached excessive sizes yet, at least from the standpoint of economic growth [36].

and comparative advantage act as limits on the size of cities, with the latter beginning to slow the growth of large cities in the U.S. over the last few decades. Many argue that our big cities are riddled by pollution, congestion, and public finance problems that are almost unsolvable. Do increases in population exacerbate these problems? Do these problems distort the size of the city that is, do they make cities larger or smaller than they would be without the problems?

Consider the problem of pollution [35]. Damages per resident will increase as population rises; therefore, the marginal damage caused by an additional person exceeds the average damage per person. Clearly residents themselves bear the damage of pollution, and they will continue to locate in the city as long as their net benefit of so doing exceeds the average pollution damage. Thus the additional person(s) will understate his true damages, and the urban area will obtain an excessive number of persons. The same principle applies to highways and congestion. People enter a highway based on average costs rather than marginal costs, and after costs begin to rise with each additional traveler, marginal costs exceed average costs. Those already on the road are forced to consume the difference between average and marginal costs, in the form of delays.

The case of the public sector distorting city size could be pursued in a number of ways, but here we shall consider the impact of jurisdictional fragmentation on metropolitan area size. Suburbanites use many public services in cities, but those living in cities use relatively few public services in the suburbs. For a number of reasons, which will be explained later in this book, cities are unable to make suburbanites pay for most of these services. To produce a given level of services, say, comparable to that in the suburbs, the tax rate on city residents is inflated because suburbanites are not paying their fair share. Clearly, it is advantageous to locate in suburbs; thus the structure of our local institutions may distort the distribution of population in the metropolitan area by providing tax havens for high-income persons. Possibly these suburbanites would opt to move to other cities if they were charged the full tab for public services.

The problems of pollution, congestion, and interjurisdictional spillovers could be classified as possible causes, or better yet, symptoms of excessive urban size. But they do not get at the heart of the matter; that is, how do we determine the optimal size of a city? A more general explanation might be that the optimal city size is reached when the additional social benefits of adding another person to the city are exactly equal to the additional social costs; that is, when the marginal social utility of adding another person is zero. Although this rule is useful at the conceptual level, empirically it would be very difficult to determine the social costs and benefits of adding more persons to a city.

Charles Leven [37] has set out on the difficult task of explaining the optimal size of cities. Leven argues that a prerequisite for identifying the optimal size is that we must develop a theory of the *urban process*, just as we have theories of the household or family. Leven identifies the urban process as one of a permanent clustering of people. Besides city size per se, it is argued that the following must be included as jointly dependent variables in the theory: (1) the spatial organization or urban places, (2) the frequency distribution of urban places by size, and (3) the spatial distribution of urban places in a larger (national) system of urban places. The spatial organization clearly characterizes a city (compare Los Angeles to New York), while (2) and (3) point up the need to consider all cities simultaneously. It is impossible to talk about the size of a city by itself, since its size in part is based on comparative advantage. Central-place theory is of little help here, it may be noted, since it considers relative rather than absolute city size distributions.

Along with the actual size of an urban place, the above three jointly dependent variables may be thought of as the *outcomes* of the urban process, according to Leven. The *mechanism* of the urban process involves the provision of economic opportunities so that people will be attracted to the area and, most important, providing the necessary facilities to accommodate the increased population. The latter point is at the base of the pollution, congestion, and interjurisdictional problems discussed earlier. Besides facilities, institutions in the urban process must be identified and their relationships to outcomes measured, if we are ever going to make explicit and efficient choices on urban size.

The Leven model of the urban process is somewhat vague, but the seeds of the basis for a general urban theory are there. Based on two simple assumptions—first that people can express their preferences about city size independent of the city in which they live, and second that we can control city size—Leven has generated a broad conceptual framework for determining whether there exists an optimal size for a city.

V. SUMMARY

In this chapter we have considered the rudiments of location theory, and found that (1) firms have a tendency to locate at the materials or market sites, and (2) central locations are especially suitable for firms serving the whole city. These factors, of course, help to explain concentration. Under empirical tests, these basic principles hold their own. Like firms, people locate where they get the greatest return, especially if they can get information.

Two models that cover simple multiplier effects on the urban economy were considered. The short-run income-determination model highlights the effects of an exogenous change in spending. Base models were discussed in detail. The theory behind the base approach is certainly lacking. In addition, secondary measures of the base are biased. Nevertheless, extensions of the base concept via the use of wage rollout models or even input–output models could be quite useful for explaining the growth process of urban areas.

The central-place and input–output models emphasize spatial and economic interdependence. The central-place model describes trading relationships between cities and their hinterlands. In general, central-place models have predicted the development of small towns quite well, but have failed when large megapolises have been considered. Input–output models emphasize the interdependence *within* an urban area, and if one extends the input–output model to include trading relationships with its contiguous areas, it can do all the central-place model does plus more. Unfortunately, input–output models are so expensive to build that they are done in the real world only on an ad hoc basis, which limits their usefulness to planners.

On the frontiers of urban growth analysis, we saw it was possible to determine the distributional impact of any given change in spending. This information is very important for policy decisions. We also found that continued urban growth may be limited if our service sectors do not increase their efficiency. Finally, we saw that an optimal city size is difficult to define, and that any model used to identify the optimum-sized city would have to explain the structure, functions, and interrelationships of all cities simultaneously.

SUGGESTED READINGS

Alonso, William. "Location Theory." *Regional Development and Planning: A Reader*, edited by John Friedman and William Alonso. Cambridge, Massachusetts: MIT Press, 1964.

Christaller, Walter. *Central Places in Southern Germany*, translation by C. W. Baskin. Englewood Cliffs, New Jersey: Prentice Hall, 1966.

Hoover, Edgar. *The Location of Economic Activity*. New York: McGraw-Hill, 1948.

Hoover, Edgar. *An Introduction to Regional Economics*. New York: Knopf, 1971.

Isard, Walter. *Methods of Regional Analysis*. Cambridge, Massachusetts: MIT Press, 1960.

Losch, August. *The Economics of Location.* New Haven, Connecticut: Yale Univ.
  Press, 1954.
Miernyk, W. H. *The Elements of Input Output Analysis.* New York: Random
  House, 1965.
Mills, Edwin. *Urban Economics.* Glenville, Illinois: Scott Foresman, 1972.
Nourse, Hugh. *Regional Economics.* New York: McGraw-Hill, 1968.
Pfouts, Ralph. *The Techniques of Urban Economic Analysis.* San Francisco, Cali-
  fornia: Chandler, 1960.
Thompson, Wilbur. *A Preface to Urban Economics.* Baltimore Maryland: Johns
  Hopkins Press (for Resources for the Future, Inc.), 1965.
Tiebout, Charles. "The Community Economic Base Study." Committee for Economic
  Development Paper #16, December 1962.

REFERENCES

1. August Losch, *The Economics of Location* (New Haven, Connecticut: Yale
   Univ. Press, 1954).
2. Edwin S. Mills, *Urban Economics,* Chapter 1 (Glenview, Illinois: Scott Foresman, 1972).
3. Edwin S. Mills, "An Aggregate Model of Resource Allocation in a Metropolitan
   Area," *American Economic Review, Papers, and Proceedings* 57, No. 2 (1967):
   197–210.
4. Edgar M. Hoover, *The Location of Economic Activity,* Chapters 1–3, 5 (New
   York: McGraw-Hill, 1948).
5. William Alonso, "Location Theory," in *Regional Development and Planning:
   A Reader,* John Friedman and William Alonso, eds., pp. 79–81 (Cambridge,
   Massachusetts: MIT Press, 1964).
6. Eva Mueller and James N. Morgan, "Location Decisions of Manufacturers,"
   American Economic Review, Papers, and Proceedings (1962): 204–217.
7. M. I. Logan, "Locational Decisions in Industrial Plants in Wisconsin," *Land
   Economics* 46, No. 3 (1970): 325–328.
8. J. F. Due, "Studies of State-Local Tax Influences on Location of Industry,"
   National Tax Journal 14 (1961): 163–173.
9. W. V. Williams, "A Measure of the Impact of State and Local Taxes on
   Industry Location," *Journal of Regional Science* 7, No. 1 (1967): 49–49.
10. Benjamin Bridges, Jr., "State and Local Inducements for Industry," *National
    Tax Journal* 18 (1965): 1–14, 175–192.
11. William J. Stober and Laurence H. Falk, "The Effect of Financial Inducements
    on the Location of Firms," *Southern Economic Journal* 36, No. 1 (1969):
    25–35.
12. Melvin Greenhut, "An Empirical Model and a Survey: New Plant Locations
    in Florida," *Review of Economics and Statistics* 41 (1959): 433–438.
13. Walter Isard, *Methods of Regional Analysis* (Cambridge, Massachusetts: MIT
    Press, 1960).
14. Ira Lowry, *Migration and Metropolitan Growth: Two Analytical Models* (San
    Francisco, California: Chandler, 1966).
15. Michael Greenwood, "An Analysis of the Determinants of Geographical Labor
    Mobility in the U.S.," *Review of Economics and Statistics* 51, No. 2 (1969):
    189–194.

16. Samuel Bowles, "Migration as Investment: Empirical Tests of the Human Investment Approach to Geographic Mobility," *Review of Economics and Statistics* 52, No. 4 (1970): 356–362.
17. Hugh Nourse, *Regional Economics,* pp. 160–161 (New York: McGraw-Hill, 1968).
18. Charles L. Leven, "Regional and Interregional Accounts in Perspective," *Papers, Regional Science Association* 13 (1964): 140–144.
19. Roger Leigh, "The Use of Location Quotients in Urban Economic Base Studies," *Land Economics* 46, No. 2 (1970): 202–205.
20. Edward L. Ullman and Michael F. Dacey, "The Minimum Requirements Approach to the Urban Economic Base," *Papers, Regional Science Association* 6 (1960): 175–194.
21. David Greytak, "A Statistical Analysis of Regional Export Estimating Techniques," *Journal of Regional Science* 9, No. 3 (1969): 387–395.
22. Wilbur Thompson, *A Preface to Urban Economics,* pp. 70–73 (Baltimore, Maryland: Johns Hopkins Press (for Resources for the Future, Inc.), 1965.
23. Harold Moody and Frank, Puffer, "The Empirical Verification of the Urban Base Multiplier: Traditional and Adjustment Process Models," *Land Economics* 46, No. 1 (1970): 91–98.
24. Walter Christaller, *Central Places in Southern Germany, 1933,* translated by C. W. Baskin (Englewood Cliffs, New Jersey: Prentice-Hall, 1966).
25. Brian Berry and William Garrison, "Recent Developments of Central Place Theory," *Papers, Regional Science Association* 4 (1958): 107–120.
26. W. H. Miernyk, *The Elements of Input-Output Analysis* (New York: Random House, 1965).
27. Anne Carter, "Changes in the Structure of the American Economy, 1947 to 1958 and 1962," *Review of Economics and Statistics* 49 (1967): 209–224.
28. Charles Richter, "The Impact of Industrial Linkages on Geographic Association," *Journal of Regional Science* 9, No. 1 (1969): 19–28.
29. K. Polenske, *Research Review* (1971): 1–7.
30. W. H. Miernyk *et al., Impact of the Space Program on a Local Economy: An Input-Output Analysis* (Morgantown, West Virginia: West Virginia Univ. Library, 1967).
31. M. Dolenc, "The Bucks County Interregional Input-Output Study," *Papers, Regional Science Association* 20 (1968): 43–53.
32. Charles Tiebout, *Southern Economic Journal* 24 (1957): 140–147.
33. Arthur Silvers, "The Structure of Community Income Circulation in an Incidence Multiplier for Development Planning," *Journal of Regional Science* 10, No. 2 (1970): 175–189.
34. William Baumol, "The Macroeconomics of Unbalanced Growth: The Anatomy of Urban Crisis," *American Economic Review* 57 (1967): 414–426.
35. Edwin Mills and David de Ferranti, "Market Choices and Optimum City Size," *American Economic Review, Papers, and Proceedings* 61, No. 2 (1971): 340–345.
36. William Alonso, "The Economics of Urban Size," *Papers, Regional Science Association* 26 (1971): 67–83.
37. Charles Leven, "Determinants of the Size and Spatial Form of Urban Areas," *Papers, Regional Science Association* 22 (1969): 7–28.

4

THE ECONOMICS OF INTRAURBAN LOCATION DECISIONS

I. INTRODUCTION

In this chapter we shall consider the location decision of firms or establishments within urban and metropolitan areas. The importance of this decision should be self-evident, for where firms locate will in large part determine future land use, residential location, and transportation decisions. The question we shall try to answer is: Once firms have chosen to locate in a given urban area, *where* in that urban area will they locate? If firms are competitors, they may repel each other; on the other hand, if firms are complementary, they may desire to concentrate. Principles of concentration and dispersion are covered in this chapter. In addition, the basic intraurban-location determinants often cited in the literature are discussed and scrutinized empirically. Upon finding these determinants to be somewhat partial, more general approaches are covered through the consideration of location models. Finally, we close the chapter with a discussion of some principles of public-facility location, a heretofore overlooked area in the field of intraurban location, but certainly a question of great importance in contemporary urban America.

Up to this point we have discussed some very general locational factors, primarily focusing on interurban location decisions. Now that our focus has changed to intraurban decisions, do these previously cited factors (that is, transportation costs, factor costs, and market location) remain valid [1]? Some do, but there are many new factors to consider. Access to inputs and markets is still important, and can be shown to be consistent with minimizing transfer costs if all other costs are given. Access-oriented sectors within cities are retail trade and similar sectors that have to be near customers. Financial districts are often located in the center of a city so that the large labor pools will be able to minimize their transport costs. Other factors that remain significant when choosing a site within (versus among) urban areas are the availability of agglomeration economies, the cost of space, and the quality of resources.

On the other hand, once a city is chosen for the location, certain "new" factors take on significance. First, the labor supply response is much greater to small variations in wage rates in a given area, whereas across urban areas labor usually must migrate to take advantage of higher wage rates. This idea can be extended to other factors of production, especially to intermediate goods. That is, if a city produces good i used by sector j in that city, the supply of i will be more price elastic than if i were produced in some far-off city.* Second, decisions external to firms are potentially significant within a given area, while across cities these externalities would probably cancel out. For example, if I locate a boutique next to a heavily traveled shopping area, but all the other shops move to the suburbs, I am in trouble. Environmental and business surroundings matter within the urban area. Zoning is often used to stabilize and homogenize areas, but it does not always work. Third, the spatial structure of the transportation system becomes very important for firm-location decisions within cities. This is important not only for the shipment of products—for example, if I produce large transformers, I want to locate near a rail line—but also for the collection of inputs. People must have a relatively efficient means of getting to work.

In general, we might argue that if a firm has competitors and its

---

* Elasticity may also depend on market organization [2].

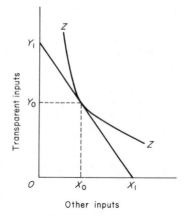

Figure 4.1   *Firm equilibrium in a two-factor market.*

markets are local, we would have to add to the criteria listed above an explanation of the interdependence effects among competitors. This problem will be considered in the next section. However, if there are no competitors and markets are local, one would probably locate in the center of the area to minimize transport costs. If transport and other costs are substitutable, one would not necessarily locate in the center. The logic of this assertion can be explained with the help of Figure 4.1.

If a firm uses transport inputs Y and other inputs X to produce a given level of output, the production recipe can be shown as ZZ. ZZ is referred to as an isoquant, since it shows alternative combinations of two inputs (X and Y) that yield the same level of output (ZZ). At any given point on ZZ, the change in output associated with a given change in an input, times the change in the amount of the input, will be equal for all inputs. Thus, by definition, as we move from one point to another on ZZ, $MP_x \; \Delta X = MP_y \; \Delta Y$, where MP denotes marginal product. If the firm has a fixed budget I, and it spends all of the budget on X, it can buy $I \div P_x = X_1$ amount of X, where P_x is the price of X. Similarly, if it buys only Y it can have Y_1 units. Thus alternative combinations of the two inputs the firm can purchase are represented by the budget line X_1Y_1.

If the firm wants to maximize its output,* given the budget constraint and factor prices, it will buy X_0 and Y_0 amounts of X and Y respectively. Why? Because if it bought more or less of either input, it could not attain

---

* If price of the output is given, this is also the profit-maximizing level of resource use.

the maximum level of output (ZZ). Notice that where X_0 and Y_0 inputs are taken, the slope of the budget line equals the slope of the isoquant ZZ. The slope of the budget line is $I/P_y \div I/P_x = P_x/P_y$. The slope of ZZ is $\Delta X/\Delta Y = MP_y/MP_x$, Now $\Delta Y/\Delta X$ is called the marginal rate of substitution (MRS) of Y for X or vice versa. Thus when the MRS equals the price ratio, the firm is at an optimal position.

How does this analysis relate to our initial question? Assume we are located in the center of the city, and for some exogenous reason we find that the price of X is cheaper in the northeast section of the city. Since the P_x reduction essentially means that our real budget increases, we could now buy more of X, more of Y, or both if we located in the northeast. If X is a normal good,* we will buy more of it. How much more? Enough to restore the equality between the MRS and the new price ratio. But what about our customers; many of them are farther away from us now that we have moved. It is possible, however, that the increase in output (supply) attained by using the cheaper input X will depress the price of the final product such that the savings in the lower cost of the final product to the consumer will exceed his increase in transport costs. So we will not necessarily lose any customers when we move; in fact, we could gain some.

Thus, when a firm has no competitors and its market is the city, it will locate where the MRS of inputs equals their price ratio, provided that inputs are substitutable. If the firm's market is national in scope, regardless of whether competitors are in the same city, the firm will attempt to choose a location that minimizes costs. The interesting case, and the one most applicable to urban analysis, is when competition exists and the market is local. We now turn to a discussion of the principles of locational interdependence, which will help us resolve this issue.

Locational Interdependence: The Case of Competitors

In the previous chapter, we showed under highly simplified assumptions that a single seller (a bakery) would locate in the middle of a linear market. Suppose two producers sell the same good on a linear market, where buyers are distributed evenly along the market. If costs are the same everywhere along the market, and prices are f.o.b. (that is, the buyers pays the price at the plant plus shipping charges), then the boundary of the market areas between these two sellers will occur where the freight rates are equal. In Figure 4.2, this point is b, since BF and EG are transport cost rays. Notice that the price at the produc-

---

* That is, if the demand curve for X is downward sloping.

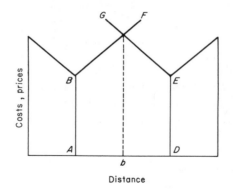

Figure 4.2   Market areas of two firms.

tion sites (AB and DE) is the same for both producers. Also, the freight
rates, shown by the slopes of BF and EG, are equal. Clearly if costs
(price) fell for one producer, his market area would increase. Similarly,
if a producer's freight charges per mile decreased, his market area would
increase. Prices and freight rates, then, can determine one's market area
and location site. But are these location sites stable? What is to keep
one seller from lowering his price to increase his share of the market,
and will the other retaliate? To answer these questions, we must consider
the interdependencies of location decisions.

Why Firms Concentrate in Space

The earliest model used to portray locational interdependence was
developed by Harold Hotelling [3]. Although the Hotelling model is
quite simple, it is a useful starting point. If buyers are evenly distributed
along a given line with perfectly price-inelastic demands for a homogeneous good produced by two sellers, and costs are the same everywhere with f.o.b. pricing, where will the two producers locate if relocation is instantaneous and costless? Obviously each producer will continue
to move toward the other to increase his share of the market until both
end up at the center. This situation is illustrated in Figure 4.3 for a
market of length AB and two firms, X and Y. At the center both firms
can serve the market equally well, and each will get half the business;
thus it will not pay either to move. Note that the prices of the good
will be equal at the center. At any point other than the center—say,

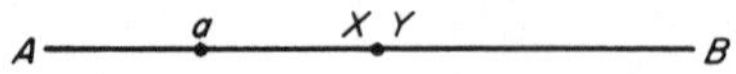

A———————•———•———————B
         a   X Y

Figure 4.3   A simple model of locational interdependence.

point *a* for firm *X*—the situation is not stable because *X* could increase his market share by moving toward *Y*. And there is nothing to stop *X*, since moves are costless.

Is the center the only possible stable solution? If no collusion occurs, the answer is yes. However, one should note, as Hotelling did, that the center is not the socially optimum location site. The quartiles of the line would be the optimal location sites from society's view, for here freight costs would be minimized to consumers; thus prices of the final product would also be minimized.

Some persons have used the Hotelling argument as a rationale for the concentration of firms; however, if one drops a few of the unrealistic assumptions, this conclusion is unfounded. For example, if demand is elastic, transport costs are a hindrance to sales, and firms will disperse toward their buyers. In the real world relocation costs are not zero, and collusion does occur; thus mutually beneficial end results for each firm can be obtained by minimizing the fighting, and sharing the market. Of course the market can be shared with firms at the center, endpoints, or anywhere in between where the firms are equidistant from their respective endpoints.

If we add a third firm to the Hotelling model, instability results, because it would always pay the middle man to go toward an endpoint. If collusion were allowed between two sellers, it would be possible for them to drive the third seller out. But under collusion agreements of either two or all three sellers, there is no guarantee that the socially optimum sites will be chosen. However, as the number of firms increases, the location choices will tend toward the optimum.

The Hotelling model and its variants are too simple to explain reality; nevertheless, they emphasize the interdependencies involved when the firm makes a decision: how will competitors react, what are their demand potentials, how far can they cut price, and so forth. Unfortunately, economists have not derived any simple models* of locational interdependence in the Hotelling spirit. Since our primary interest in viewing competitors selling in the same market is to determine whether they will concentrate or disperse, it may be useful to merely explain those factors that affect concentration and dispersion. Melvin Greenhut [5] has shown that the following factors affect the concentration of firms in space:

(1) price elasticity of demand;
(2) freight rates as a share of total selling price;

* There has been a lot of work in this area, however. Much of it is reported in Robert Dean *et al.* [4].

(3) shape of the marginal-cost curve;
(4) uncertainty about one's competitors;
(5) population densities;
(6) the possibility of price discrimination.

We have already considered the effect of price elasticity of demand on concentration. As elasticity increases, the forces of concentration weaken, other things being equal. Similarly, if freight costs become a greater share of price, firms will disperse, *ceteris paribus*. Two of the remaining four factors cited above may be explained easily. As uncertainty about rivals increases, it will pay to move to the center of the market, where overall risks are minimized. And as population density increases, the possibility of concentration of firms obviously increases.

If marginal costs are constant, as Hotelling assumed, and if f.o.b. prices are charged, then the addition of the freight charge to the marginal cost curve increases the price to the average buyer by one-half of the freight charge when the demand curve for the product is linear. This constant-marginal-cost case is shown in Figure 4.4. Curve DR is marginal to the demand curve DD. Given the constant marginal cost curve MC_1, the profit-maximizing price is $\frac{1}{2}(OA + OD)$. Now if the freight increase is represented by an increase in marginal costs to MC_2, at this point the profit-maximizing firm would charge a price equal to $\frac{1}{2}(OB + OD)$. Thus it follows that the increase in price equals $\frac{1}{2}AB$, which of course is half of the freight increase. So we can argue that if the marginal-cost curve is constant, increases in freight rates have no effect on concentration or dispersion.

If the marginal cost curve is rising, however, the addition of freight charges to marginal costs will increase price such that more than half

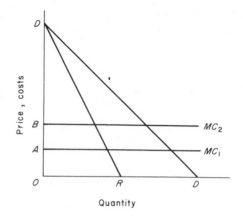

Figure 4.4   *Freight absorption under constant costs.*

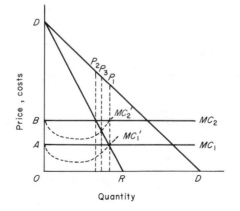

Figure 4.5 *Freight absorption under increasing costs* [5].

of the freight charges can be absorbed by the average buyer. This case is shown in Figure 4.5. Given the analysis from the constant-cost case in Figure 4.4, we know that the price charged before the freight increase was P_1; after the increase the price rose to P_2. We can draw a curvilinear MC_1 curve denoted as MC_1', beginning at A and cutting the constant MC_1 curve where DR cuts MC_1. Now by drawing the new curvilinear marginal-cost curve (MC_2') parallel to MC_1, we can see that the profit-maximizing price will be P_3. Since P_3 is less than P_2, the seller absorbs more than half of the freight increase under rising marginal costs. If the seller absorbs over half of the freight increase, there will be pressure on him to locate more centrally. Alternatively, if marginal costs are falling over the relevant range of output, the amount of freight absorption on the part of average buyers will be less than half of the freight charge, and the seller will probably seek a less central location.

Given the price elasticity of demand and shape of the marginal-cost curve, the assumption of f.o.b. pricing makes it imperative for firms to locate near their customers. What would happen, however, if firms could discriminate against nearby buyers by charging them effectively higher prices than more distant buyers? Recalling from basic economics that markets are traditionally divided by differences in price elasticity, we know intuitively that a seller can discriminate against buyers who have low price elasticity of demand because such buyers cannot obtain substitutes easily. If everyone in the city has a given demand for a product, such as DD in Figure 4.6, it is possible to show that discrimination against nearby buyers is profitable [5, pp. 157–159]. DR is the curve marginal to DD, and represents marginal revenue. Marginal costs are constant, and shown by EF. Now a profit-maximizing firm produces

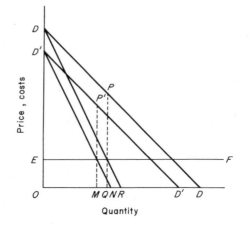

Figure 4.6 *Spatial price discrimination* [5].

where marginal revenue equals marginal cost, or where *DR* cuts *EF*. The price associated with this intersection is *QP*, and the quantity is *OQ*. Clearly, if all buyers were located at the production site, we would find $PQ = \frac{1}{2}(OD + OE)$ charged. But buyers are scattered across the area, and they pay the net mill price plus freight; thus sellers view the distant buyer as having demand curve *D'D'*, where *DD'* is the transport cost of the distant buyer. The marginal revenue curve associated with *D'D'* is *D'N*; thus the profit-maximizing price charged to the distant buyer is $P'M = \frac{1}{2}(OD' + OE)$. Clearly the nearer buyer is discriminated against by the amount $\frac{1}{2}DD'$.

Thus, when the demand curve decreases in elasticity as price falls, as occurs along any linear demand curve, the effect of freight or transport costs is to increase elasticity for the more distant buyers, in the eyes of the firm. The greater elasticity may be visualized in Figure 4.6 by noting that *P'M* is closer to its marginal revenue curve than is *PQ*. The ability to discriminate against nearby buyers discourages dispersion because distance becomes less significant; a firm will not be likely to lose many customers by taking a central location.

II. THE BASIC DETERMINANTS OF INTRAURBAN
LOCATION DECISIONS AT THE FIRM LEVEL

Thus far we have considered the similarities and differences between inter- versus intraurban location decisions, and some principles of locational interdependence. At this point it may be useful to lay out some of the basic determinants of intraurban location for a single firm: accessibility, external economies, taxes, and land costs. Thoughout this section we shall assume that the locations of all other firms are given and fixed. This will enable us to focus on the firm by itself.

As stated earlier, accessibility is always important in choosing a location. Given the existing and expected structure of transport facilities, one will choose the site that is most accessible to inputs, buyers, or both if possible. The importance of access will vary across sectors. To retail trade firms producing lower-order goods and services, access is of paramount importance. Thus we see shopping centers of all sizes, and many single stores, located near residential areas. Similarly, restaurants abound in entertainment districts and near large arenas so that people can have easy access to complementary goods. Not all facilities go to the customer (that is, decentralize) in order to provide maximum access, however. Libraries and governmental offices take on central locations in order to maximize their access to all of the public. And of course customer access has little meaning to firms producing for national markets; yet it is quite clear these firms must choose a location that is accessible to their inputs.

External economies are a major determinant of location decisions within urban areas. External economies are factors exogenous to a given firm that lower that firm's per-unit costs of production. We have already discussed the existence of external economies in the form of agglomeration advantages and input–output linkages in earlier chapters. These factors lead to the clustering of industries within certain areas of the city. There is another type of positive externality associated with certain manufacturing and service sectors in large cities that we have not discussed. Many industries, such as printing, publishing, fashions, toys, and advertising, are made up of rather small firms that must be able to tap a common pool of facilities at almost a moment's notice. To meet these needs, New York City and other large cities are inevitable locations of such firms [6,7].

Robert Lichtenberg polled manufacturing firms in New York City for 1954, and found that external economies were the major determinant of location, while transport costs ranked second [6, p. 139]. Nationally, transport costs were the major determinant of locational sites, and external economies were of only minor importance. Lichtenberg found that those firms locating on the basis of external economies were primarily small, single-plant firms producing a highly unstandardized product with fluctuating and uncertain demands. Many of the firms in a given sector clustered together to use common space, facilities, and supplies.

This trend of locating small firms in large cities has begun to be reversed with the implementation of more capital-intensive processes and standardized products produced in many of the sectors listed above. High-speed communications and transportation networks have been substituted for the old face-to-face contact activity. Thus we might expect the new firms entering the publishing, printing, toys, and fashion sectors to locate outside of the larger cities in a horizontally integrated plant. One of the reasons that may cause firms to seek a suburban location is the relatively low taxes, which we turn to next.

Although we cannot prove that taxes were a significant factor in interurban or interstate location decisions (see Chapter 3) many firms choose sites *within* metropolitan areas that carry the highest level of public services per tax dollar expended. As our analysis on factor price changes showed earlier in this chapter, if the price of an input declines, one can buy more of that input or other inputs or both. Clearly a firm has an impetus to seek a site having a low price of governmental services.

Youn and Beaton [8] tested the importance of property tax rates on the location decisions of manufacturing firms in 25 cities of Orange County, California. Standardizing for land characteristics and prices, the authors found that high property taxes were significant deterrents to locations in the cities covered. Once a firm chooses to locate in a given area, its markets (revenues) are more or less fixed; thus to maximize profits its problem becomes one of minimizing costs. Therefore, we would expect high costs of governmental services to have a negative impact on the growth of firms in a given metropolitan area, other things being equal.

The Price of Land and Location Decisions

The final locational determinant we shall consider is the price of land. As one might expect, the price of land varies inversely with distance from the center of any city. For example, vacant land in the city of Boston was selling at $3.50 to $4.50 per square foot in 1970. Ten to 15 miles out during the same time period, along the industrial Route 128, prices were $1.15 to $1.30 per square foot. And 25 to 30 miles out along Route 495, vacant land was selling for $0.70 to $1.00 per square foot. Obviously if a firm desires cheaper land, it will have to give up access to the central city. Economists have built elaborate models to explain where a firm will choose its site in relation to the center of a city, and it might be useful for us to consider one of these here.

William Alonso [9] has shown that one can establish an equilibrium firm location site with respect to distance from the center of the city. Alonso assumes:

(1) a centralized city exists, with consumers in the center;
(2) firms maximize profits;
(3) the product price is given, with no interference from spatial competitors;
(4) the price of land varies inversely with distance, and all land is of equal quality except for access to the center;
(5) all other factors that may affect the rent of a site are ignored.

Given these assumptions, as a firm opts to move away from the center of the city, its revenues decline, operating costs increase (because of poorer accessibility), but rents decline. Thus movement away from the center involves the substitution of increased transport and other costs plus falling revenue for reduced rents. There should be some price of land the firm is willing to pay at varying distances from the center that will yield the same level of total profits. If we can find that price which is consistent with actual land prices and highest profit levels, it will then be possible to determine the optimal location site of the firm in relation to distance from the center of the city.

Alonso shows the equilibrium position for the firm graphically with the help of bid-price curves. Bid-price curves show how the price of land must vary with distance for a firm to attain the same level of profits. Bid-price curves have the following properties:

(1) *single-valued*—Only one price is bid at each distance from the center for any given level of profits.
(2) *downward slope*—As a firm moves out from the center, if the savings in land costs are exactly offset by the loss in revenue plus the increase in operating costs, then to keep the same level of profits, land prices must fall.
(3) *lower curves denote higher profits*—If we assume the MRS between land and other inputs is a constant, as the price of land declines at any given distance from the center, profits must rise.
(4) *do not intersect*—If bid-price curves clearly represent different profit levels, it would be illogical for them to intersect.

In Figure 4.7 we have three linear bid price curves (BPC's), where BPC_1 denotes a higher level of profit than BPC_2, and so on. These three curves are only part of a family of BPC's facing each firm. They are drawn linearly to simplify the diagram. The actual price of land with respect to distance from the center is denoted by curve P_L; thus the equilibrium location site for the firm would be OX_1 miles away from the center of the city O. The equilibrium is stable under the assumptions given, because if the firm faced P_L and it chose a site closer

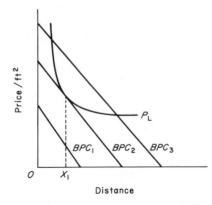

Figure 4.7 *Single equilibrium location for a firm.*

to the city, the slope of P_L would exceed the slope of BPC_2. In this position, the savings in rent from moving farther away from the center would exceed the loss in revenue plus decrease in operating costs; thus the firm would move toward X_1. If the firm went beyond X_1, the forces would operate in the exact opposite manner to push the firm inward until it reached X.

In evaluating the Alonso model, it is clear that many discontinuities exist in P_L for any city in the real world; therefore, more than one equilibrium site may exist. This situation is depicted in Figure 4.8, where OX_1 and OX_2 are equilibrium sites, and a sharp jump occurs in P_L between X_1 and X_2. If another firm desired to locate at distance X_1

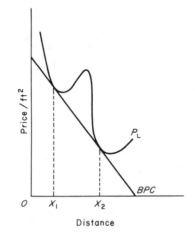

Figure 4.8 *Multiple equilibrium location sites for a single firm.*

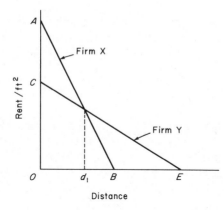

Figure 4.9 *Two-firm ceiling-rent analysis.*

from the city in Figure 4.7, it is not clear which firm would win out
if we viewed the city as a straight line emanating from O.

This latter issue may be resolved by using a more simplified model
developed by agricultural economists, known as ceiling-rent curves [10].
Ceiling-rent curves show the maximum amount of rent per unit of land
a firm can pay with increasing distance from the city center and still
earn a normal profit. If land markets operate perfectly, land goes to
the highest bidder. AB represents the ceiling rent bid by firm X in
Figure 4.9, and CE represents the ceiling-rent curve for firm Y. Given
that land markets operate perfectly, firm X will locate within Od_1, and
firm Y will locate outside of Od_1. Note that both firms bid the same
rents at Od_1. Thus, to resolve the issue of two firms vying for the same
position, we require linear ceiling curves that (1) have different slopes
and (2) intersect. If firm X's ceiling rent curve was linear, but Y's was
nonlinear and cut X's curve in two places, it would not be possible
to establish a unique locational area for Y. This case is shown in Figure
4.10. Firm Y could locate up to Od_1 miles from the center, or beyond

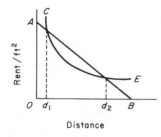

Figure 4.10 *Linear and nonlinear ceiling-rent analysis.*

Od_2 miles. Thus the slope of the ceiling-rent curve is very important. In general, the slope will depend upon the increase in transport costs with distance, and the substitutability of land for nonland inputs.

Summary

Access, external economies, taxes, and the price of land all have some effect on the location decision of firms within urban areas. How strong each factor is in specific decisions depends upon the nature of and demand for the product(s) produced by the firm, as well as the firm's production function. It should be kept in mind that all of these factors are interrelated. For example, access has a fairly strong relationship to the price of land, as we saw in the preceding section. External economies are also tied to access. For example, almost every sizable shopping center has at least one restaurant that is easily accessible. Accessibility is a key to the restaurant's location, but the success of the shops in attracting customers (and employees), a factor external to the restaurateur, determines in large part the success of the restaurant.

III. MODELS OF INTRAURBAN LOCATION DECISIONS

Although the discussion of intraurban location decisions thus far has been informative, we have done little more than identify a number of key factors, depending on the situation of the firm relative to its markets and competitors. With the exception of the Alonso model, which is untestable in its present form, we have not covered any *general* models of intraurban location. In the remainder of this chapter we hope to bridge this gap. We shall begin with some models of firms selling in local markets, then turn to firms with national markets, and finish our discussion with an inquiry into public-facility location.

Central Place as a Location Model

In the previous chapter, we explained how urban areas are composed of a hierarchy of central places. The origin and size of a central place are determined by the threshold and range concepts, respectively. The threshold occurs for a given product when demand warrants production; that is, when under given technology and demand conditions, the firm can earn normal profits. The range of a good or service is synonomous with the radius of the market area of the central place. The range is primarily determined by transport costs and spatial competition on the part of other firms.

For any given good or service, there will be a number of central places in any city. The number will be inversely related to the order of the good and the size of the city. For any city of given size, there are more grocery stores than mink shops. If we know the number and size of central places for a given product, and the factors that change the number and size of central places, it is possible to predict whether a new firm will originate production. If we can predict that the number of market areas for a product will increase, there is probably a good chance that a new plant will locate in the city. Exactly where it will locate depends on a number of factors, such as the spatial pattern of existing establishments, commuting patterns, and population densities.

The number and size of central places or market areas in a city are determined by, among other factors,* (1) changes in demand, (2) reactions of competitors, and (3) changes in transport costs. Each of these factors will be discussed in detail, so that we can better explain and predict the number and size of central places for a given product.

To determine the demand curve and size of the market area facing a single seller, we make the following simplifying assumptions:

(1) The product is sold at a single production site for a given price p, and consumers pay the f.o.b. price $p + t_r$, where t_r is a constant transport rate per mile.
(2) Consumers are uniformly distributed over the city with identical demand curves for the product.

Thus the individual demand g will be a function of p and the distance d from the production site,

$$g = f(p + t_r d) \tag{4-1}$$

This demand function can be represented by a demand curve that will cut the vertical axis at a price so high that persons at the production site will buy no quantity. This point may be referred to as $p_{\max}$, denoting the maximum price. Similarly, where the individual demand curve cuts the horizontal axis, we have the maximum quantity taken.

The last consumer in the market area is at boundary r_p; thus the market area has radius r at price p of

$$r_p = \frac{p_{\max} - p}{d} \tag{4-2}$$

---

* The reader may want to refer to our discussion of central-place models in the previous chapter.

There is an inverse relationship between given changes in p and resultant changes in r and thus the size of market areas; that is, if price increases, the radius declines. If one assumes no spatial price or other competition, the aggregate demand facing a single producer can be found by adding up all of the individual demands across space.

How are prices actually determined in central places or market areas? To answer this question, we follow the great pioneering work of central-places and location theory by August Losch [11]. Consider the equilibrium price of a single producer in the long run under conditions of free entry. If we have the demand assumptions stated earlier, and further assume no spatial competition, a profit-maximizing firm faced with spatial-demand curve D_{r_1p} and per-unit costs AC will produce output level OQ_1 and charge price Op_1, as shown in Figure 4.11. The output level is decided by the point at which marginal revenue equals marginal cost, but the marginal curves are left out of Figure 4.11 to minimize the clutter. For price Op_1, the producer has a circular area of effective demand, which is his market area, with radius r_1p. With excess profits of cp_1ab being earned, new firms will enter the overall city market until equilibrium is attained at price Op_2 and output level OQ_2. The effect of the entry of firms on each seller in the city is to cause his demand curve to be lowered, since each seller loses customers at his boundary. Thus, at equilibrium, all sellers are faced with Dr_2p. At OQ_2 under Dr_2p, r_1 exceeds r_2, as the student can assess by substituting

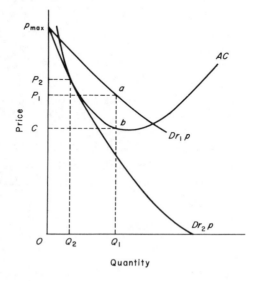

Figure 4.11 *Pricing and the size of market areas* [12].

the higher price (OP_2 rather than OP_1) into Equation (4-2). Thus the size of market areas is reduced when equilibrium is attained.

So free entry can result in smaller market areas, yielding the greatest number of firms possible under the assumed conditions. Losch argued that smaller areas are in society's interests, because transport costs would be minimized. However, Denike and Parr [12] have shown that if restricted entry is enforced by the government, it is clear that Losch may have erred. If firms are kept out, market areas can increase to (at least) a radius of r_1. Thus production occurs at a greater scale, and firms can charge a lower f.o.b. price. The resultant benefits must be compared with the increased costs of transportation borne by outerlying customers as the market area expands under restriction. Denike and Parr have also shown that as market size decreases (due to free entry), the shape tends toward a hexagon; whereas with increased size (due to restricted entry), the shape is more likely to be a circle. Since circles would not fill up all the space in the city, customers in the interstitial areas would not be served.

Thus society is faced with a paradox in choosing whether or not to restrict entry. On the one hand; it can allow free entry, which (1) reduces the transport costs and (2) makes the product available when it would not have been, to a few customers. This is done at a cost of less output produced less efficiently for almost all of society. On the other hand, if entry is restricted, the majority of society can be benefited at the expense of a rather small minority. If restriction is instituted by some other means, such as collusive tactics on the part of existing firms in the industry, it is difficult to say that any of society would be better off.

In retrospect, we have found that easy entry can reduce the size and increase the number of central places for a given product. Thus easy entry allows more firms to locate in a given city as the city grows and expands over space. There could be a real cost to society, however, in that scale economies may not be able to be realized.

Now that we have shown how demand or prices and conditions of entry explain the number and size of central places, it remains to consider the impact of changes in transport costs. We can begin our analysis with the Loschian framework again, and assume that equilibrium has been reached as in Figure 4.12. Now if there is a decrease in transport costs, to consumers faced with f.o.b. pricing this is the same thing as an increase in their real income, which could increase their demand for the product, say to D'. With the increase in demand, new firms enter the industry and market areas decline as the old equilibrium is once again attained. Note that we now have more firms located in the

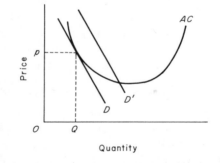

Figure 4.12   *A change in demand and market areas.*

city, but the average output is the same as before because customers can now buy more because of their higher real income. In short, a reduction of transport costs has caused market areas to become smaller, and the number of firms to increase.

This conclusion is surprising in that we usually think of more efficient transportation systems enlarging market sizes. For example, as freeways are built leading out of heavily urbanized areas, people living in the fringes can get to shopping areas in the city faster; thus we would expect the size of the shopping area's market to increase.

The "catch" in the analysis presented above is that the increase in real income brought about by the reduction in transport costs may not be spent on the consumption of more transportation, at least in a net sense. Transportation services may be inferior goods; that is, as their price decreases people may buy fewer units. Edgar Hoover [13] has considered the impact of changes in the prices of transport services on the size of central places, and he found two interesting conclusions:

(1) For small urban areas, transport improvements lead to smaller market centers. Thus the Loschian model would probably predict well for small towns outside of metropolitan areas.
(2) For larger and more developed urban areas, improvements in transport result in larger market areas with agglomerations of firms.

Clearly, the impact of changes in transport costs on the number and size of market areas will depend upon the size of the city.

Empirical Tests of the Central Place Model

Geographers and planners have performed most of the theoretical and empirical work on central-place models. Although many elaborate theoretical extensions have been made with the model, from an economic location standpoint, little progress has been made. Although it is not possible to say exactly *where* a firm will locate in a city or one of its subcenters, we can calculate the number of stores a subcenter of a given size can service. Then if we find empirically that fewer stores exist in that subcenter, we might forecast that new stores will enter and locate somewhere in the subcenter.

Berry and Garrison [14] did a study of 33 small urban centers in Snohomish County, Washington in which they used a model that could predict the number of stores of retail and service activities. Their model was

$$P_i = A(B)^{N_i} \quad (i = 1, \ldots, n, \quad n = 33)$$
$$(j = 1, \ldots, M, \quad m = 52)$$

where P_i is the population level of the ith urban center N_j is the number of stores for activity j in the ith center, and A and B are parameters to be estimated statistically. Berry and Garrison found values for A and B for 52 types of retail and service activities.

The threshold population for any given j would be the value of P when $N = 1$, given A and B. If one computes A and B, and if P is substituted into the equation, a forecasted value of N can be obtained and compared to the actual value of N for any urban center outside of the sample used to calculate A and B. We would assume, of course, that the cities within the sample and the city under question had similar spatial and socioeconomic structures. To the extent that this assumption is realistic, any positive differential between the forecast and actual N should reflect the possibility of new stores entering the activity, *ceteris paribus*.

Berry and Garrison noted that the value of B could be used to determine whether scale economies occur as the number of stores increase in a given activity. For example, the threshold population for barber shops was found to be 386, and the value of B for barber shops was 2.39. Thus if an urban center went from one to two barber shops, these two shops could service $384(2.39)^2 = 2254$ persons. Clearly, as the population of an urban center increases, the average size of stores will increase and take advantage of scale economies.

The Berry–Garrison model is rather crude and simple, but it still is useful. Certainly population density rather than population would have to be used if the model were applied to urban centers in a metropolitan area. A more fundamental problem is the formulation of the model itself: as the model is stated, changes in the number of stores would independently affect the population levels. Is it not the other way around? A more reasonable formulation would have population independently affecting the number of stores in a given activity.

J. D. Forbes [15] has tested a model of the following form:

$$N_j = AP^B \qquad (j = 1, \ldots, m, \quad m = 35)$$

with 1963 data for all SMSA's in the U.S. For 21 of the 35 activities, B was found to be statistically different from unity. If $B < 1$, then market-area size increases as population rises. Computationally, this is because as B decreases, N decreases. And for a given population, as N decreases, stores serve larger markets. Activities for which B was less than 1 included department stores, fish markets, grocery stores, and gas stations. Since market size increases with $B < 1$, it is probably safe to infer that these activities are experiencing scale economies. Fruit and vegetable stores, bakeries, candy shops, and meat shops had values for B greater than unity; thus their market areas decreased as population rose. Scale economies are probably not significant in these activities. We may conclude, then, that it is possible to forecast the number of stores in retail activities by means of population levels. However, it is not clear, for any given activity at the city level, that population alone can explain the number of stores. Certainly more research in this area is needed.

Shopping Behavior Models

Prospective locators in any given subcenter of an urban area often base their decisions on the level of prospective demand, or the total attractive forces of the subcenter. One of the popular models used to measure attraction is the gravity model, discussed in the preceding chapter as an explanation for migration among cities. W. J. Reilly formulated his famous Law of Retail Gravitation in 1929 [16], which says that a city or subcenter attracts any given customer located in its hinterland in proportion to its size and in inverse proportion to the square of the distance between the customer and subcenter. As a corollary of this law, one can identify the boundary (b) between two centers (x and y) as the locus of points where

$$\frac{P_x}{d^2 b_x} = \frac{P_y}{d^2 b_y}$$

That is, where the ratio of size, as measured by the population P, to the square of the distance is the same for two centers, the customer is indifferent between the two centers and is thus on the boundary between them.

Reilly's law is really a special case of the general gravity model, which may be formulated as ·

$$I_{ij} = A \frac{P_j^{\alpha}}{d_{ij}^B}$$

where I_{ij} is the probability of interaction between individual i and retail center j, P_j is the attractive force in j, measured here by population, and d_{ij} is the distance from i to j. The α, A, and B are parameters to be estimated. Reilly, of course, argued that B would be about 2. Clearly the value of this general gravity model depends on its ability to predict, since it has little explanatory value in comparison to many of the models discussed thus far.

Many criticize the general gravity model because it cannot explain retail decentralization. It is also argued that external diseconomies in downtown or other highly active retail centers, such as congestion, crime, and high rents, cannot be accounted for. The first criticism is probably well grounded, since until suburbanization of retail activities begins in a new area, past shopping patterns that would be used to estimate α and B would be misleading. On the other hand, once a node of shopping facilities is established, any additional shops could be readily predicted with the gravity model. The diseconomy criticism does not have a very strong basis. Obviously if a center is not attractive, the value of α can be forced to be less than 1. If congestion is a major problem, this means it will take any given individual a longer travel time, which is another way of saying distance has increased. Thus one would raise the value of B to account for congestion.

A more appealing model, at least conceptually, of whether or not an individual will be attracted to any given store has been developed by Baumol and Ide [17]. Their model calculates the expected net benefits of shopping at a given store. In general, net benefits will vary positively with the number of items N available at the store, and inversely with the distance D in miles to the store. The net benefit B_n function is written by Baumol and Ide as

$$B_n = wp(N) - v(C_dD + C_n\sqrt{N} + C_i)$$

where (1) w and v are subjective weights for the benefits and costs respectively, (2) $p(N)$ is the probable satisfaction or gross benefit function, represented by N, and (3) costs are represented by C_d, C_n, and C_i, which stand for transport costs per mile, actual shopping costs, and the costs of opportunities forgone respectively for the ith individual. On the costs side of the net benefit function, C_d is multiplied by D to give total transport costs. Actual shopping costs (C_n) depend upon how many stores one goes to; thus C_n is weighted by the square root of the number of stores N. The opportunity cost of one's time is the same, regardless of how far one travels or to how many stores he visits. Thus C_i is not weighted by N or D.

What are the implications of the Baumol–Ide model? First, the minimum N required to attract a given shopper increases with D. This can be seen by holding the benefit function $p(N)$ constant at any minimum N, and increasing D. The result, of course, is that costs rise and net benefits decline. Second, the maximum distance any shopper would travel to a given store is found by setting B_n equal to zero and solving for D. If one does this,* he will find that the maximum distance will increase as w or $p(N)$ increases, or C_d declines. That is, if my expected benefits increase, or my distance-related costs decline, I will be more willing to shop in a given area.

In general, the Baumol–Ide model says that consumers choose shopping areas on the basis of the spatial location and number of items offered at each store. By comparing values of B_n for alternative shopping areas, an individual will choose his actual shopping site where B_n is maximized. So if an entrepreneur could empirically determine the B_n function for many individuals in alternative areas, he could choose the optimal location site. It should be quite clear to the reader, however, that this model is next to impossible to implement empirically in its present form. Its importance rests in explaining the shopping decision of an individual, and thus providing the basic information needed for an entrepreneur to make a rational location decision, *ceteris paribus.*

The Move to the Suburbs

As we have stated earlier, a profit-maximizing firm selling in national markets will locate within any urban area at that site which minimizes its costs. Suburbs often have cheaper land, easy access to highway and rail facilities, and enough space for a horizontally integrated production process. Although the final evidence is not in as to which of these factors is more important in attracting firms to suburbs, the data show that most of the growth in the past few decades has not been in central cities. Table 4-1 shows that the suburban areas have taken an increasing percentage of employment in sectors that sell locally as well as nationally.

* If we set the B_n function equal to zero and solve for D, we obtain

$$D = \frac{W}{vCD}\, p(N) - \frac{1}{C_d}\, (C_n\, \sqrt{N} + C_i)$$

TABLE 4-1

Suburban Ring Share of SMSA Employment and Population for Selected Years[a]

	1948 (%)	1954 (%)	1958 (%)	1963 (%)
Employment				
Manufacturing	33.1	38.6	42.0	51.8
Wholesale trade	8.2	14.5	20.7	28.6
Retail trade	24.7	30.6	37.2	45.4
Selected services	15.2	21.6	26.1	31.3
Population	36.0	43.5	48.2	54.3

[a] John Kain, "The Distribution and Movement of Jobs and Industry," in *The Metropolitan Enigma*, James Q. Wilson, ed., p. 27. (Cambridge, Massachusetts: Harvard Univ. Press, 1968.)

A number of empirical studies have attempted to explain the flight to the suburbs, but almost amazingly few have been successful in finding statistically significant results. Leon Moses and Harold Williamson [18] tested a model of the relocation of old plants or the birth of new plants in the Chicago area between 1950 and 1964. The authors hypothesized that firms moved outward because of lower land prices, access to transport facilities, and many other a priori variables. Their results were generally poor, except they found that most firms were attracted to zones having manufacturing complexes, which may be a solid vote for agglomeration effects.

Raymond Struyk [19] has attempted to explain intrametropolitan location decisions in Boston, Minneapolis, and Phoenix. In all cases, be the firms old or new, Struyk found that the majority of chosen sites were outside of the central city areas. Moreover, firms (especially the smaller ones) tended to move short distances. Interestingly, the location patterns of relocating old firms were quite different from those of new firms.

Michael Goldberg [20] tested two hypotheses for manufacturing, transportation, and wholesale trade establishments in Santa Clara County, California between 1962 and 1965:

(1) An inverse relationship exists between the size of a plant and the density of the area in which it locates.
(2) There is a positive relationship between growing and moving, and growing plants move to outlying areas where there is room to grow.

Both of these hypotheses have as an underlying basis the idea that large firms internalize external economies, and that they do so by moving to suburbia. Goldberg found that both hypotheses were statistically significant, but that each relationship was quite weak.

Finally, the Youn and Beaton study of locations in 25 cities of Orange County, California, referred to earlier [see p. 80] found that as the capital assets per acre in a city rose, firms did not locate there. This implies that location decisions in these cities were pulled toward suburban, relatively undeveloped areas. The term undeveloped here does not mean an area without public facilities such as transportation and utilities. The authors found that firms did not move to locations where the price of land was lowest, which implies that facilities were readily accessible. This implication is justified, since the price of land was strongly correlated with access to freeways.

Urban Public Facility Location

One of the more neglected but increasingly important areas of intraurban location analysis is the location decision for public facilities. Where should the police and fire stations, the library, or city hall be located? These institutions are not profit-maximizers, so it is rather difficult to apply traditional economic analysis to their locational choices. Nevertheless, we shall see that a number of basic locational principles discussed earlier in the context of the private sector are applicable when one considers the location of public facilities.

One can categorize public facilities into two classes—point patterns and networks [21]. Point patterns are illustrated by distributive services, such as post offices, libraries, hospitals, and police and fire stations. Like the ordering of central places, one finds a hierarchical system of facilities for many of these types of service. Services that need continuous connections in space, such as utilities and highways, are examples of networks. Our concern here is with the decision-making process used to develop the point patterns of distributive services.

Any governmental decision process is constrained by: (1) the problem of learning the true preferences of society, which is exacerbated because market prices for governmental services do not exist; and (2) normal allocation problems, even if one is given a reasonable facsimile of society's tastes. Within these constraints, there are two opposing forces that inevitably permeate the public-facility location decision—economies of scale and advantages of dispersion. Which of these forces wins out? One answer lies in the type of service under consideration. For example, the concept of consumer choice is effectively inoperative in the location of police and fire stations, and the (direct) price charged for these services is zero. If the theory of consumer choice were applicable here, rational people would opt to have these facilities close to their homes, and they would reveal their preferences by paying a higher price for these services. But since we do not charge prices (directly) for police and fire services, people cannot reveal their preferences.

The locations of facilities in reality are no doubt a compromise of political and other technical factors. On the other hand, consumers do have a vote in the location of some facilities, such as libraries. Larger libraries offer more services and are usually centrally located. If these varied services are not being utilized, smaller facilities can be erected closer to the population by having branches, at least where budgetary constraints permit. The level of jurisdication making the decision will also affect the outcome of the scale–dispersion struggle. City, county, metropolitan, and federal institutions all have different constituencies and budgetary constraints, and therefore may be expected to act differently in facility-location decisions.

Manfred Kochen and Karl Deutsch [22] have considered the problem of centralization and decentralization of public facilities in detail. Using a Hotelling-type model of a city as a straight line, the authors concluded that developing cities would have centralized facilities, while larger, more developed cities would require decentralized forces. These conclusions are based on the hypothesis that consumers desire to minimize travel costs, and that demands are evenly distributed along the line. A relaxation of the even-demand-distribution assumption, as one might expect, leads to an increased number of facilities. But after considering many distributions of population and facilities, based on cost minimization, the authors concluded that uneven spatial distribution of demand moderately favors centralization, or else it leaves the number of facilities unchanged. When uneven demand distributions were allowed to vary over time, it was found that slight decentralization would occur, the degree being dependent upon the relationship between peak and average demands.

In retrospect, it is difficult to say at the conceptual level where the optimal locations of public facilities would be, unless we work with an unrealistically simple model. It is clear, however, that alternative location sites carry different cost tags; thus public decision-makers have dual questions that must be answered simultaneously: where can we locate the total system of facilities so that (1) per-unit costs of production are minimized and (2) distribution or consumer collection costs are minimized?

Summary

In this section we have considered a number of models of intraurban location decisions. The central-place model was covered in detail, with the finding that prices, entry conditions, transport costs, and city size all have a significant impact on the number and size of market areas. Although these factors per se were not employed in the empirical models covered here, very simple models relating population to the number of stores could predict threshold demand levels and the existence of economies of scale for retail stores. Shopping-behavior models were viewed as being useful to potential retail locators. Although suburbanization of firms is quite evident from real-world data, empirical studies have not filtered out the most significant causal factors behind this trend. Finally, we saw that there is a tradeoff issue between minimizing production costs (and thus centralizing) versus minimizing transport costs to the consumer (and thus decentralizing) in choosing the location site(s) and number of public facilities.

SUGGESTED READINGS

Alonso, William. *Location and Land Use*. New Haven, Connecticut: Harvard Univ. Press, 1964.

Greenhut, Melvin, *Plant Location in Theory and Practice*. Chapel Hill, North Carolina: Univ. of North Carolina Press, 1956.

Hoover, Edgar. *An Introduction to Regional Economics*. New York: Knopf, 1971.

Leahy, W., McKee, D., and Dean, R. *Urban Economics*. New York: Free Press, 1970.

Lichtenberg, Robert. *One-Tenth of a Nation*. Cambridge, Massachusetts: Harvard University Press, 1960.

Losch, August. *The Economics of Location*. New Haven, Connecticut: Yale Univ. Press, 1954.

Richardson, Harry. *Regional Economics*. New York: Praeger, 1969.

REFERENCES

1. Edgar M. Hoover, "The Evolving Form and Organization of the Metropolis," in *Issues in Urban Economics*. Harvey Perloff and Lowson Wingo, Jr., eds, pp. 237–248 (Baltimore, Maryland: John Hopkins Press, 1968).

2. Benjamin Chinitz, "Contrasts in Agglomeration: New York and Pittsburgh," *American Economic Review, Papers, and Proceedings* 51, No. 2 (1961): 279–289.

3. Harold Hotelling, "Stability in Competition," *Economic Journal* 28 (1929): 41–57.

4. Robert Dean, William Leahy, and David McKee, eds., *Spatial Economic Theory*, Parts II and III (New York: Free Press, 1970).

5. Melvin Greenhut, *Plant Location in Theory and Practice* (Chapel Hill, North Carolina: Univ. of North Carolina Press, 1956).
6. Raymond Vernon, *Metropolis 1985* (Cambridge, Massachusetts: Harvard Univ. Press, 1960).
7. Robert Lichtenberg, *One-Tenth of a Nation* (Cambridge, Massachusetts: Harvard Univ. Press, 1960).
8. Y. P. Youn and C. R. Beaton, "Effect of Property Taxation on the Location of Manufacturing Activity," *Annals of Regional Science* 3 (1969): 67–75.
9. William Alonso, *Location and Land Use: Toward a General Theory of Land Rent,* pp. 42–58 (Cambridge, Massachusetts: Harvard Univ. Press, 1964).
10. Edgar S. Dunn, Jr., "The Equilibrium of Land-Use Patterns in Agriculture," *Southern Economic Journal* 21 (1954–1955): 173–187.
11. August Losch, *The Economics of Location,* translation by W. H. Woglom (New Haven, Connecticut: Yale Univ. Press, 1954).
12. Kenneth G. Denike and John B. Parr, "Production in Space, Spatial Competition, and Restricted Entry," *Journal of Regional Science* 10, No. 1 (1970): 49–63.
13. Edgar Hoover, "Transport Costs and the Spacing of Central Places," *Papers, Regional Science Association* 25 (1970): 255–274.
14. Brian Berry and William Garrison, "A Note on Central Place Theory and the Range of a Good," *Economic Geography* 34 (1958): 304–311.
15. J. D. Forbes, "Central Place Theory—An Analytical Framework for Retail Structure," *Land Economics* 48, No. 1 (1972): 15–22.
16. W. J. Reilly, "Methods for Study of Retail Relationships," Univ. of Texas Bulletin 2944, Austin, Texas, 1929.
17. W. J. Baumol and E. A. Idle, "Variety in Retailing," *Management Science* 3 (1956): 93–103.
18. Leon Moses and Harold Williamson, "The Location of Economic Activity in Cities," *American Economic Review, Papers, and Proceedings* 57, No. 2 (1967): 211–222.
19. Raymond Struyk, "A Progress Report on a Study of Intrametropolitan Location of Industry," presented at meeting of Committee on Urban Economics, Cambridge, Massachusetts, Sept. 11–12, 1969.
20. Michael Goldberg, "Intrametropolitan Industrial Location: Some Empirical Findings," *Annals of Regional Science* 3 (1969): 167–178.
21. Michael Tietz, "Toward a Theory of Urban Public Facility Location," *Papers, Regional Science Association* 21 (1968): 35–51.
22. Manfred Kochen and Karl Deutsch, "Decentralization and Uneven Service Loads," *Journal of Regional Science,* 10, No. 2 (1970): 153–173.

5

LAND USE

I. INTRODUCTION

Land is a factor of production, used by households, businesses, and the public sector. As such, the demand for land is derived from the demand for the output of these three sectors. In the short run, the supply of land services is fixed and nearly perfectly inelastic. Thus the demand for land is the major determinant of its price. And prices, of course, determine how land is allocated among users.

There are basically four types of use for land in urban areas:

(1) commercial, which includes all forms of businesses and private institutions, be they profit-making or nonprofit;
(2) residential, consisting of all housing facilities (except hotels, motels, and so on);

(3) public, made up of land owned, leased, or rented for public uses such as schools, streets, and parks;

(4) waiting, a term that denotes vacant land that is "ripening" for a higher use.

Surprisingly, the last category comprised over one-fifth of the land in cities of over 100,000 persons in 1970 [1]. Focusing on the private sector only, the type of land use for any given parcel will be determined by the relative bids of businesses, residents, and speculators. Which wins out, and the determinants of these bids, is the subject matter of this chapter.

Two additional comments are in order before we begin. First, one should keep in mind the close relationship between location decisions and land use. If a firm wants to locate in a given area of a city on an empty parcel, assuming there are no permanent zoning constraints, it can often do so because it can outbid competitors (such as residents) for the land. And once a firm erects structures on the parcel, the land use becomes permanent for all intents and purposes, since buildings last a long time. So location decisions, by firms and persons as well, play an important role in land-use patterns. Indeed, one could argue that location and land-use decisions are made simultaneously.

Second, we must keep in mind that land is an asset, which earns returns over many years. Similarly, bonds, stocks, and machines are assets. Because uses of land are so permanent—that is, returns are earned over many years—when we speak of the value of land we are really speaking of the *capitalized* value of land. The capitalized or present value of any asset that yields a fixed return from now until doomsday is given by the formula

$$PV = \frac{A}{i}$$

where PV is the present value, A is the fixed return, and i is a discount rate, which reflects the opportunity cost of the asset. The PV formula may be used to determine the demand price of any asset. For example, if I could always get $10,000 for renting a piece of land, and I had to pay 5 percent interest to get a loan to buy that piece of land, I would be willing to pay $10,000/0.05 = $200,000 for the land. If the asset is urban land, however, its present use will probably not yield a constant return over the years. Moreover, its use may change in some finite time period. To find the present value of the land under these conditions, we use

$$PV = \frac{A_1}{(1+i)} + \frac{A_2}{(1+i)^2} + \frac{A_3}{(1+i)^3} + \cdots + \frac{A_t}{(1+i)^t}$$

if the land is expected to stay in its present use for t years. Now we can let the returns A_t take on different values over time, and the same is possible for the discount rate. *PV* in this case is often referred to by economists as the present discounted value of land. Note that in both formulas, if the discount rate decreases, the present value of the asset increases. Returning to our demand-price example, we are merely saying that as the cost of borrowing decreases, we are willing to pay a higher price for a piece of land. So land values are really prices of the lands services generated over time, and the *price of land* is the present value of the return from those services over the expected life of the service. Rent, on the other hand, is the price of these services in any specific time period.

II. GENERAL URBAN LAND-USE MODELS

Before analyzing the determinants of the use of any given parcel of land in the city, it may be useful to get a birdseye view of how some economists and planners see the overall pattern of land use in our cities. In this section we shall cover three macroscopic or general land-use models: (1) the concentric zones developed by E. W. Burgess [2], (2) the radial-sector theory of Homer Hoyt [3], and (3) the multiple-nuclei model of Harris and Ullman [4].

Concentric Zones

According to Burgess, a city expands from the center in the form of concentric zones. The effect is very similar to that obtained by throwing a stone into a pool. Figure 5.1a illustrates the concentric-zone pattern of land use in a city. Activities in the concentric-zone model are grouped in five successive zones around the central business district (CBD), which is composed of office buildings, hotels, museums, department stores, and so forth. The first zone, labeled 1 in Figure 5.1a, is a wholesaling area, where warehouse and storage facilities are located to provide easily accessible supplies for the businesses downtown. The second zone is a transitional one, often with a mixture of low-quality or slum housing and scattered businesses of many varieties. The third zone is composed of low- and middle-income residences, primarily housing industrial workers. Upper-income single-family residences makeup the fourth zone, while high-income suburban commuters live in the fifth or last zone.

Since the center is the seat of activity, as it grows and expands outward there is pressure on each successive zone to expand more or less proportionately. Thus we have a succession of land uses over time. Hous-

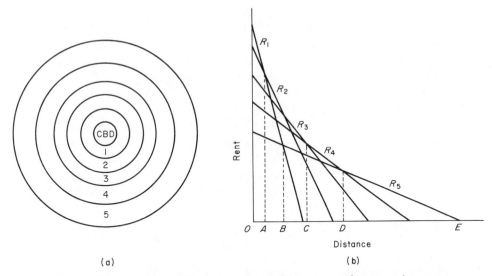

Figure 5.1 (a) *Concentric zones;* (b) *ceiling rents and concentric zones.*

ing will "filter down" from higher- to lower-income families. If for some reason the city's population declined, however, the outer zones would remain intact while the second or transitional zone would recede into the wholesaling and central-business-district zones. This situation would lend itself to a contraction of the central business district and an extension of the slum or blighted area of the city.

The work of R. M. Haig [5] provides an economic explanation of the concentric zones. Haig argued that people desire to minimize the costs of friction of overcoming space. In a city having a single center, friction costs will include transportation costs and rent. These two factors are inversely related, of course. If people and businesses preferred to be near or at the center and competition existed in land markets, we would find the uses of land decided according to the highest bidder, as shown in Figure 5.1b. R_1 through R_5 show the ceiling rents bid by the five classes of users described earlier for the land around the central business district at O. Thus wholesalers bid R_1 and use land as far as OA from the center (O) of the city. People and firms in zone 2 bid R_2 and use land between A and B. One can obtain the concentric zones of Figure 5.1a by circumscribing circles with the radii OA, OB, OC, OD, and OE.

It may seem to the reader that two logical inconsistencies occur in Figure 5.1b. That is, if everyone prefers to be near the center, how can low-income families in zone 2 (AB) outbid high-income families in zone 5 (*DE*)? This can be explained as follows. In the transitional zone, the discounted present value or price of land is very high, since speculators hold the land in its present use waiting for huge capital gains when the land is transferred to a higher use. During this waiting period, there is little if any incentive for speculators to keep up the structures on the land; thus rents or the price paid for land services for a given year will be low enough for low-income families to afford the housing. The subdivision of old houses into many apartments also helps to increase the rent per unit of land, keeping the speculators well-off during their waiting period.

William Alonso [6] argues that higher-income persons have a stronger preference for the size of the parcel of land they buy than for distance. Since large sites are cheaper in the outerlying areas, higher-income people trade off larger estates for increased commuting costs. Accessibility for higher-income persons is an inferior good, with a negative income elasticity.

The basic criticism of the concentric-zone model is that it does not explain land-use patterns in the real world. More specifically, the zones are not even and continuous in real-life cities. Heavy manufacturing industry is excluded.* Rent-bid functions are not independent among firms; thus true competition for sites is questionable. Constraints such as zoning are unaccounted for. Although most of these criticisms have some grain of truth in them, the concentric-zone theory, developed in the 1920's, still stands as a remarkably accurate overall view of land-use patterns in many of our larger cities. We shall see that the other two general models are really modifications of this model.

Radial Sectors

Homer Hoyt developed the radial-sector model to explain residential land-use development, although the logic can be applied to any type of use. According to the model, a circular city is composed of sectors of similar types of land use radiating outward from the center. Figure 5.2 gives an illustration of a city having four types (A thru D) of land uses around the CBD. Sectors A and B could be devoted to business and light manufacturing, while C and D refer to low–middle- and higher-income residential areas, respectively.

The similarity of land uses within each sector is ensured by rents

---

* Hoover notes that this is logically consistent with the Burgess model; heavy industry is not attracted to the center of the city because its customers are not local (although its suppliers may be, which would be an attractive force), and its has large space needs, which attract it to outside areas [7].

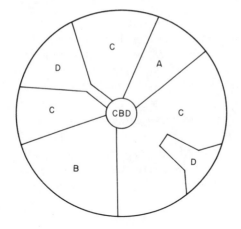

Figure 5.2 *Radial sectors.*

bid by the users and by topographical conditions. For example, agglo-meration forces will attract firms, thus allowing them to bid higher rents for land in sector A or B. Similarly, good transport routes to the city center will attract residents, who can offer higher rents, since their com-muting costs will decline the closer they locate to the highway. Thus sector D in Figure 5.2 extends inward toward the CBD. The local geog-raphy of the city also provides natural walls between land uses. Houses can be built on hillsides more easily than shopping centers can.

Like Burgess, Hoyt attempted to expand the dynamics of land-use succession in cities. Hoyt, however, did not picture the process as another stone being thrown in the pool; that is, the impetus did not come from the center of the city. Instead, the highest-income families located at the periphery, given an increase in their purchasing power, would opt to buy more land and housing services. This was accomplished by the movement of higher-income families farther from the center. Lower-cost housing would now filter down to relatively lower-income families, with the impact of the filtering diminishing with distance. Thus changes in neighborhoods are gradual, but continuous, and the changes originate in the D sectors of Figure 5.2.

Hoyt also noted that the high-quality housing sector usually begins along the best transport lines, then extends out beyond suburbia, and possibly the center of its force may turn back toward the city center if luxury accommodations are available near the central business district. It would seem, then, that Hoyt's model describes the overall develop-ment of many single-centered metropolitan areas quite well. Yet, many criticisms have been made of the model.

The major criticism of Hoyt's model is that it overemphasizes the importance of high-income residential areas as the basic catalyst in the process of land-use changes. Little is said about the nonresidential sectors, and their potential effect on land use. For example, consider the movement of a number of firms producing standardized products into the low-income and transitional sectors. This may be an attractive force for many low- and middle-income residents, which would dampen the catalytic power of the high-income residents, and possibly slow down considerably the filtering process. Another criticism is that free markets are implicitly assumed, which does not square with the real world; restricted markets may prove to halt the filtering process. Blacks and other easily identifiable socioeconomic groups are still discriminated against in housing markets, for example.

Despite these criticisms, the Hoyt model is useful. It builds on the concentric-zone model, bringing the latter closer to reality by explaining how land-use patterns follow sectors or similarities of uses. These sectors are probably fairly cohesive over time, for as moves are made, families and firms will choose the path of least resistance, which undoubtedly will mean a new location within their own sector.

Multiple Nuclei

One of the major shortcomings of the previous two models is their assumption of a single central business district. Although this assumption generally holds true for many of our major eastern cities, some western cities, notably Los Angeles, are spread out over vast areas with many nuclei or subcenters.* Even cities having single centers have numerous subcenters throughout the overall urban area.

Hoover [7, pp. 317–318] cites a number of types of subcenters, which help explain why subcenters originate:

(1) subcenters based on central-place activities, such as shopping centers, which were described in detail in the previous chapter;
(2) subcenters based on transport nodes or terminals;
(3) subcenters based on major agglomerations or single units, such as industrial facilities, sports stadiums, or universities;
(4) former small towns, which often become major subcenters in metropolitan areas;
(5) subcenters that develop because of natural advantages of their sites.

Once a given subcenter exists, concentric zones and/or radial sectors may emanate from its center in various patterns. The allowance of many

---

* Hoover, [7] notes that in 1968, 48 of the 233 SMSA's in the U.S. had at least two names, such as Minneapolis–St. Paul.

nuclei within the city permits compatible agglomerations of land use, which are important if the city is to maintain its functions. For example, manufacturing firms can locate together near rail lines and suppliers. Finance, insurance, and real-estate offices can select sites away from the manufacturing complex. Clearly, zoning laws in fact ensure that similar land uses or sectors will potentially exist.

The multiple-nuclei hypothesis privides an interesting snapshot of the city at a given point in time. To qualify as a major general theory of urban land use, it must be refined to the point where it can at least give a more specific explanation of land-use changes over time. This may, however, be asking too much of a general model. In its present state, the model is probably more realistic than the concentric-zone and radial-sector models, although many of the characteristics of the latter two models are included in the multiple-nuclei hypothesis.

III. THE DETERMINANTS OF SPECIFIC LAND USES

In the previous section we reviewed three models of land-use patterns considering the city as a whole. It is now time to ask ourselves how a specific parcel of land will be used. Will it go to commercial usage? Or will residents use the land? Under what conditions will it remain idle or vacant, awaiting a higher use? These questions will be considered in this section, using a simplified analysis whereby we assume away the public sector for the most part. In this way, we can take existing governmental constraints (location and patterns of streets, freeways, schools, parks, and so on, as well as zoning and building codes) as given, and focus on the basic determinants of land use.

A Simple Paradigm of Urban Land Markets

Let us begin our analysis by considering a simple but instructive model of urban land markets developed by Ira. S. Lowry [8]. The land market is a point of contact between real-estate owners and persons who desire to buy, rent, or lease property for their residences or businesses. The way this market operates will take us a long way in explaining how land is utilized.

Consider any city whose land is divided up into a number of sites. Each site may or may not have structural characteristics consistent with a given use. At the end of every transaction period, users will reassess the advantage of their present site by considering the present discounted value of net benefits of all sites in the city. Thus they will establish some price that they would be willing to pay for their own and all

TABLE 5–1

Demand Prices for a Five-User, Five-Site City

User	Site				
	1	2	3	4	5
1	$ 5	$8	$ 8	$10	$12*
2	6	2	13*	4	5
3	8	9*	4	6	6
4	12*	5	1	2	3
5	7	5	9	11*	10

other sites. These demand prices are shown in Table 5-1 for a five-user, five-site city. In Table 5-1, user 1 bids $5 for site 1, $8 for site 2, and so forth. Obviously, the user is equally well-off at any of the sites if he pays his demand price. Assume that the demand prices in Table 5-1 are known to all owners of the respective sites. Each owner would check his column of bids and deal with the highest bidder. The highest bidder may be the existing tenant, the owner himself, or a third party. Whatever the distribution of users is at the outset, the new distribution at the beginning of the coming transaction period is shown by the asterisks: sector 1 will use site 5, sector 2 will use site 3, and so forth.

Although the illustration in Table 5-1 is very simple, it easily could be made more realistic by expanding the number of sectors and/or sites. A solution can easily be found, regardless of whether the number of users equals the number of sites or not. The only condition for an identifiable solution is that no user bid the highest price for more than one site. If this happened, bargaining between the owners and users would establish the solution.

Many will argue that this model is unrealistic. The typical user does not calculate a demand price at the end of each transaction period for every site. He probably considers only his own site and possibly one or two alternatives. Furthermore, negotiations are shrouded by secrecy. Users would never want to let owners know their demand prices. And contracts between users and owners do not all expire simultaneously, so that users are not all looking or "in the market" at the same time. Withstanding these criticisms, the simple paradigm illustrated above is a useful model for explaining how land is allocated among users. Alterations in site characteristics will occur over time, but these changes will be reflected in new demand prices, which may (or may not) cause a reallocation of land among users.

How are the demand or bid prices arrived at? Although the remainder of this section will be addressed to this question, we can cover the general arguments here. If the prospective user is a business, its demand price will be determined by:

(1) characteristics of the business, such as its production function and the demand for its product;
(2) characteristics of the site, including access, structures, amenities, and needed improvements;
(3) the location of the site with respect to competitors or complementary establishments.

One should notice a parallel between these factors and those discussed in the previous chapter on intraurban location. With appropriate alterations in these three factors, we could explain the demand price for residents; that is, under (1) we would be interested in their preferences and income levels, and for (3) we would want to know the neighborhood characteristics of the respective sites. The determinants of demand price by speculators would include the speculators' expectations as well as the factors listed above for businesses. The present-value formula described earlier is a basic tool for speculators and businesses.

Over time, changes in the factors outlined above will cause changes in demand prices; thus land may be reallocated among users. Clearly, even if site characteristics and all other locations are given, one could get a new set of bid prices for a business, and potentially a change in land use if the demand for land changes. In the remainder of this section, we shall analyze the determinants of specific land uses in more detail.

Commercial Land Use

Land is like any other factor of production; thus a profit-maximizing firm in a competitive product and factor market will buy land up to the point at which the additional revenue from using another unit of land is exactly offset by the additional cost. The additional revenue attributable to any factor is called its marginal revenue product. The marginal revenue product is equal to the marginal revenue obtained by selling another unit of output times the marginal product of the factor.

We know that in a competitive product market, price is constant; thus marginal revenue is also constant and equal to price. The marginal product of a factor is the addition to total product or output of using another unit of that factor. We know that if the other factors are fixed,

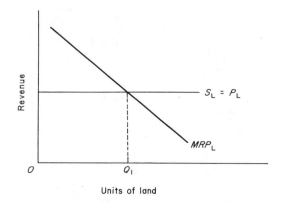

Figure 5.3 *Firm equilibrium in a single-factor market.*

as more land is used, its marginal product declines. This is the familiar law of diminishing returns. Thus if marginal revenue is constant, and marginal product declines, the marginal revenue product of land will decline as we use more units of land, *ceteris paribus*. The declining marginal revenue product (MRP) schedule shown in Figure 5.3 can represent the firm's demand schedule for the factor land.*

In a competitive factor market, the firm can buy all of the input it wants at the same price; thus the marginal cost of hiring another unit of land is the price of land P_L. Thus the firm will hire OQ_1 units of land if it desires to maximize profits. If it hired fewer than OQ_1 units, it could add more to its revenues than to costs by hiring additional units up to OQ_1. Clearly, OQ_1 is an equilibrium level.

The marginal-productivity theory is indispensable for explaining *how much* of any factor a firm will hire. In a city, however, we also have to consider where (spatially) the land units will be purchased. In the preceding chapter we used a bid-price-curve model to establish where the firm would locate in relation to the center of the city. We assumed that all buying occurs in the center of the city, unless one is willing to incur transport costs to get to outlying firms. Let us turn to a similar model and consider in more detail the determinants of the slope of the bid-price curve.†

Consider a single-centered city, and a firm with product price given

---

* Technically speaking, the MRP schedule is the demand schedule only if the firm uses a single factor. It can be easily proven, however, that when more than one factor is considered, the demand schedule for any given factor will slope downward [9].

† This section relies on Hugh O. Nourse, *Regional Economics* [10].

and all factor prices given except for rent. If the firm locates near the center of the city, its revenues will be higher, since it will be more accessible. Farther out from the center, the firm will have to incur additional selling costs in order to attract customers; thus revenues net of selling costs will decline with distance from the center.

If the firm is located at the center, the maximum rent it can pay will occur where total revenue TR equals total cost TC. Clearly, as the possible rent increases, TC will increase until just normal profits are earned. This maximum rent can be called ceiling rent, as we noted in the previous chapter. Now as a firm moves out from the center, its costs decline because of lower prices of land; thus, again where the lower TR equals the lower TC, we obtain the ceiling rent for a firm x miles from the center. The rents bid x miles from the center (R_x) will be less than the rent bid at the center (R_c), because nonland costs become greater as we move away from the center. So if we plotted R_c and R_x and additional rents farther from the center, we would obtain a downward sloping curve as in Figure 5.4. Our remaining task is to explain the slope of the rent-bid curve, and the factors that shift the curve. In this way, we can explain some of the determinants of the demand prices discussed in the paradigm earlier in this chapter.

Three factors affect the slope of the rent-bid curve. First, the more it costs in advertising and other inducements to attract the same number of customers at x miles as one had at the center, the steeper the rent-bid curve. Second, the greater the productivity of land, the steeper the curve. And finally, the slope is steeper if land and nonland factors are poor substitutes. These last two factors are not inconsistent. As land productivity increases, output rises under a given budget, and if the increase in selling costs exceeds the increase in revenue, one can bid only a lower rent at a given distance from the center. If land is a poor substitute

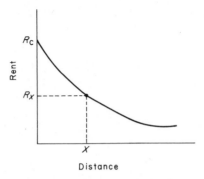

Figure 5.4 *Rent-bid curve.*

for other factors, it costs more to produce a given level of output; thus again one can bid only lower rents.

What factors shift the rent-bid curve? Clearly, changes in the demand for or the supply of the product produced by the firm will shift the rent-bid curve. For example, if demand increases, product price will rise, and the firm can pay a higher rent. Similarly, if a more effective technique of advertising is used, costs will decline, which will increase the curve. If the price of a factor rises, however, costs rise and the curve shifts downward.

Although we have considered only a firm selling its output within the city, the reader should have no problem in applying these principles to a firm exporting its product. In this case, revenues are constant over space. Labor costs will increase as one moves away from the single-centered city, but land costs per unit will decline. Thus the slope of the rent-bid curve of the exporting firm will depend on these two factors and the substitutability of land for nonland factors. Clearly, the greater the increase in wage rates and the less substitutable land is for other factors, the steeper the slope of the rent bid curve. As in the case of the nonexporting firm, any change in demand or supply for the product will shift the exporting firm's rent-bid curve.

Residential Land Use

Unlike firms, which maximize profits, residents are assumed to maximize utility. We can use the Alonso model covered in the preceding chapter for the firm to explain how the rent bids of residents are arrived at. As in the section above on firms, we are primarily interested in the slope of the rent-bid curve, and factors that shift the curve.

Assume that we have a household attempting to locate near the highest-quality school district in a given city. This district is surrounded by somewhat less high-quality districts. All quality levels are fixed. Thus the marginal utility of access to the highest-quality district declines with distance from that district. We further assume that the location of all other residents is fixed. Under these conditions, households bid lower rents as they get farther away from the high-quality school district.

There is some tradeoff between reductions in rent bids and increases in distance from the desired school district in obtaining the same total level of utility. These isoutility curves will have the following properties:

(1) They are single-valued; that is, only one price is bid for each parcel as one moves away from the high-quality school district.
(2) The curves slope downward.

(3) Lower curves represent higher utility.
(4) The curves do not intersect.

As with firms in the previous chapter, there is a family of isoutility curves for each household (U_1, U_2, and U_3 in Figure 5.5). Where the slope of the lowest isoutility curve equals the slope of the actual price of land, one can find the location site of the resident with respect to the highest-quality school district (represented by O in Figure 5.5). This site is Od_1 units from that district in Figure 5.5. The rent paid is Or_1.

What factors determine the slope of the isoutility curves of Figure 5.5? Essentially the preference structure of households determines how steep the slopes will be. For a given income, level of taste, and price of substitute goods, the curves will be steeper for households that prefer access to O more strongly than other goods. In addition, if transport costs declined to zero under the given assumptions, households could bid a higher rent for land at a given distance from the desired district. In the diagram, this would have the effect of rotating the isoutility or rent-bid curves rightward at the top and leftward at the bottom; thus the equilibrium position would be closer to the desired district. In general, inward shifts of the isoutility curves would occur if the household's income increased, tastes changed toward access, or if the price of substitute goods increased.

Would our model give any different results if we considered the more traditional case of residential land use with respect to a single-centered city? Not really, although we may want to cover a few finer points. As we found in our initial coverage of central places, any change in transport costs may or may not move one farther away from or closer to the center. Clearly, as transport costs decline, one's real income in-

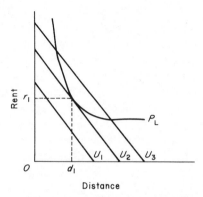

Figure 5.5 *Single household equilibrium location.*

creases. According to Muth [11], higher incomes increase the demand for space. Of course, higher incomes also increase the cost of commuting. If the former outweighs the latter, which Muth has found in U.S. cities, then increases in income will lead to movements away from the central city.

In summary, residents bid for land on the basis of utility maximization. Given the income and preferences of households, increases in rent are traded off against more access to a desired location. Bid rents for a given parcel of land will change with changes in demand on the part of the household.

Empirical Studies of Urban Land Values

Now that we have a more detailed view of how businesses and residents bid for land, it may be interesting to see whether or not these models hold up in the real world. The reader should understand that our models are of the partial- (rather than general-) equilibrium variety; that is, we looked at commercial land-use bids, holding all other uses constant. Similarly, we considered residential bids, holding other uses constant. Thus our models as they stand are difficult to test empirically, but the spirit of the models can certainly be tested.

One of the major findings of the rent-bid analysis is that land values will decline with distance from the center of the city. In addition, we argued that characteristics of the site and the surrounding area were important. E. F. Brigham [12] has tested a linear model of this type for the city of Los Angeles, using a sample of land values along three rays emanating from the central business district. He found the slope of the rent-bid curve for all users to be between −0.5 and −0.9. In other words, a 1 percent increase in distance units from the center was associated with a 0.5–0.9 percent decrease in land values. This is rather remarkable, since Los Angeles is said to be a highly decentralized city.

Edwin Mills [13] has performed some interesting tests of the relationship between land values and distance over a long time period. As a city grows and expands over time, our models would argue that rents would rise downtown, while the slope of the rent-bid curve should decline if transportation improvements do in fact "cause" people to locate farther from the central city. Using data for Chicago land values in 1836, 1857, 1873, 1910, and 1928, Mills estimated a simple least-squares relationship between land values and distance for each of these years. Mills found that the rent at the center steadily increased during the 92 year period. With the exception of 1857, the slope of the rent–distance relationship steadily declined. Finally, the ability of distance alone to explain the variation in land values declined markedly over the period. This is to be expected in an expanding city.

Mills also attempted to relate residential land values to distance from the city center for a contemporary period, 1966. He also accounted for site characteristics and zoning practices. The results were statistically insignificant. Although there are probably many reasons for the poor results from this residential model, one could be that his estimates of residential market values were in error. One way of sidestepping this problem is to use an estimate of the size of physical structures used on the land, which is probably highly correlated with land value. Using floor space per acre, Mills found a significant negative relationship with distance using 1959 Chicago data, not only for residential land but also for commercial, manufacturing, and public land.

Our final note of interest from the Mills' study is that the strongest results obtained showed a nonlinear relationship between land values or floor space per acre and distance. Since the rent-bid function, given the demand for the product, is derived from the production function of the firm, this finding is clear evidence that the production functions of businesses are also nonlinear. Clearly, land is substitutable for nonland inputs as one moves away from the central city and vice versa.

Harold Brodsky [14]] was more successful in explaining residential land values than Mills, although Brodsky's study area was census tracts in Washington, D.C. Besides distance, Brodsky used two site character-istics—density and income of the population in each tract. As expected, Brodsky found that distance and income were negatively and positively related to land values, respectively, whether the latter was measured on a square-footage or per-person basis. Density, on the other hand, was positively related to land values per square foot, but negatively related to land values per person. Clearly, in more densely populated areas, land costs are shared; thus on a per-person basis the inverse rela-tionship has a logical basis. All of the Brodsky results were statistically significant and nonlinear in form. Thus households are able to substitute land for nonland items in their utility functions as they move away from the center of the city.

In short, the results of empirical tests of the rent-bid models, although incomplete and imperfect, show that the models do have explanatory power.

IV. CHANGES IN LAND USES

Up to this point, we have argued implicity that land would be con-verted from one use to another if the demand price or rent bid of one user, say A, exceeded that of another potential or the existing user, say B. There is nothing wrong with this view, except that it offers very little of the behind-the-scenes action, which is important to understand if we want to learn how land is used over the long run. In addition, we have focused primarily on the land market from the buyer's side. If I own a parcel, what factors must I consider in renting or selling that parcel to users? When is the optimal time to convert my land from one use to another? In this section we shall attempt to answer these questions. We shall also consider how land at the boundary of a city is converted from agricultural to nonagricultural use. This will show not only how land uses change but also how boundaries are shifted.

The Income Expectations Approach

An owner faced with renting, leasing, or selling his land naturally desires to maximize the income from the transaction. If the land is rented or leased, the income will be taken over a period of years; therefore, we will be interested in the discounted present value of this earnings stream. Clearly the size of this stream is determined largely by the expectations of the owner. Theoretically, land uses will change until the present values are maximized for each owner. This is nothing more than the simple paradigm discussed earlier. One question we have failed to answer, however, is: What considerations does the income-maximizing landowner make in deciding to change the use of the land? Clearly landowners do not have published tables such as the illustration in Table 5-1; thus they must figure out on their own what the highest and best use for their land is. This is why expectations are so important.

Consider a parcel of rural land, located near an urban area, which earns a constant annual income A. In its next-best alternative use, the parcel could earn i percent per year. If the parcel were to be sold for an urban use, and an idle or ripening period occurred, then the discounted present value of this parcel would be [15]

$$PV = \frac{A}{i} + \frac{CG}{(1 + i_{cg})^t} \tag{5-1}$$

where CG represents the capital gains from the urban use, i_{cg} is the discount rate for the capital gains, and t is the number of years A will continue before CG is received. If no idle or ripening period occurred between the change in uses, and A was already borne for the present and final period, the formula for the discounted present value would be

$$PV = \frac{A}{i} + CG \tag{5-2}$$

Clearly if *CG* is not greater than zero, one would not sell his land for the urban use, given that he is an income-maximizer.

What would happen to this model if a ripening or idle period occurred whereby income or losses occurred during the ripening stage? Leaving the land idle will reduce *CG;* thus the correct measure of *CG* is the value of the gain in the year of transition less the reduction of income during the ripening period. Alternatively, if the land has an interim use, we would add the resultant net income to the *CG* when the change-over takes place. We are assuming, of course, that capital gains are realized when the transition occurs.

Thus we can explain the transition of land uses based on income expectations. But often, sellers will develop the land themselves rather than let it remain idle. To include this developmental cost in the model above, the cost could be treated exactly like the cost of idle land. A more interesting question to the seller who decides to develop his land first is: When should he develop the land? What is the optimal development date, that is, the date that will maximize his gain?

Any profit-maximizer will improve a given parcel up to the point at which the additional revenues obtained by hiring more units of capital are exactly offset by the additional capital or construction costs. This principle applies to any land improvement. For example, if one wanted to know how high to build a skyscraper, he would continue upward until the discounted value of future returns from another story would exactly equal the additional cost of another story.

This simple principle of profit maximization can also be used to show intuitively the conditions under which a developer can determine the optimal date of development.* Consider a *bare* parcel that will be sold for a higher use in the future. Our problem is to figure out when to develop the land, much as a wine maker or tree grower has to determine the optimal maturation period. The answer to our problem is that we would develop the parcel when the increase in its value was exactly equal to the discount rate. Recall that the discount rate represents the opportunity cost of the site. Since appreciation is the only return we would get from holding the bare site idle, the market mechanism, if operating efficiently, will drive the increase in value into equality with the rate of return on the next-best alternative use—or what we call opportunity cost. When this occurs, the optimal date is at hand. Note that this rule is nothing more than the marginal revenue–marginal cost criterion found in any economics text.

How would a tax affect the optimal development date? Assume the tax is a fixed percentage *k* of the value of the parcel. In this case,

* For those who have background in calculus, this discussion is developed in Donald C. Shoup [16].

we would develop when the increase in value is equal to the discount rate *and* the tax rate, or algebraically,

$$\frac{PV'}{PV} = i + k \tag{5-3}$$

where PV' is the increase in the discounted present value of the parcel. Notice that the tax causes the rate of appreciation to increase, although the tax *decreases* the value of the land. Clearly, the latter largely explains the former, since the denominator on the left-hand side of Equation (5-3) is smaller. An interesting conclusion of this consideration of taxes is that, contrary to what most textbooks claim, taxes may have nonneutral effects on resource allocation [16, p. 39]. In other words, the optimal date of development may vary according to the level of k; thus the level of resources allocated to the construction sector will also vary.

We can also consider the effect of using the site for a low-order interim use before development to its highest use. Many sites are used as parking lots or varied purposes before they are developed. In this case, the marginal cost of the site is reduced by the net return earned in the interim use; thus the optimal date for development will be given by

$$\frac{PV'}{PV} = i + k - r \tag{5-4}$$

where r is the rate of return derived from the interim use. Clearly r reduces the rate of appreciation in the parcel, primarily because it increases the PV of the parcel.

In retrospect, we have established conditions under which land would be changed from one use to another, based on the expected income from the uses. We have also shown the conditions for choosing the optimal date of redevelopment if the seller decides to improve the land. Although these models are useful for explaining the process of land-use changes, one should be aware of the implicit assumptions and shortcomings of the models. For example, uncertainty plays a large role in real-estate markets; thus owners will have a difficult time projecting A into the future. True discount rates are not easy to identify, and they vary among persons. Expectations can change overnight, causing a reevaluation of A and i. And the growth rates of (true) land values are not as well known as biologically established growth rates of trees or wine; thus the conditions for the optimal improvement date are difficult to identify.

In spite of these shortcomings, the income-expectations model is a very important tool for explaining changes in land use. We shall see throughout the remainder of this book that changes in expected income, and thus land uses, can often result in families losing their houses, or even whole neighborhoods being done away with. Clearly, this section is very important for those who want to attain a more than superficial understanding of contemporary intraurban problems and their solutions.

The Economics of City Boundary Changes

In the previous section we showed how rural land could be changed into urban land, if certain conditions were met. Our primary focus was on the decision-making criteria of the owner of the land. One of the missing elements in the income-expectations approach is space. In this section we shall cover a model developed by Richard Muth [17], which will show not only why land-use changes may occur but also how the boundary of the city shifts with land-use changes.

Assume we have two sectors using land, an urban sector and a rural sector. Both sectors have given production functions, which relate land and nonland inputs to their respective outputs. For simplicity, we can assume that nonland inputs are labor, whose price is the wage rate. Now if we have a single-centered city, we can argue that the price of land declines with distance from the center, as we have shown earlier. Finally, the demand function for the urban and rural sectors' products is given.

If the two sectors in our model were residential and agricultural, it would not be surprising to find the boundary at *b* miles from the center of the city, as shown in Figure 5.6. With the assumptions presented above, it is possible to show in detail how changes in rent bids will occur, and thus resultant shifts in land use and the boundary. Our model is similar to the single-sector models covered earlier in the sections

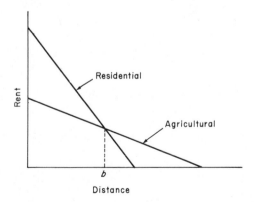

Figure 5.6 *The city boundary in a two-sector model.*

on commercial and residential land use, except that now we are considering two uses simultaneously.

Figure 5.7a shows traditional demand and supply curves in the second quadrant for sector 1. That is, demand is a function of product price, given income, tastes, and the price of substitutes. Supply is also a function of price, as well as factor prices and the boundary. The boundary in a circular city gives us the radius of each sector's land area. Thus, using simple rules from plane geometry, we could determine the land area. To obtain the aggregate supply of any use, we merely multiply output per unit of land times the land area. As demand and supply change for product 1, equilibrium prices will trace out the rents R that the sector will bid for land. Thus we would need a diagram such as that shown in 5.7a for each sector. Rents, of course, are positively related to price. Clearly, if P_1 rises, sector 1 can pay a higher rent. If the wage rate and supply for each sector (S_1 and S_2) are given, we can draw the boundary in Figure 5.7b as a function of the ratio of rents bid between the two sectors. The boundary is fixed under these conditions thus a bar is placed above b. Clearly b is a positive function of R_1/R_2, for if sector 1 is the urban sector, and 2 is the rural sector, an increase in R_1 would move the boundary outward. Rents, of course, will be inversely related to distance from the market, as we have shown elsewhere. Wages will also be inversely related to rents, which is obvious.

It is now possible to figure out the impact of any exogenous change, such as changes in tastes, wages, or technology, on the rural–urban landuse pattern and boundary. For example, assume that tastes change such that the demand for sector 1's services increases. If we start from a point of equilibrium, the impact of the increase in demand can be shown in Figure 5.8. In Figure 5.8a, the increase in demand to D_1' results

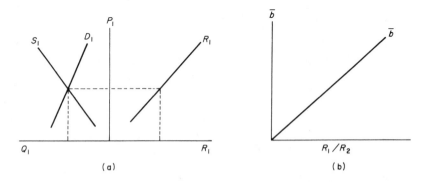

Figure 5.7 (a) *Equilibrium product price and rents in a two-sector model;* (b) *relative rents and the city boundary in a two-sector model.*

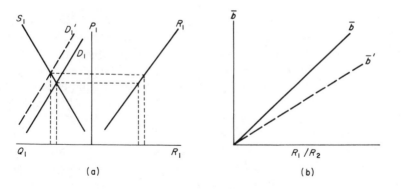

Figure 5.8 (a) *Effect of an increase in product demand on price, output, and rent;* (b) *effect of an increase in product demand on the city boundary.*

in a greater P_1 and Q_1, and higher R_1 bid. The increase in R_1 will cause the boundary to shift out from $\bar{b}$ to $\bar{b}'$ in Figure 5.8b. Thus, in the rural sector, the supply of the product will diminish, so P_2 and R_2 will rise. The student is urged to use a pencil and piece of paper to draw the diagram for sector 2's response. The result, then, of an increase in demand for sector 1's output is that the boundary moves outward while the rents for both sectors increase.

If the demand for 2's output increased, with 1's demand remaining constant, the boundary would shift closer to the center of the city. An interesting case is when both demands increase simultaneously; if this occurs, the shift in the boundary is determined by the relative price elasticities of the two sector's products [17, p. 17]. If the demand for sector 1 is elastic, while 2's demand is inelastic, a very great increase in 1's demand relative to 2 would be required for the boundary to move out. Thus if sector 1 is housing, and sector 2 is agriculture which sells its products solely in the local market, it is not clear that increases in income or population in the city will necessarily lead to an expansion of residential land use.

The student should work through alternative exogenous changes and find the resultant boundary and land-use pattern.

Empirical Studies of Changes in Land Use

Both the income-expectations model and the rural–urban conversion model are difficult to test empirically in their present forms. Nevertheless, a number of studies of land-use changes have been made that more or less corroborate the principles discussed in this section.

For example, Clonts [15] developed a model to explain rural land

values in an area undergoing rapid urbanization near Washington, D.C.
Land values were hypothesized to be related to variables consistent
with the concepts of capital gains and ripening stages; thus the model
is a test of the income-expectations approach. Land uses studied were
residential and other rural or ripening uses. Since the influence of urbanization, as measured by access and amenities, significantly affected land
values, Clonts concluded that shifts in land use and capital gains were
important determinants of the value of rural land.

Michael Rancich [18] studied the changes in land values of outlying
vacant and agricultural land in the Green River Valley area of metropolitan Seattle between 1956 and 1966. Rancich found that accessibility,
clustering of uses, and the timing of development had an important
impact on these land values at the fringe. The building of new freeways
in the area, as expected, sent land prices soaring. The size of the parcel
also seemed to be important, since the greater the size, the more options
the owner has in its future uses.

A study of the determinants of the price of vacant land in the North
Philadelphia area between 1945 and 1962 was conducted by Adams
et al. [19]. The authors hypothesize that land values are related to
access, legal restrictions (zoning), taxes, and the amenities of the land.
They expect that land would appreciate at a rate equal to the sum
of the discount rate plus the tax rate, which is just what we argued
earlier in terms of the optimal development date. The authors tested
their land-value hypothesis for residential as well as commercial (and
industrial) land uses. The results showed that for residential land, the
long-run price trend followed the normal return or discount rate. The
net return was 7.7 percent, which the authors argued was very close
to the discount rate. The appreciation of property values in land to
be used for commercial and industrial purposes was very high (16 percent), and after accounting for taxes, amenities, and so forth, the rate
did not fall. Assuming that a normal return (discount rate) in this case
is less than 16 percent, one might conclude that the development of
the land was not anticipated, possibly because of market imperfections.
Clearly, if the market was operating optimally, the appreciation rate
of land values would exactly equal the net rate of return on the land.

V. LAND USE POLICY

Policy in urban areas is effectuated by government. The economic
rationale for having a government, and thus policy, is to provide a helping hand when the market mechanism (price system) breaks down or

fails outright. When the price system fails, resources are not allocated efficiently. Economists say there is an efficient allocation of resources · toward the production of any good or service when the price of the good P equals the marginal cost MC of the good. Why? Because P represents the additional value of attaining another unit of the good, and MC represents the opportunity cost of the resources in producing another unit of the good. So if society desires to maximize its value or utility from any good, that good should be produced up to where the $P = MC$. If $P_x > MC_x$, society is saying it desires more x; thus more resources will be allocated to the production of x until $P_x = MC_x$. On the other hand, if $MC_x > P_x$, society is saying it values other products more highly than x; thus resources will be allocated out of the production of x and into their next-best alternative.

Besides efficient resources allocation, governments also affect the distribution of income. Although Musgrave has argued that only the federal level of government should actively seek to redistribute income [20], local governments clearly alter the income distribution by their taxation and expenditure policies. Thus equity considerations are important in the assessment of land-use policies. For example, if the local government taxes everyone to build new highways, but not everyone directly uses the new highways, there is a redistribution from nonusers to users.

In this final section of the chapter, we shall consider some of the tools used by government to alter land-use patterns. In addition, we shall also take a look at some of the effects of urban renewal on land usage, and resultant changes in resource allocation and the income distribution.

Tools of Land Use Policy

There are many tools that local governments can use to alter land use policy: zoning and building codes, fire and safety ordinances, tax and expenditure policies, and government takeover of private land. In this section we shall consider just three of these tools—zoning, taxation, and expenditures.

Zoning occurred in the late nineteenth century in New York City, as we saw in Chapter 2. Zoning means that certain geographical areas are constrained in the type and number of structures that can be placed on the land. Clearly, zoning freezes the use of land in the short term. There is an economic rationale for zoning, however, and it involves the $P = MC$ criterion explained earlier. If I invest my lifetime earnings in a fine home, and someone is allowed to come along and build a noisy, dirty gas station beside my house, I am in trouble. Certainly the value of my home will decline. But the gas station owner does not have to consider this decline in his decision-making process. He considers only his own private costs. If he considered social costs as well as his own private costs, there would be an inequality between his P and MC; that is, $MC > P$. In this case, fewer resources would be devoted to gas station production; thus he would probably not locate his station beside my house.

In this gas-station illustration, the station owner produces a negative externality that I am forced to consume. This lowers the utility of my property or causes me grief. To prevent such problems, areas are zoned so that similar uses are grouped together as much as possible throughout the city. Residential, commercial, and industrial zones are used, with many subcategories under these three general zones. At the borders of zones, however, one will always find negative (and positive) externalities abounding; thus an inefficient allocation of resources results in these transition areas.

In general, zoning has a positive effect on resource allocation; that is, it "restores" the $P = MC$ equality that might not occur if zoning were nonexistent.* It may also be argued that zoning tends to cement the existing distribution of income, since it acts to freeze existing land uses.

One of the major tools used to raise revenues at the local level is the property tax. In a static model in which the supply of land is perfectly inelastic, variations in the property tax do not affect the price or quantity of land. Only economic profits or rents are affected. Thus property taxes are said to have a neutral effect on resource allocation and land use. But we know, from our earlier discussion in this chapter on the optimal development date of land, that in a dynamic setting taxes are not neutral, since they cause land to appreciate faster. This accelerated increase may or may not bring about a quicker change in land use, depending upon the expectations and (risk) preferences of the speculator. Over time, then, it is possible that taxes will raise P, thus causing more land to be bought up by speculators because $P > MC$.

On the equity side, many [22] argue that increases in land values in cities are primarily the result of public decisions (such as the building of new roads, schools, utility lines, and so on); thus the public should capture the benefits of these increases through taxing the increases and distributing the revenues equitably. Presently, the property tax at local levels is regressive that is, low-income persons pay a higher share of

---

* For an alternative view based on an analysis of a city (Houston) without zoning laws, see Bernard Siegan [21].

their income in property taxes than higher-income persons do. This inequity has been clearly established for decades [23], yet governments have done little to change the situation. Netzer argues [22, pp. 191–199] that we need to restructure the emphasis of the tax from buildings to land. High taxes on buildings destroy incentives for new or maintenance-type construction. Low land taxes may prolong the holding of land in its present use by speculators. Thus, to get a more efficient allocation of resources and a more equitable distribution of income, Netzer says we should tax land more heavily. A major problem of this policy prescription is the difficulty one would face in divorcing increases in value due to land versus those due to the structures on the land.

Property taxes also present equity problems at the urban–rural fringe. As urbanization spreads, farmers who continue to raise crops and find their property values rising have to pay much higher taxes. Speculators or persons holding alternative investments do not have to pay increased taxes annually, because of capital-gains provisions. Clearly an inequity exists here. Blase and Staub [22] found the property tax to be regressive with respect to farm size for seven rural Missouri counties outside of Kansas City.

In summary, property taxes can affect the allocation of resources and thus land use over time. In practice, property taxes serve to redistribute income from the "have-nots" to the "haves." Moreover, existing tax laws seem to favor speculators, which probably serves to reduce the supply of land available for use at any given moment of time. This causes the price of land to rise, and causes a reallocation of resources away from the $P = MC$ optimum. In short, property taxes seem to exacerbate the problems government is supposed to solve!

What about the other side of the government coin—expenditures. How do they affect land-use patterns? It should be rather obvious that many expenditure decisions have a direct effect on changes in land use. For example, new highways lead to new commercial and residential districts. If the particular highway goes to the suburbs, most of the development usually occurs in the outerlying area. However, land prices in the city are affected; thus changes in land use there may occur. For example, Goldberg has shown [25] that improvements in highway transportation lead to an expansion of urban land uses at the fringe, and concomitantly a decline in aggregate economic rents or profits in the city. Let us consider his model briefly.

If the demand for land is given and elastic, as the supply of land increases in the city because of transportation improvements, the price of land falls. Note that neither aggregate rents nor land values need fall. The reduction in price brings an increase in total revenue;

thus aggregate land values rise. For any individual landowner, however, profits decline because of the reduction in the price of land. In the short run, each firm, on the average, will cut back its output. With the expansion at the fringe, the total output of the land industry increases, of course. This means an increase in the demand for construction resources needed to develop and improve the land. The combination of higher construction costs and lower land prices results in lower aggregate profits or economic rents; thus a reallocation of resources may occur.

Goldberg tested the model outlined here by comparing land values in a region that had undergone highway transportation improvements with those in another region that did not have any major highway improvements. San Francisco's land values increased by only 1.3 percent between 1930 and 1956, whereas Marin County, which was opened up by the Golden Gate Bridge, experienced property value increases of 162.4 percent over the same period. Similarly, Contra Costra County's property values rose 141.7 percent after the opening of the San Francisco–Oakland Bay Bridge. Clearly the real price of land fell in San Francisco; thus, according to the models discussed earlier in this chapter, land-use patterns changed.

Urban Renewal

Although urban renewal has been going on for decades, the decay present after World War II brought the federal and local governments into the picture in a major way. The primary goal of the governments' urban renewal program is to eliminate blight and slums. Often this involves changes in land use, especially if former slum residential areas are transformed into commercial areas. By the power of eminent domain, government takes the land, improves it in many cases, and sells it to developers. Residents who have to be removed often end up on the short end of the stick.* Land developers get the parcels at a fraction of the real cost to society; thus urban renewal is clouded by gross inefficiencies and inequities. To illustrate this point, we shall consider the impact of bringing higher-income housing to the central city [27].

Traditional rent-bid analysis by income class would show a land-use pattern similar to that in Figure 5.9 for American cities. This figure assumes that access is an inferior good. For some persons, however, such as those without children, the income elasticity of demand for access may outweigh the income elasticity for space. If urban-renewal programs lead to new luxury apartments and condominiums downtown,

---

* For an excellent evaluation of urban renewal, see Jerome Rothenberg, *Economic Evaluation of Urban Renewal* [26].

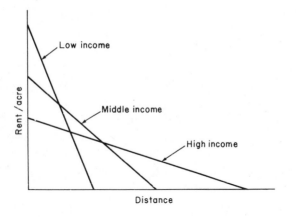

Figure 5.9   *Rents bid by income class.*

such persons will be likely to move into the city. In this case, the bid curves may be like those shown in Figure 5.10. The curve for the higher-income household would be kinked. Clearly the low-income families cannot find housing at the rents they are accustomed to paying. They must either pay the higher prices or move outward. But they do not have as much space now, so density will increase, which further raises the price of land. The result is similar to the findings of the property tax: instead of helping the market to operate more efficiently, government often makes the problem worse. Developers pay understated prices for improved land at the expense of the rest of society and especially the poor.

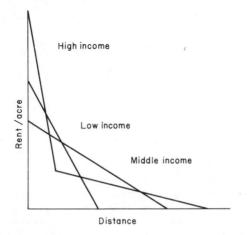

Figure 5.10   *Impact of urban renewal on land use: a kinked high-income rent-bid curve.*

VI. SUMMARY

In this chapter we have considered the determinants of and changes in urban land uses. We began our discussion with three general models of land-use patterns, which gave us an overall view of land use in the city. Next we covered the determinants of land uses in some detail. We argued that land will go to the highest bidder; thus profit-maximizing firms and utility-maximizing individuals will locate in the city, where they maximize their respective objective functions. Changes in land use were explained by an income-expectations model, as well as a more general two-sector model. In the areas of land-use policy that we have covered, it is not uncommon to find that policies are exacerbating rather than solving problems.

SUGGESTED READINGS

Alonso, William. *Location and Land Use.* Cambridge, Massachusetts: Harvard Univ. Press, 1964.

Edel, Matthew, and Rothenberg Jerome. *Readings in Urban Economics.* New York: Macmillan, 1972.

Hoover, Edgar. *An Introduction to Regional Economics.* New York: Knopf, 1971.

Muth, Richard. *Cities and Housing.* Chicago, Illinois: Univ. of Chicago Press, 1969.

Netzer, Dick. *Economics and Urban Problems.* New York: Basic Books, 1969.

Netzer, Dick. *Economics of the Property Tax.* Brookings Inst., 1966.

Nourse, Hugh. *Regional Economics.* New York: McGraw-Hill, 1968.

Perloff, Harvey, ed. *The Quality of the Urban Environment,* Baltimore, Maryland: Johns Hopkins Press (for Resources for the Future, Inc.), 1969.

Richardson, Harry. *Regional Economics.* New York: Praeger, 1969.

Rothenberg, Jerome. *Economic Evaluation of Urban Renewal.* Brookings Inst., 1967.

REFERENCES

1. Ray M. Northam, "Vacant Urban Land in the American City," *Land Economics* 47 (1971): 345–355.
2. E. W. Burgess, "The Growth of the City," in *The City,* R. E. Parks and E. W. Burgess, eds. (Chicago, Illinois: Univ. of Chicago Press, 1923).
3. Homer Hoyt, *The Structure and Growth of Residential Neighborhoods in American Cities.* U.S. Federal Housing Administration (Washington D.C.: Government Printing Office, 1939).
4. Chancy D. Harris and Edward L. Ullman, "The Nature of Cities," *Annals of American Academy of Political and Social Sciences* 242 (1945): 7–17.
5. Robert M. Haig, "Toward an Understanding of the Metropolis," *Quarterly Journal of Economics* 40 (1926): 179–208.

6. William Alonso, *Location and Land Use: Toward a General Theory of Land Rent*, pp. 101–109 (Cambridge, Massachusetts: Harvard Univ. Press, 1964).
7. Edgar Hoover, *An Introduction to Regional Economics*, pp. 309–310. New York: Knopf, 1971).
8. Ira S. Lowry, "Seven Models of Urban Development: A Structural Comparison," in "Urban Development Models," pp. 121–146. Highway Research Board, Report 97, 1968.
9. C. E. Ferguson, *Microeconomic Theory*, 3rd ed., pp. 398–402 (Homewood: Irwin, 1972).
10. Hugh O. Nourse, *Regional Economics*, pp. 96–110 (New York: McGraw-Hill, 1968).
11. Richard F. Muth, *Cities and Housing: The Spatial Pattern of Urban Residential Land Use*, pp. 29–34 (Chicago, Illinois: Univ. of Chicago Press, 1969).
12. E. P. Brigham, "The Determinants of Residential Land Value," *Land Economics* 41, No. 4 (1965): 325–334.
13. Edwin Mills, "The Value of Urban Land," in *The Quality of the Urban Environment*, Harvey Perloff, ed., pp. 489–497 (Baltimore, Maryland: John Hopkins Press (for Resources for the Future, Inc.), 1969.
14. Harold Brodsky, "Residential Land and Improvement Values in a Central City," *Land Economics* 46, No. 3 (1970): 229–247.
15. Howard A. Clonts, Jr., "Influence of Urbanization on Land Value at the Urban Periphery," *Land Economics* 46, No. 4 (1970): 489–497.
16. Donald C. Shoup, "The Optimal Timing of Urban Land Development," *Papers, Regional Science Association*, 25 (1970): 33–44.
17. Richard Muth, "Economic Change and Rural-Urban Land Conversions," *Econometrica* 29 (1961): 1–23.
18. Michael Rancich, "Land Value Changes in an Area Undergoing Urbanization," *Land Economics* 46, No. 1 (1970): 32–40.
19. F. G. Adams *et al.*, "Undeveloped Land Prices During Urbanization: A Micro-Empirical Study Over Time," *Review of Economics and Statistics* 50, No. 2 (1968): 248–258.
20. Richard Musgrave, *The Theory of Public Finance*, Chapter 1 (New York: McGraw-Hill, 1959).
21. Bernard Siegan, *Land Use Without Zoning* (Lexington, Massachusetts: Lexington Books, 1972).
22. Dick Netzer, *Economics and Urban Problems* (New York: Basic Books, 1969).
23. Dick Netzer, *Economics of the Property Tax* (Washington, D.C.: Brookings Inst., 1966).
24. Melvin G. Blase and William J. Staub, "Real Property Taxes in the Rural-Urban Fringe," *Land Economics* 47, No. 2 (1971): 168–174.
25. Michael A. Goldberg, "Transportation, Urban Land Values, and Rents: A Syntheses," *Land Economics* 46, No. 2 (1970): 153–162.
26. Jerome Rothenberg, *Economic Evaluation of Urban Renewal* (Washington, D. C.: Brookings Inst., 1967).
27. Matthew Edel, "Planning, Market or Warfare?—Recent Land Use Conflict in American Cities," in *Readings in Urban Economics*, M. Edel and J. Rothenberg, eds., pp. 134–151 (New York: Macmillan, 1972).

HOUSING

I. INTRODUCTION

The importance of housing for urban dwellers can hardly be over-stated. Spatially, housing structures consume a large share of land in cities. In terms of cost, housing services represent a significant share of most persons' budgets. Americans spend over $100 billion per year on housing.* The value of residential structures and their sites makes up nearly one-third of the national wealth.

Housing is a product that has unique characteristics when compared to other products. First, it stays in one place. Thus the value of housing will be affected in large part by the neighborhood in which it is situated. Second, housing is a very durable good, often lasting between 50 and 100 years. It should come as no surprise, then, that over 90 percent

---

* Included here are rents, mortgage payments, utilities, furniture, domestic help, and other household expenditures [1].

of the housing services consumed in a given year come from the existing housing stock. Third, housing is such a bulky commodity that it usually requires on-site construction, in the open, which means that weather and other factors can hamper the production process. This problem is exacerbated because housing structures come in so many varieties and forms. Finally, housing is quite expensive in relation to average incomes. For the vast majority of persons, the price of a dwelling unit represents a multiple of their yearly income; thus people are *forced* to borrow, or enter the rental housing market. The latter is the most important rental market in the economy.

In this chapter we take a rather close look at urban housing markets. The determinants of the demand for and supply of urban housing will be covered from conceptual and empirical standpoints. The latter information will be especially useful for a discussion of housing policy. In addition to the coverage of housing markets and the impact their imperfections have on resource allocation as well as the distribution of income, we shall cover such topics as slum formation and racial discrimination in housing. Finally, a detailed inventory of housing policies is made, and the effectiveness of each policy is assessed, where possible.

II. HOUSING MARKETS

Before we begin our discussion of the demand and supply side of urban housing markets, it will be useful to review a few of the general characteristics of all housing markets. There are two markets in the housing sector: (1) the market for housing services, which everyone is in, and may be viewed as a consumer's market; and (2) the market for the stock of housing structures, which is principally composed of investors. Of course every homeowner is in both markets. Certainly these two markets are related, in that the variations in the stock of housing will lead to similar changes in the level of housing services consumed. For example, if I own my own home and increase its size by adding another room, the size of the housing stock has increased and I can also consume more housing services. It is important to keep in mind that changes in the stock of housing occur not only through building new or demolishing old housing but also by expanding or depreciating the existing stock.

Demand

The quantity of housing services demanded, like that of most other goods or services, is related to the price of those housing services, income, and other factors such as the formation of new households and one's spatial relationship to the city center. The latter is especially important in urban housing markets, for we know from our analysis in previous chapters that access can play an important role in the location decision of residents.

The demand for housing stock is clearly derived from the demand for housing services, for if the stock did not provide any services it would have no value in housing markets. If housing markets operate efficiently, the price of housing services per year should reflect the costs or expenses of using a given unit of housing for that year; that is, depreciation, taxes, maintenance, repairs, and any net return.

In the short run the housing stock is more or less given, and changes in the quantity of housing services demanded will be reflected by changes in the price of housing services. In the long run, however, changes is the housing stock can occur; thus any long-run analysis of housing services must also consider changes in the housing stock. What are the signals that change the stock of housing in the long run, and thus the available quantity of housing services?

If markets operate efficiently, in the long run the desired stock of housing will equal the actual stock of housing. At this equilibrium point, the rate of return on the marginal unit of the stock is exactly equal to the rate of expenses of owning that unit. In other words, marginal revenue just covers marginal cost. This situation is shown in Figure 6.1a, where MR_H is the rate of return on the marginal unit of the stock of housing. The rate of return on any unit equals the price of housing services P_h divided by the price of that unit of housing stock P_H. The rate of expenses on the marginal unit of the housing stock is depicted by MC_H in Figure 6.1a; the rate of expenses is defined as the sum of expenses (depreciation, taxes, maintenance, repairs, net return) divided by P_H.

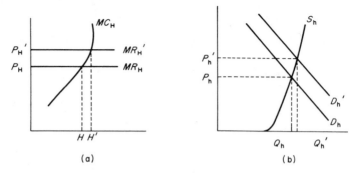

Figure 6.1 (a) *The housing-stock market under increased demand;* (b) *the housing-services market under increased demand.*

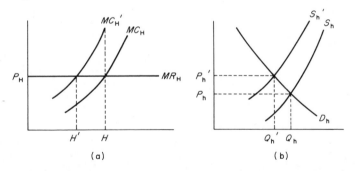

Figure 6.2 (a) *The housing-stock market under increased costs;* (b) *the housing-services market under increased costs.*

Any factors that change the rate of return or the rate of expenses will alter the actual stock of housing. For example, if net immigration into the city occurs, the demand for housing serivces will increase, as shown in Figure 6.1b. This will raise P_h to P_h', but it will not have any appreciable effect on the quantity of housing services Q_h, since the latter is more or less given in the short run. Any increase in P_h, however, other things being equal, will increase the rate of return on housing. Thus in Figure 6.1a MR_H will increase. Investors will now see that there are profits to be made in housing markets, since at the old equilibrium level of housing stock H, MR_H' exceeds MC_H. Alternatively, this situation can be described as one in which the desired stock of housing H' exceeds the actual stock of housing H. Additional housing will be added to the stock until the rate of return equals the rate of expenses; that is, until the desired stock of housing equals the actual stock. This addition in Figure 6.1a is equal to HH'.

As another example, suppose maintenance and repair costs increased, as we find is happening in most cities today. If we begin from an equilibrium situation, any increase in expenses, other things being equal, will cause the rate of expenses to exceed the rate of return on housing. This situation causes a shift in the MC_H curve as shown in Figure 6.2a to MC_H'. Now the actual stock of housing exceeds the desired stock H'. Under such circumstances, we can expect housing units to be undermaintained until the desired and actual stock are equal. This decrease in housing stock via undermaintenance will decrease the supply of housing services in Figure 6.2b and drive up P_h.

Supply

As we stated earlier, the vast majority of housing available for rent or purchase is second hand. In 1968, new housing starts (including both single- and multifamily dwelling units) increased the total number of dwelling units in the U.S. by 2.6 percent. By 1970 the rate of increase was only 2.1 percent. New construction, then, does not significantly change the size of the available stock during any given time period. Although mobile homes have represented over one-fifth of the new housing starts since 1969, mobile homes are still only a few percentage points of the total stock of dwelling units.

As in the case of most economic goods, the quantity of housing supplied is positively related to the price of housing, other things being equal. As we saw in the previous section, if the price of housing service rises, *ceteris paribus*, suppliers will increase the stock of housing over the long run if they are profit-maximizers. Supply may be increased by building new structures or adding to existing structures. Our focus here will be on the former.

Contrary to popular belief, construction costs do not represent an overwhelming majority of new home costs. In fact, recent evidence shows that only 55 percent of new single-family home costs are construction costs (materials and labor) [1]. Almost as surprising, construction costs only comprised roughly 60 percent of the cost of new apartment buildings. Nearly 25 percent of the cost of a new single-family home goes for developed land. Since the average price of new single-family homes now exceeds $25,000, it is safe to say that many urbanites in SMSA's pay over $5,000 for developed land when they purchase a new house. Of the construction outlays, materials often cost nearly twice as much as labor. Clearly, as the price of resources increases, the supply of new housing will decrease, causing the price of new housing to rise, *ceteris paribus*.

The Concept of Filtering

What is the housing supply situation in urban areas? Many urban economists and real-estate experts argue that the majority of new homes are built at or near the periphery of urban areas, primarily for those in middle and upper income classes. After these persons enter their new homes, the old homes are said to filter down to lower-income persons. This filtering-down theory has received a fair amount of attention by urban economists. The concept has intuitive appeal, in that we can see in most communities that the low- and lower-middle-income classes seem to live in second-, third-, and *n*th-hand housing, while the upper-income classes seem to spread out farther and farther in relatively new housing.

Traditionally, filtering has been defined in terms of changes in the real value of an existing unit of the housing stock. The argument that connects the availability of second-hand and older housing to lower-income groups of the city implies that the real value of a given housing unit declines over time. Thus lower-income groups will be able to afford that unit. This argument, then, asserts that housing always filters down. It is quite possible, however, for housing to filter up (that is, for the real value of a unit to increase), especially if markets work efficiently.

Let us see how housing can filter up. We know that in any city at a given moment of time the stock of housing is fixed. The price of housing services derived from any unit of the stock will be determined by the amount of services that unit offers, among other things. We can assume that the amount of services is proportional to the size of the unit. Now if excess demand exists for a unit of given size, rational suppliers would allow slightly larger housing to filter down by reducing maintenance and repair expenditures. Similarly, units slightly smaller than the given size in excess demand would be filtered up through increased maintenance, so that entrepreneurs can capture the (expected) excess profits inherent in the excess-demand condition. Thus housing may filter up and down in the same market simultaneously! What in fact happens in any given urban housing market is, of course, an empirical question.

Empirical Studies of Housing Markets

Thus far we have dealt mostly with housing markets at the conceptual level. It is important to understand whether or not these housing models have empirical validity, not only for academic reasons, but also for policy purposes. That is, if the desired stock of housing exceeds the actual stock, do we find an increase in the housing stock forthcoming? This depends on the price elasticity of supply. If the long-run price elasticity of supply is found to be very low, say close to zero, then our model will have little explanatory value. This elasticity information would be very useful, however. For example, if we desired to subsidize housing of the poor to help them consume more housing services, we would know that this policy alone would be incorrect. Why? Because if the price elasticity of supply is very low, increased demand from the subsidies would only serve to drive up prices. Alternatively, if the income elasticity of demand for housing by low-income persons is found to be quite small, a policy of income subsidies to solve the housing problem of the poor would not be very efficient. In this section we will take a look at the findings of a number of empirical studies of demand and supply to obtain a better idea of how urban housing markets actually operate.

Demand: Price and Income Elasticities

Table 6-1 presents a summary of evidence on price and income elasticities of demand for owner-occupied and rental dwelling units. One of the first studies of housing demand was completed by Richard Muth [2]. Muth estimated a demand relationship for aggregate nonfarm housing with 1915–1941 data, assuming that the actual stock of housing equaled the desired stock of housing at the end of each year. His demand model related the per-capita amount of housing stock to the real price of housing, the per-capita permanent income, and the interest rate.

Muth found that the price and income elasticities were slightly greater than 0.5; however, he did not believe that these were the true elasticities, since there is not complete adjustment between the desired and actual stock of housing at the end of each year. When a noncomplete adjustment process entered the model, the price and income elasticities increased to about 0.9. Interestingly, Muth found that the adjustment

TABLE 6–1

Summary of Demand Elasticity Studies

Source of data	Price elasticity	Income elasticity	Years(s)	Area
Owner-occupied single-family homes				
Muth	−0.9	0.9	1915–1941	U.S.
Uhler	—	1.0–0.6	1964	U.S.
Reid	—	1.7	1950	30 large U.S. cities
Reid	—	1.6	1950	43 large U.S. cities
Winger	—	1.0	1962–1964	SMSA's
Lee	—	0.8	1959, 1961	523 nonfarm households; U.S.
Maisel	−0.9	0.7	1966	100 observations from 29 SMSA's
Rentals				
Reid	—	1.0	1950	30 large U.S. cities
Reid	—	0.8	1950	43 U.S. cities
Lee	—	0.55	1959, 1961	164 nonfarm U.S. households
de Leeuw	−0.7–1.5	0.8–1.0	1960	19 SMSA's

between the desired and actual stock of housing would be only 90 percent complete after six years.

Although the Muth findings are based on rather old data, they represent one of the few housing-demand relationships estimated with time-series data. Of those studies based on cross-section data, some interesting information on income elasticities was obtained by Russell Uhler [3]. Uhler related the value of owner-occupied housing (based on 1964 Survey of Consumer Finance data) to current household income and the age of the household head. It is common knowledge that housing expenditures as a share of total income decline as the latter grows. That is, the average propensity to consume housing decreases as one's income level rises, at least at relatively high income levels. What is not known well, however, is the marginal propensity to consume housing across income size classes. Uhler found that marginal propensity to consume decreased as one moved to higher income classes.* This information is very important for policies that attempt to raise the housing standards of lower-income persons by some form of income subsidy. That is, if we found that the marginal propensity was near zero for low-income families, it would not be efficient to use income subsidies to solve the housing problems of the poor. Uhler found that the marginal propensity exceeded unity for those in the lowest two income classes only. Thus it follows that income subsidies may be a useful method for solving the housing problems of the poor.

Unfortunately, the Muth and Uhler studies used aggregate data for the U.S.; therefore it is not clear whether the findings are directly applicable for explaining housing markets in urban areas. We do have a number of checks on aggregative findings, however. In a monumental study of urban housing markets, Margaret Reid used 1950 census data for 30 large cities and found the income elasticity of demand to be 1.7 [4]. Using an alternative sample of 43 cities for 1950 collected by the Bureau of Labor Statistics, Reid estimated the income elasticity to be 1.55. Employing 1962–1964 FHA data for SMSA's, thereby (more or less) standardizing for variations in credit terms, Allen Winger found the income elasticity to be around 1 [5]. Interestingly, Winger had data for old as well as new housing units. The income elasticity for the former was 1.10, while for new homes the elasticity was 0.82. This is expected, if for no other reason, because there are more existing homes than new homes in the housing stock of SMSA's.

Although there are many biases in each of the studies discussed, it seems that the income elasticity is around 1.0, if one is willing to accept

---

* The classes were $2625, 4100, 5500, 7200, 8250, and 10,400.

estimates based on aggregate data either for the U.S., for SMSA cities, or for census tracts. If individual-household observations are used, the elasticity is lower, as shown by Lee and Maisel [6, 7].

Turning to rental markets, Margaret Reid found income elasticities of 1.0 and 0.8, respectively, for her 30- and 43-city samples based on 1950 information. Frank de Leeuw noted that Reid and others had biases in their elasticity estimates [8]. After correcting those biases, de Leeuw found the income elasticity to be between 0.81 and 0.99, using a sample of SMSA's for 1960. de Leeuw's finding for the price elasticity of demand shows a range from -0.7 to -1.5.

In reviewing the empirical evidence on demand elasticities, it is clear that estimates vary according to whether the data are of the time-series or cross-section type, and whether the data represent aggregate, inter-urban, or intraurban housing markets. Nevertheless, there are some discernible patterns in Table 6-1:

(1) The price elasticity of demand is probably greater for renters than home-owners. Thus if we wanted to set up a policy to increase the supply of housing, it would be more efficient to operate through rental rather than single-family owner-occupied housing markets.
(2) The income elasticity of demand is near unity for both single-family homeowners and renters, thus to enable people to consume more housing services, income subsidy schemes would be useful in nearly any housing market.

These estimates of the price and income elasticities of demand will be very useful when we discuss housing policy later in this chapter.

Supply

Until recently, very little empirical work had been done on estimating supply relationships. Muth's work on nonfarm housing, discussed earlier, included a supply model whereby the primary determinant of supply price was not quantity but the prices of (labor) resources. In general, economists and others have relied on vacancy rates to explain short-run excesses of supply. As expected, vacancy rates and housing prices are inversely related; thus tight markets are also "explained" by means of vacancy rates. In the long run, of course, vacancy rates are not a good measure of housing markets, since new homes are constructed and old homes are removed from the housing stock.

As argued earlier, urban economists seem to feel that filtering may be the real process of supply in any given city. Unfortunately, the majority of work done on filtering models has been theoretical rather than empirical. Empirically, it would be useful to establish the direction, magnitude, and pattern of filtering, for the supply of housing available to lower-income families may be determined basically by this filtering process. Donald Guy and Hugh Nourse performed a test on filtering for two cities in the St. Louis area recently [9]. In both towns, Guy and Nourse followed the occupants in a selected group of houses from 1918 through 1969, using R. L. Polk data on the occupational characteristics of those living in each respective house. By finding the average incomes provided by various occupations the authors could determine whether successive occupants had higher or lower incomes. If the income of the new owner exceeded that of the old owner, the house was said to filter up, and vice versa. Using this rationale, housing was found to filter down very slightly in Kankakee, Illinois, while in Webster Groves, Missouri just as many houses filtered up as down.

Although there are a number of methodological assumptions in the Guy–Nourse study that might lead one to have reservations about their approach to measuring filtering, it is clear that they have broken new ground in testing the filtering hypothesis. The old notion that, over time, housing filters down from high- to low-income families does not necessarily hold, at least in the two towns considered. More evidence on this issue would be very useful in explaining and predicting the past and future supply of housing for low-income persons, which is an important contemporary policy question.

Turning to empirical studies of housing supply in the rental market, a cross-sectional model of 39 SMSA's was done by Frank de Leeuw and N. F. Ekanem with 1967 data [10]. The authors argued that in the long run, the rents would be higher in those cities having greater marginal costs of renting housing services. These costs, of course, are determined by the prices of incremental inputs. Using these hypotheses, de Leeuw and Ekanem found that the long-run price elasticity of supply ranged from 0.3 to 0.7, depending on the magnitude of the rental under consideration. Higher rentals had the greater elasticities. Although the authors took care in noting potential biases in their elasticity estimates, it is clear that if their estimates are "in the ballpark," then the efficacy of solving housing-shortage problems by means of subsidies is jeopardized. With inelastic supply curves, rental subsidies may do little more than to drive up the price of rental services.

III. HOUSING-MARKET IMPERFECTIONS AND THEIR IMPACTS

In the previous section we discussed a model of housing demand based on the assumption that housing markets operate more or less perfectly. That is, we argued that if differences in the rate of return and rate of expenses occurred, in the long run more or less housing would be added to the stock, depending on whether the desired stock was less than or exceeded the actual stock of housing. Implicitly, we assumed that people could express their preferences for housing services, and suppliers could easily meet those preferences. Are these assumptions consistent with the real world? The empirical findings discussed thus far do not give us a clear answer to this question.

To answer this question, let us look in detail at what conditions are needed to have perfectly competitive housing markets:

(1) The market must have many buyers and sellers.
(2) The sales volume of each individual seller must be very small compared to aggregate sales.
(3) Neither buyers nor sellers may collude.
(4) Both buyers and sellers must have easy entry into and exit from the market.
(5) Buyers and sellers must have more or less perfect knowledge of prevailing bids, and will act accordingly to maximize their utility and profits, respectively.
(6) No artificial restrictions may be placed on demand or supply or on other prices that affect demand and supply (that is, the price of substitutes and resources, respectively).
(7) Housing services must be homogeneous.

No doubt the first three competitive conditions are met in most urban housing markets, although some persons argue that if sellers do not in fact collude, they act as though they do. But conditions (4) through (7) do not hold for all segments of the population. There are many reasons for this:

(1) Despite new laws against segregation, certain minority groups still have difficulty entering certain spatial housing markets in urban areas.
(2) Obviously both buyers and sellers do not have perfect knowledge of supply and demand curves, respectively.
(3) Artificial restrictions in the form of income tax deductions for homeowners result in a greater demand for housing by those able to buy their own homes, thereby resulting in a smaller available supply of housing services for lower-income people.
(4) Similarly, federal tax programs of accelerated depreciation and the heavy reliance of local governments on property tax often lead to longer lives and less maintenance of low-quality housing, thus restricting the supply of housing services from the stock of low-quality structures.
(5) Although government public-housing programs have clearly increased the supply of housing stock, urban-renewal programs have decreased the stock.

(6) Rent-control programs have restricted the supply of housing services, if not to all users in a given city, at least to those immigrants who came after rent controls were put into effect.

Items 3 through 6 show that government provides many artificial restrictions that operate on both the demand and the supply sides of the housing market.

The Problem of Externalities

Even if the imperfections just listed did not exist, the market could easily fail in bringing about an efficient allocation of resources toward the production of housing because of the problem of externalities. As we noted earlier in this chapter, the value of any given housing structure is determined by, among other things, the characteristics of the neighborhood in which the structure is located. Therefore, if I own a house, the value of my house is affected not only by my own maintenance and repair policy but also by the maintenance and repair policies of my neighbors. Clearly, if I am a profit-maximizer, it will always pay me to undermaintain my property. Why? Because the rate of return will always be higher (on an expectations basis) if I assume that others will maintain, since if they do, my property increases in value at a zero outlay on my part.* So a single owner, acting alone, will always have rational reasons for undermaintaining. Of course if everyone undermaintains, the housing stock will be smaller than it would have been without the externality; that is, there will be an underallocation of resources toward housing as long as the externality persists.

This negative externality or neighborhood effect that results in an underallocation of resources toward housing maintenance or production is most prevalent in areas of concentrated, low-quality housing. We often refer to such areas as slums. It may be useful as well as interesting to consider the formation and economic consequences of slums, since slums do result (in part) from market imperfections. After our consideration of slums, we can turn to a similar and related problem more directly tied to market imperfections—racial segregation and discrimination in housing markets.

The Formation and Economic Consequences of Slums

Although economists do not agree on the causes of slums, they do more or less agree on what a slum is—a concentration of low quality,

---

* For a more detailed explanation of this argument, see Otto Davis and Andrew Whinston [11].

blighted structures that yield very low levels of housing services. Obviously, there are many noneconomic characteristics of persons and the overall communities of slum areas that are of major importance in helping explain the formation and perpetuation of slums, but we can concentrate only on the economics of the process.

I think it is possible, without doing a great amount of injustice to the urban economics profession, to assert that there are two general schools of thought on how slums originate and what the logical policy conclusions are to do away with slums. For want of better names, we shall call these two schools the traditional and the nontraditional.

Slums: The Traditional Argument

Economists have traditionally argued [12] that slums form because as older housing filters down to increasing numbers of lower-income and minority groups near the business districts of cities, externalities and market imperfections more or less ensure that (1) landlords will undermaintain their structures, and (2) low-income persons will continue to live in these low-quality housing areas. Let us consider this statement in more detail.

As cities grow and expand, we have found a tendency for the newer housing structure to be built at the periphery. It is not difficult to see a sort of reverse concentric-ring explanation of filtering in housing markets. If this filtering market worked reasonably well, the supply of older housing available to lower-income and minority groups that often locate near business districts of cities would no doubt be ample. In other words, even as more inmigrants enter the city (and demand therefore increases) the response of supply due to filtering should more or less keep prices constant. Empirical evidence shows, however, that the price of housing services has risen steadily in slum areas. Clearly one of the following situations is at work: (1) demand increases are outstripping supply increases, (2) supply is constant and demand is rising, or (3) demand is more or less constant but supply is decreasing.

Historically, as we saw in Chapter 2, and even in the past decades, huge streams of inmigrants have been associated with poor housing conditions in certain sectors of our cities. It seems safe to assume, then, that demand has been increasing in slum areas, since census data show that inmigration is still continuing into low-quality housing areas of most major cities. In addition, it is also probably safe to say that persons causing the increase in demand are often characterized by having low incomes and being members of minority groups. To complete our discussion of why slums form and persist, then, it remains to cover the supply side of the market.

Slumlords, or owners of low-quality housing in slum areas, find it profitable to undermaintain and thereby reduce the stock of housing. One of the major reasons, of course, is the negative externalities or neighborhood effect discussed earlier, which results in a breakdown of the market mechanism. In simple demand and supply terminology, slumlords help create excess demand for slum housing by undermaintaining their structures, thus causing further increases in the price of these housing services. Given that low-income and minority groups have few if any substitutes for slum housing near the business districts, their demand for slum housing will be inelastic. So if demand is inelastic and price increases because of a decrease in supply through undermaintenance, total revenue will rise; thus with less maintenance (and thereby lower or constant costs and greater revenues) profits are higher.

There are market imperfections that also cause slums to be more profitable than they otherwise would be. Federal income-tax laws, for example, provide for accelerated depreciation schemes, which can result in sizable reductions in the landlord's taxable income. Under such schemes, the landlord is allowed to depreciate the property completely when in fact there may be many years left in the useful life of the property. Given the continual increase in demand for housing in slum areas, if the landlord has completely depreciated the property, he can still sell it and make a handsome capital gain. Why would a buyer purchase the undermaintained property? Because he can also depreciate the property in an accelerated fashion, and through undermaintaining (and rising demand) he can maximize his return on the housing. The effect, then, of accelerated tax provisions is to make existing property *no less* profitable than new property, given that the old property does not have to be maintained. The result is, of course, that old property (slum housing) is kept in existence much longer and at an increasingly lower quality level than it would be if the accelerated tax provision did not exist. Slums persist.

The supply of low-quality housing services is also restricted and perpetuated by local property-tax practices. It pays me to undermaintain, for then my property taxes will be lower. Clearly, if I do maintain or even expand my property, I will do so only if the additional revenues exceed the additional cost. Since property taxes are an increased cost, it is possible that they may prohibit profit-maximizers from increasing the supply of housing services (which suppliers would have done without the tax). With property taxes, suppliers will obviously choose less capital-intensive uses of the land; or, in other words, they will undermaintain.

In summary, the traditional argument on slum formation begins with the filtering down of older housing in areas near business districts of cities that face a more or less increasing demand for housing services on the part of low-income and minority groups. Externalities cause undermaintenance of housing structures, and tax-law provisions not only perpetuate the undermaintenance practice but lengthen it as well. The result is that low-income and minority groups pay higher prices for fewer and lower-quality housing services.

Slums: The Nontraditional View and a Critique

The alternative view [13,14] of slum formation is that slums form basically because of poverty or the low income of the inhabitants of blighted areas. The nontraditionalists take exception with almost all of the traditional views. For example, they do not accept the undermaintenance argument, since they argue that this does not explain why some landlords do in fact maintain their structures. Second, it is argued that the filtering down of older housing toward the central business districts results in a movement of persons to outlying areas; thus demand for housing does not increase in a net sense. Instead, for a given stock of housing, the prices rise on the outer areas of the city, at least relative to central areas. Third, the traditional view that externalities will result in continually undermaintained properties is attacked on the grounds that it would be in the interests of single owners to obtain contiguous properties or for cooperatives to form among continguous owners.

According to nontraditionalists, the shortcomings of the traditional view of slums can also be illustrated by showing that it is inconsistent with, or fails to explain that:

(1) Slum housing is expensive relative to its quality.
(2) Urban-renewal projects continually lose money.
(3) Housing quality in urban areas has increased over the past decades [13, pp. 121–125].

At this point it may be useful to see how well the nontraditional views stand up; that is, do these criticisms have a firm basis? Turning to criticisms of undermaintenance first, it is quite possible that *some* landlords do keep up their properties, especially in areas where there happens to be an excess supply of housing. But single-family homeowners of limited means often find it difficult to borrow funds for upgrading their own homes. Because of the impact of negative externalities on slum housing prices, borrowing funds for the acquisition of contiguous properties is also difficult. Cooperative agreements would provide a basis for obtaining funding only if banks could somehow be guaranteed that the cooperative arrangement was permanent, which is not probable.

Whether or not the net demand for housing rises or falls as older housing filters down to the center of the city is an empirical question for any given city. For the postwar period in northern cities, it is clear, however, that net inmigration of blacks and other minority groups has caused a net increase in the demand for low-quality housing. Surely in the wake of this continual increase in demand, price would rise and one would *expect* to find slum housing to be expensive, in relation to its quality. Since urban-renewal projects have reduced the supply of low-quality housing, it is almost certain that price increases have occurred.

Why is it that urban-renewal projects lose money? First, in very few cases do we find urban-renewal projects providing housing services for those low-income persons the projects displace. These displaced persons must find low-quality housing nearby in order to be close to their jobs. Thus we find a conversion of the properties near the renewal site to low-quality housing. Of course these nearby low-quality housing districts are a negative externality from the view of the commercial business that may bid on the renewal sites, causing a lower bid than one might get without the externality.

Another reason for urban-renewal projects ending up in the red is that rent–distance functions seem to flatten over time. In other words, as markets move outward in cities, rents bid in central areas become relatively lower. Given this phenomenon along with (1) the fact that most projects take nearly a decade from start to finish and (2) the heavy costs of planning, demolition, and improvements involved in most urban-renewal projects, it is no wonder that most projects lose money.

The argument that housing quality in cities has increased over past decades is not necessarily inconsistent with the traditional view of slum creation and perpetuation. Clearly, slums may not only exist but also expand in any given city, while the overall quality of housing increases. This is because it is possible that the increase in the stock of nonslum housing may exceed the increase in slum housing in the city. Whether in fact the housing quality has increased is a moot point. If one measures housing quality by the number of bedrooms, baths, garage stalls, fireplaces, and so on, it is fairly clear that the quality has increased. However, the U.S. Bureau of Census has used a set of highly questionable and subjective criteria for defining low-quality or dilapidated housing.*

---

* Housing is called low quality or substandard if it lacks any plumbing facilities (hot running water, private bath or shower, and private flush toilet), while dilapidated housing is defined as housing that does not provide safe and adequate shelter.

Since nontraditionalists define the rise of high-quality housing as a fall in the percentage of low-quality or substandard or dilapidated housing, it is important to keep the definitional issue in mind. There is no question, however, that census data show substantial decreases in the percentage of substandard housing units in our metropolitan areas between 1950 and 1970. Until better measures of housing quality are derived and used, I think it is difficult to say much about changes in housing quality.

It is important from the student's standpoint to assess both views on slums rather closely, for the efficacy of housing policy hangs on the outcome. If one sides with the nontraditionalist view, income subsidies will more or less solve the problems of slums, for supposedly people will have the means to move out of the central areas and purchase higher-quality housing. This assumes that minorities can overcome discrimination and other constraints, which is the next question we shall consider. The traditionalist, on the other hand, would argue that income subsidies, under existing tax institutions and extramarket imperfections (externalities), would on the whole merely find their way into slumlords' pockets in the form of higher rents.

Discrimination and Segregation in Urban Housing

Thus far in this section on market imperfections we have inventoried a list of market and extramarket imperfections, and have covered one result of these forces—the formation and perpetuation of slums. One of the factors that could cause slums to continue in existence longer than they otherwise would is the restriction of nonslum housing to minority groups. Clearly any restriction of supply causes prices to be higher than they would be otherwise, *ceteris paribus*. Since housing discrimination is typically defined as a situation in which people pay higher prices for a unit of given quality, it is not difficult to see that greater ability to pay may not be a cure-all for ending slums. One further introductory point: segregation and discrimination are not necessarily the same phenomenon. Segregation occurs if groups in fact live closer together than one would expect if all members of every group were randomly distributed throughout the city. People may pay higher prices to live near others in their same income or ethnic group, but this higher price does not necessarily result from a restriction in supply. It may be due to one's preferences, which would negate discrimination for that person.

One of the most heated topics in urban economics is the issue of racial discrimination in the housing markets. Although housing discrimination has been outlawed in most areas since the 1950's by so-called fair-housing legislation, discrimination is still a very lively topic. One of the earlier issues in this area that still exists among many laymen today is that the movement of nonwhites into previously all-white areas will cause property values to fall. How might this occur?

If whites prefer not to live next to nonwhites, then we would expect the demand for housing to decrease in the integrated area, at least as far as whites are concerned. If this were the end of the analysis, for a given supply, housing prices would in fact decrease. But obviously, one must also consider the increase in demand caused by the movement on the part of nonwhites. If nonwhites prefer to live in integrated areas, it is quite possible that the net effect of integration on price may be positive rather than negative. Empirical studies in fact show this to be the case in many cities.

This fear of a drastic decrease in the value of one's home on the part of whites in previously segregated areas has led to and been caused by the old practice of "blockbusting." That is, real-estate agents buy housing at lower prices from whites (who are fearful that their housing value will fall if nonwhites enter their neighborhood) and sell it at much higher prices to nonwhites.

It is possible, of course, to have a movement of whites out of an area with only a threat of integration on the part of a real-estate agent. By instilling fears in people's minds that they had better sell now and get a reasonable price rather than have to sell later at a very low price, real-estate agents may get whites to move out, thus causing prices to fall. There are constraints, however, on the potential success of the threat hypothesis: (1) the white's income level, (2) the availability and price of substitute housing in all-white areas, and (3) interest rates for both nonwhite and white borrowers.

The major question that must be answered in the areas of racial housing discrimination is: What factors determine whether a sale is made to a nonwhite in a (potentially) newly integrated area? If this question could be answered and the price of the sale recorded, one could go a long way in explaining a major share of discriminatory practices. Economists have built a number of models, both theoretical and empirical, in an attempt to get a better understanding of the overall discrimination process and its ramifications. In the next few pages we shall consider some of these models.

Models of Discrimination

Simple logic tells us that if real-estate agents decide to collude and not sell to nonwhites, they can succeed as long as someone does not break the collusive agreement. With competition, of course, nonwhites could buy at unrestricted lower market price. Given the blockbusting and threat tactics discussed above, two important questions we might consider are: (1) Under what conditions will a sale be made to a nonwhite in a previously all-white area? (2) Will collusion on the part of the sellers affect the price? One model used to shed some light on these questions has been called "the prisoner's dilemma" [15]. Let us see how this model works.

Consider an all-white area of homes owned by noncolluding profit-maximizers. Two adjacent homes are soon to become vacant, and a nonwhite attempts to rent from one of the owners. Assume that rents will rise if an owner rents to nonwhites, while costs remain constant. In addition, a nonwhite is willing to pay this higher price only if he is the only nonwhite. If *both* vacant homes are rented to nonwhites, *both* nonwhite families will only pay rents below those that whites are presently paying. Finally, if only one of the homes is rented to a nonwhite, then a white will rent the remaining vacant home only at a very low price. Under these assumptions, the owners are caught in the prisoner's dilemma.

Table 6-2 will help us clarify the dilemma. If both owners refuse to rent to nonwhites, they will each receive $100 from whites. Now if owner 1 rents to a nonwhite and owner 2 rents to a white, the latter owner will not find this situation to his liking. Clearly owner 2 can increase his rents by $10 if he rents a a nonwhite. This competition will result in both renting to nonwhites and earning $90, even though each would prefer the other to rent to a white. Alternatively, if collusion occurred, each would rent to a white, although, again, each would prefer

TABLE 6–2

Prisoner's Dilemma Model[a]

	Owner 2	
Owner 1	Rent to white	Rent to nonwhite
Rent to white	$100, 100	$80, 110
Rent to nonwhite	110, 80	90, 90

[a] Smolensky, Becker, and Molotch, "The Prisoner's Dilemma and Ghetto Expansion," *Land Economics* Vol. XLIV (November 1968) p. 421.

to rent to a nonwhite, provided the other rented to a white. Thus under competition or collusion, each owner perceives himself as being not as well off as he could be.

The important point to learn from the prisoner's dilemma model is that if it explains real life, then we can expect collusion to occur; nonwhites will be restricted from moving into previously all-white areas. Smolensky, Becker, and Molotch tested this model in the Chicago area and found that only a small percentage of either owners or agents saw themselves faced with the prisoner's dilemma. Thus we would expect nonwhites to have little trouble buying housing services in white areas, but this is not the case in practice.

Benjamin Cohen [16] has shown that by slightly changing the numbers of Table 6-2 it is possible to stay within the assumptions of the dilemma but show that collusion need not occur to *prevent* nonwhites from entering a white neighborhood. If the $110's in Table 6-1 are lowered to $102, and the $90's are raised to $97, our dilemma conditions are still satisfied. But now if each owner acts to maximize the minimum profit he can make, he will always rent to a white, for he will get at least $97 whereas by renting to a nonwhite he takes a chance on getting only $90.

Although economists have developed many other more sophisticated models besides the prisoner's dilemma model to explain racial discrimination in housing markets, the most popular approaches have assumed that two housing markets exist—one for whites and the other for nonwhites—and that whites prefer to live near whites only, but nonwhites prefer to live near whites. Given these assumptions, if nonwhites were found to pay higher prices for comparable housing, it would be difficult to prove that payment of the higher price was not consistent with their preferences. Needless to say, such a situation does not preclude the existence of price discrimination. This difficulty could be partially solved, however, if one could explain the price of housing in a given city, standardizing not only the bundle of housing services consumed by whites and nonwhites alike but also the socioeconomic characteristics—here a proxy for preferences.

A number of empirical studies have been performed that in fact do attempt to explain the discrimination markup or price premium paid by nonwhites as a result of the dual housing markets for whites and nonwhites. In the past these studies involved comparing housing costs between whites and nonwhites for similar dwellings. Recently, more sophisticated statistical models have been used to explain the impact of race on housing prices in large cities. For example, R. Ridker and J. Henning [17] related the median value of owner-occupied homes to characteristics of the houses, their neighborhoods, and race, using data for St. Louis. They found that in 1960, single-family homes in nonwhite areas cost 5–8 percent more than comparable single-family homes in white areas. Using more or less the same methodology, R. Muth found that in 1950 and 1960 blacks paid 2–5 percent higher housing prices than whites in the south side of Chicago [13, p. 239]. More recent (1967) evidence on St. Louis was obtained by J. Kain and J. Quigley [18]. For renters the markup was found to be 7 pecent, while for homeowners a markup existed but its size was not reported. In general, most studies find that nonwhites pay approximately 5–10 percent more for housing services.

Not all economists agree that a positive statistical relationship between being nonwhite and the price of housing necessarily indicates discrimination. Muth, for example, expected to find a negative relationship between nonwhites and expenditures on housing. He argues that the price elasticity of demand for blacks is at least equal to (but probably greater than) unity. Therefore an increase in the price of housing to blacks would result in lower total expenditures for housing by blacks. In other words, price discrimination would result in lower expenditures for housing by nonwhites. Muth rationalizes the positive relationship he found between blacks and the value of housing in Chicago on the grounds that: (1) there are higher operating costs involved with black housing than with white housing, and (2) rentals paid by blacks include a disproportionate percentage of utilities and furniture.

The work of F. de Leeuw, mentioned earlier in this chapter, provides an independent estimate of Muth's contention that nonwhites have a price-elastic demand [8]. For nonsingle-person families de Leeuw found that the price elasticity for nonwhites fell between 1.11 and 1.18. For all nonwhite families, the price elasticity was 0.97. Thus it is possible that empirical studies that purport to show a racial markup of 5–10 percent may be biased (upward), at least in rental markets.

The Impact of Discrimination in Housing Markets

Although urban economists have directed a great deal of attention to the existence and magnitude of racial (price) discrimination in urban areas, few (with the exception of John Kain) have devoted much time to other costs and ramifications of discrimination. Moreover, little has been done in analyzing the various forms of nonprice racial discrimination in urban housing markets. In this section we shall consider both of these issues. We begin with a few examples of the effects of segregated housing markets in cities.

Segregated urban housing markets make it difficult for blacks and other minority groups to get and keep jobs in suburbia, where most new jobs are opening up (see Chapter 2). Efficient public transportation service is often not available to new plants and employment centers from central cities; thus distance may represent a severe cost to those in segregated areas. Distance also plays a role in that blacks and other minority groups often have less information than suburban whites about job openings in suburbs. Finally, employers located in suburbia *may* discriminate against blacks because of retaliation by white customers for bringing blacks into previous all-white neighborhoods. Alternatively, employers may feel little pressure not to discriminate against prospective black employees.

John Kain tested the impact of these three arguments on black employment in Chicago and Detroit [19].* He found that each factor was significantly related to the location of black employment. In other words, housing discrimination does (adversely) affect the spatial distribution of black employment. In addition, Kain found that continued sub-urbanization is worsening the employment situation for urban blacks.

Joseph Mooney examined the impact of metropolitan decentralization and the exodus of jobs to the suburbs on black employment across the 25 largest SMSA's and generally found the same results as Kain [21]. However, Mooney found that the spatial separation of blacks was of secondary importance when compared with the effect of the aggregate demand on black employment opportunities. That is, increases in aggregate demand for all workers in a given metropolitan area would solve the employment problem of segregated blacks a lot more quickly than integrated housing markets.

Continual segregation in housing markets not only adversely affects employment opportunities of blacks and minorities. In addition, blacks have a lower probability of owning a home, no doubt because of dual housing markets in urban areas. This is significant in terms of the welfare of blacks, because they cannot take advantage of the many tax breaks provided to homeowners, nor do they have a fair chance to build equity.

Kain and Quigley found in their St. Louis study that for a given sample of whites and blacks with similar characteristics, blacks had a 9 percent lower probability of home ownership than whites. Of course this lower probability could be due to differences in preferences for home ownership between blacks and whites, or variations in wealth positions of blacks and whites.

Kain and Quigley, however, felt that supply restrictions on the part of white owners or real-estate agents could be of major importance

---

* For an interesting alternative model, see Paul Offner and Daniel Saks [20], plus Kain's "Rejoinder" [19, pp. 161–62].

in explaining the difference in home-ownership probability between blacks and whites. Using a sample of 18 metropolitan areas, they found that the supply-restriction hypothesis accounted for over two-thirds of the difference between the actual and the expected home-ownership rates. The authors' estimate of the costs of the limitations blacks face in homeowners' markets is conservatively placed at 30 percent; that is, if the supply restrictions were nonexistent, blacks would pay 30 percent less for their housing services.

IV. HOUSING POLICY

Up to now we have focused mainly on the operations of housing markets. We have found that housing markets have many imperfections, and that these imperfections have an impact not only in allocating resources but also in determining the distribution of income. In general, the objective of housing policy is to restore allocative efficiency in housing markets. To argue, however, that the goal of housing policy is to be neutral, at least when one considers the income-distributional effect of policy, could be foolhardy; we shall soon find out that most housing-policy tools tend to favor higher-income families.

It may be fair to say that the primary goal of national and local policymakers is to make sure that everyone has sound and sanitary housing available at a reasonable cost. The unwillingness to provide housing at below-market prices in many cities, however, allows one to attack the "reasonable cost" portion of the preceding sentence.

Policymakers and even economists often cite evidence such as that presented in Table 6-3 to "prove" that their goals are being realized. Table 6-3 shows that the share of housing units without complete plumbing facilities fell drastically between 1960 and 1970. However, logic tells us that homes with complete plumbing facilities may not be in sound and/or sanitary condition. Clearly we need better operational definitions of safe and sanitary housing.

We do know that in the past few decades a good deal of poor quality housing has been permanently removed from many of our central city areas. For example, in 1968, the Douglas Commission argued that government programs had led to the demolition of about one million dwellings, most of which were inhabited by low-income persons. Urban renewal and federal highways took about two-thirds of the units, with the remainder going for public-housing space and miscellaneous reasons. The important issue of whether or not everyone obtains safe and sanitary housing in view of these demolitions is: What has happened to the overall stock of sound dwelling units per family, especially in the central

TABLE 6-3

Percentages of Occupied Housing Units by Availability of Plumbing Facilities, 1960 and 1970[a]

	Blacks		Whites	
	With all plumbing facilities	Without all plumbing facilities	With all plumbing facilities	Without all plumbing facilities
1960				
U.S.	59	41	88	12
Metropolitan areas	76	24	94	6
Central cities	79	21	93	7
Outside central cities	61	40	94	6
1970				
U.S.	83	17	95	5
Metropolitan areas	93	7	97	3
Central cities	95	5	97	3
Outside central cities	83	17	98	2

[a] U.S. Department of Commerce, Bureau of Census, BLS Report No. 394, p. 91.

city? Unfortunately, the question cannot be answered until more of the 1970 census data are available. We do know, however, that the number of occupied housing units in central cities increased from 10.7 million in 1960 to 12.8 in 1970. How low-income families fared in this situation is not yet known.

The present federal housing policy is based in the Housing and Urban Development Act of 1968. This policy has a goal of "a decent home and suitable living environment for every American family," which is to be achieved by 1978. Present plans are to add 28.2 million dwelling units to the 1968 stock of 65.6 million units. Six million of the new units are to be for low-income families, which, if built, will be ten times more low-income units than were built in the previous decade. However, the record as of Fall, 1973 and prospective plans of the Nixon Administration cast grave doubts on whether anything but a modest fraction of these goals will be met.

Let us take a look now at some of the actual tools used to effectuate policy in the past and present. Particular attention will be placed on how each of these tools affects the housing problems of low-income and minority groups, for they seem to be the ones who have been unable to obtain safe and sanitary housing.

Housing Policy Tools

Building and Housing Codes

Most cities have laws or codes pertaining to standards that housing units must meet. These standards are not only for the safety of those presently living in the structures but are also for the protection of prospective buyers and renters. Most persons are not intimately familiar with acceptable structural properties for housing units, so the government attempts to protect consumers from potential fraud.

In general, codes specify in meticulous detail the materials and methods one can use in constructing a unit. Often this may result in holding back on the utilization of new techniques, unless the code is changed regularly. The impact of rigidity in the code is that the supply price of housing may be greater than it would be if the new techniques were employed. We are assuming, of course, that codes are in fact followed.

One of the bitter complaints in slum areas is that housing codes are not enforced, so that persons are forced to live in unsafe and unsanitary housing. However, if codes were enforced, the increased maintenance costs of slum dwellings would be passed on to the consumer in the form of higher rents. Therefore, authorities often see themselves in a dilemma when it comes to code enforcement in slum areas.

Taxes

Housing markets are directly affected by local taxes as well as federal income tax provisions. Turning to local property taxes first, the tax on housing falls on the owner or tenant (or both). Owners suffer a loss as a result of property taxes but the loss is less than the full amount of the tax because of deductible clauses in the federal income tax laws. If renters have an inelastic demand for housing, they will pay the major burden of local property taxes, because landlords will raise rents and pass the cost on to the tenants.

In relation to money income, local property taxes have been found to be regressive. If the deductibility of state and local taxes is accounted for in one's measure of income, the property tax becomes even more regressive. In 1959, the Survey Research Center of the University of Michigan found the mean ratio of residential property taxes to income for all families in the U.S. to be 2.1 percent. All families having incomes of less than $5000 paid a greater share of their incomes in taxes, while all families whose incomes exceeded $5000 paid less than 2.1 percent of their income in residential property taxes [22].

Clearly local property taxes adversely affect the allocation of resources and the distribution of income. The continued use of such taxes is based primarily on their ability to generate income. If urban areas are to solve their slum problems, some alternative revenue-generating source will have to be found, since property taxes are disincentives to the maintenance and improvement of existing structures, as well as to the construction of new structures.

Federal tax provisions are a clear incentive for persons to own their own homes rather than rent. Present laws allow complete deductions of state and local property taxes, as well as mortgage interest. The tax breaks are greater for those having higher incomes; thus these provisions cause the distribution of income to be less equal than it would have been otherwise. For those who can take advantage of the provisions, the price of housing is less per unit; thus a greater allocation of resources toward housing is made. Henry Aaron has estimated that the total tax savings to homeowners in 1966 due to mortgage interest and the property-tax deductions was approximately $2.9 billion [23].

Landlords receive a benefit from the federal tax laws in the form of accelerated depreciaton clauses. As we noted earlier, in our discussion of slums, the impact of allowing owners to depreciate their property faster than the property in fact is used up is to cause more rapid turnover in ownership. Moreover, given an increase in demand for housing in slum areas, accelerated depreciation clauses can result in perpetuating the life of slum properties. Thus accelerated depreciation clauses, which lower the effective tax rates for landlords, clearly affect the allocation of resources towards housing and the distribution of income.

One "nonprovision" in our federal tax laws provides a surplus of $4–6 billion per year for homeowners. Since we fail to tax the imputed rental income to homeowners, their taxes are less than they would be otherwise. Aaron [23] has estimated that if one assumes a yield on homeowners' equity of 4–6 percent, the tax savings amount to $4–6 billion. Aaron found that the benefits of this treatment accrue primarily to upper-income homeowners. Thus a misallocation of resources and an unequal distribution of income are the result of our failure to tax imputed rental income of homeowners. This finding is especially interesting in view of our avowed interests in helping lower-income groups obtain reasonable housing services. Favorable tax treatment (or nontreatment) does not seem to be on the side of lower-income persons, as we have seen in this inventory of tax provisions. The remainder of the tools we shall cover, however, are supposed to help solve the housing problem of the poor. It is to be hoped that these tools can neutralize, if not negate the adverse effects of tax policies.

Subsidies

Although building codes and taxes do not necessarily deal directly with the housing problems of the poor, most housing subsidy programs were set up to help solve the housing needs of low-income persons. The Federal Government has rental and interest subsidy programs for low-income tenants and homeowners, while experimental programs in income subsides are also being employed. Some states (Massachusetts, for example) have family-assistance plans that allow a welfare family a lump-sum payment each month. Whether the income-subsidy plan will result in the consumption of more housing depends on the marginal propensity to consume housing services. The latter depends on one's preferences for housing versus other goods.

From a consumer welfare standpoint it is rather simple to show that rental or interest subsidy programs may be inefficient when compared to income subsidies. If a consumer buys housing and other goods, and the prices of housing and other goods are given along with the consumer's budget AB, he will maximize his utility if he buys OH_1 units of housing and OG_1 units of other goods in Figure 6.3. If the person has a free choice of how much additional housing he wants to buy, and if the government reduces the price of housing to him by means of a rental or interest subsidy, his new budget line will be AC. Now he will consume more housing and more other goods (OH_2 and OG_2) at his new equilibrium point. Of course the government could give the person an income subsidy ($A'B'$) that could make the person just as well off, as shown by point J. The cost to the government (measured in other goods) of the housing subsidy is DH_2, while the individual

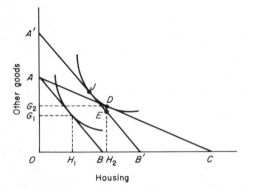

Figure 6.3 *The welfare effects of an income subsidy versus a rental or interest subsidy.*

could have been just as well off with a smaller (income) subsidy EH_2. Thus DE represents the misallocation of resources brought about by subsidies that affect the price of housing.

Just because the housing-subsidy program is inefficient when compared to income-subsidy programs does not mean we should scrap our housing-subsidy programs. Local policy makers often argue that we cannot give income subsidies because people may opt to spend *all* of their increase in income on nonhousing goods and services. But previous studies have shown that the income elasticity of housing for low-income families exceeds unity; thus these fears have little basis. If we did away with housing-subsidy programs and *replaced* them by income-subsidy programs, the savings would be 10–15 percent, according to estimates of H. Aaron and G. Von Furstenburg [24].

The present housing-subsidy programs of the Federal Government go beyond the limited FHA and VA programs of the past. From the Housing and Urban Development Act of 1968 we now have the "235" plan. This plan was originated to help persons having annual incomes between $3000 and 8000 who desire to buy a home, provided that the person has a dependable income source. The 235 plan essentially pays monthly mortgage payments above one-fifth of the family's income. Although the 235 plan has been far more successful than the rental-subsidy programs [25], the plan has a built-in bias. Although persons pay a lower effective interest rate under 235, the actual interest paid by the enrolee and government is determined in the private markets at FHA rates, since the mortgages are made by private sources. This policy means that the enrolee builds up less equity than he would if he got a direct government loan at low interest rates, given that the person contributes the same amount from his given income. Thus present interest-subsidy techniques are not helping individuals build financial security as much as they could, which is supposedly one of the major benefits of homeownership.

Opponents of the interest-subsidy plan have argued that having lower-income families move into their neighborhoods will cause property values to decline. Although the evidence is not in yet on the potential impact of the 235 plan, we do have some research findings on this issue. For example, Robert Schafer compared housing values in a development financed by interest subsidies against a control area in Los Angeles [26]. Schafer found that property values near the development increased slightly more than property values in the control area. The opponents may not have a strong argument.

An additional subsidy program is rental supplements, which have been part of our federal housing policy since 1965. Tenants can get the Federal Government to pay the difference between their monthly rent and one-fourth of their income (less $300 yearly deduction for each dependent) as long as the housing is owned by nonprofitable or limited-dividend (6 percent) institutions. To be eligible, however, the family must have an income near the poverty level, or alternatively, at a low enough level to qualify them for public housing.

Like the interest subsidy programs, rental supplements have not made a great impact in urban housing markets. One of the primary objectives of the rental-supplement plan was to help families get to a position where they could purchase housing outside the ghetto areas. Since recent data show that 93 percent of those families utilizing the rent supplements earned incomes of less than $4000 per year, it is clear that these families are impoverished and cannot be expected to make great strides in the labor markets [25, p. 59]. Another objective was to place families in areas outside of blighted neighborhoods, but more than two-thirds of the families have remained in the slum areas.

Although this program and the interest-subsidy program reach less than 100,000 families per year across the country, they are important because, other than public housing, they are the only programs that serve low-income families.

Rent Controls

Whereas subsidies attempt to work within the market mechanism, government has sometimes decided to control housing markets. During the Second World War most large cities employed rent controls, because the demand for housing near military and defense bases grew immensely while the building materials and labor that ordinarily would have responded to the increase in demand were diverted to war use. Thus, to (supposedly) help the poor man, rents were frozen at their prewar level. After the war, almost every city except New York ended the controls. Recently other cities (such as Cambridge, Massachusetts) that have tight housing markets have joined New York with this type of policy. During the early part of 1973, the Congress was strongly considering a rent-control law that would apply to the 48 largest cities in the country, in reaction to the huge increases in rent landlords made after President Nixon's Phase II price control was lifted.

Economists have traditionally argued against rent controls, at least beyond more than a few years of use. Controls are popular with tenants, of course. Like any other price control, rent-control programs restrict resource allocation in rental markets. Figure 6.4 shows the result of rent controls on resource allocation. In a rising rental market, we find an excess demand for rentals; thus rents are set at R_c, where the quantity

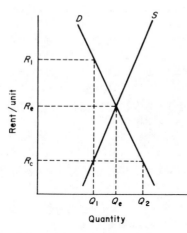

Figure 6.4 *Rent controls and resource allocation.*

demanded is Q_2 but the quantity of rentals supplied is Q_1. If rents were allowed to rise to equilibrium, we would find suppliers offering $Q_1 Q_e$ more units for rent. At this small level of output Q_1, some families will have to forgo rental housing. Note also that at Q_1 people are willing to pay a much higher price than R_c; that is, they would pay R_1; thus it would not be surprising to see payoffs made by those attempting to obtain controlled housing.

Rent controls do provide temporary relief for tenants, but they can adversely affect rental housing consumers in the long run. Landlords may be able to earn a higher return elsewhere; thus supply response is questionable. Maintenance in controlled apartments has always been a problem. Inefficiencies result when large families become small over time, but remain in their large apartments. Inequities occur in that new tenants seeking space may have to take more expensive, uncontrolled apartments if the supply of controlled apartments is limited.

The best empirical evidence we have on the effects of rent controls comes from the New York City experience. Through 1965, New York City's housing market was fine—the stock of housing was increasing, population was decreasing, and housing expenditures per dollar of income were constant [27]. Since 1965, vacancy rates have fallen drastically, apartments are being undermaintained and even abandoned, and new construction has declined drastically. In uncontrolled units (70 percent of the total apartments in 1968) prices have soared. The Rand Corporation and New York City have attempted to figure out the causes of the changes in New York City's housing market, and especially the role played by rent controls.

Thus far it seems that rent controls have been directly responsible for a good share of the undermaintenance policy followed by landlords. At present, little is known about the relationship between the controlled and uncontrolled markets. However, there are some explanatory studies that suggest that controls do not appreciably alter the amount of housing services consumed. Joseph DeSalvo [28] has shown that the 1.2 million households living in controlled units would pay $2.2 billion to live in uncontrolled housing, whereas they pay $1.4 billion to live in controlled housing. That is, presently controlled households could accept an increase in rent of $800 million. DeSalvo also found the aggregate subsidy paid to those in controlled units to be about $800 million; thus he concluded

> . . . that if tenants of controlled housing were to pay full market rents on dwellings they occupy, they would, on average, be paying about the same as their counterparts who live in uncontrolled housing. The implication is then that tenants of controlled housing consume neither substantially more nor substantially less housing than similar families who live in uncontrolled housing; the principal difference is that 'controlled' tenants pay considerably less than the market value for the housing they consume. [28, p. 227]

Edgar Olsen [29] recently published a study which more or less corroborates the DeSalvo findings. Considering New York City in 1968, Olsen found that families in controlled housing consumed 4.4 percent less housing services than they would have without the controls. However, these same families consumed 9.9 percent more nonhousing goods. Olsen also found that poor families received much greater benefits than nonpoor families, as expected.

Although the DeSalvo and Olsen studies show only slight (if any) reduction in the quantity of housing services consumed under rent controls, it is difficult to say whether or not controls have worked in New York City. Since 1965, it is clear that rent controls have not been a *solution* to the housing problems of lower-income persons. But then controls are not necessarily supposed to be.

Public Housing

Public housing has been with us since World War I. The program is for low-income, but not necessarily poverty-stricken families. The general nature of the program is for the Federal Government to pay for initial capital costs, while local housing authorities own and operate the housing, which consists entirely of apartment dwellings. Rents are set below market prices, and revenues go toward maintaining and repairing the structures. Until recently, federal law required that for every new or rehabilitated public unit started, a substandard or unsafe unit in the city had to be demolished. Thus it is not surprising that federal programs have had little positive impact on the net increase of dwelling units in most cities.

Theoretically, public housing does not necessarily offer the level of satisfaction for individuals that rent or income subsidies can because one is often forced to consume more housing than he actually desires. Recalling our earlier discussion using consumer utility theory, in Figure 6.5 we find a consumer maximizing his satisfaction at X if he buys housing services in free markets under a given budget constraint and prices. Now if a housing price subsidy is made, the rational consumer attains a new equilibrium—point Y. Consider a public-housing program that forces the consumer to take H_p level of housing or lose the subsidy. We see that this level of housing puts the individual on a lower indifference curve (U_2). The budget line AC is representative of a public-housing program, since tenants pay below-market rates. But one faced with budget AC would prefer to be at Y; therefore, unless H_p is reduced, we will have an overallocation of resources toward housing for individuals. In other words, public-housing programs may be very costly for what they in fact provide.

Besides perpetual administrative and production problems, the major problem facing the public-housing program is one of excess demand. In New York City during 1968, the Douglas Commission found that 762 applications existed for every vacancy that arose. Over all cities there is probably at least one family waiting for every unit that becomes vacant. Since people have to wait so long to get a unit, there is probably a downward bias in any estimate of the excess demand if the estimate is made from waiting lists. Clearly some more efficient and equitable system of allocating scarce public housing space than waiting lists and biased local authorities is needed.

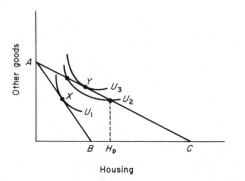

Figure 6.5 *The welfare effects of public housing.*

Given its inherent problem, public housing still provides substantial benefits for those involved. Robert Bish [30] has estimated that in 1965 the direct aggregate benefit to families of public housing units was $197 million. By direct benefit, we mean the difference between the estimated market value of the unit and the actual rent paid for the unit. Although low-income families received the majority of the benefits, Bish found that in no income class ($0–1000, 1000–1999, 2000–2999, and so on) were as many as 5 percent of the families eligible for public housing served. The value of changes in housing consumption ($135 million) was less than the total direct benefits of public-housing programs, according to Bish.* The difference between $197 and 135 million, or $62 million, represents increased consumption of other goods.

Not only should we consider the benefits of public housing, but costs are clearly important. Bish estimated that on a per-unit basis, the market rent of public housing would have been $75 per month. According to some estimates, private producers spend $5000–7000 to build housing that rents at this price. On the other hand, public housing cost over $10,000 per unit in the 1950's. This higher cost may be attributed to expensive land and methods of financing. These problems are being overcome, however, because adjustments have been made to solve them. One of the changes in policy has been to build public housing outside the core city areas, in the suburbs where jobs are available. Higher-income suburbanites oppose this policy, however, since they consider only the potential private costs to themselves when evaluating the program change.

Urban Renewal

Urban Renewal began in 1949, when the major emphasis of housing policy shifted from the construction of new dwellings to the renovation of whole neighborhoods. Our effective goal was changed from housing the poor to raising property values and tax yields in the blighted and slum areas of our cities. To be sure, *one* of the goals of urban renewal is to provide decent, safe, and sanitary housing. However, the Douglas Commission found that through 1968 over 400,000 more units had been destroyed than had been built. As a result, low-income families have

* As long as the individual housing outlay is the same in public housing as it was in private housing, total direct benefits will always be equivalent to increases in the value of housing consumption. If, however, the tenant resides in public housing and reduces his housing outlay (which occurred for all income classes in 1965), direct benefits will exceed increases in housing consumption. Note that this argument is not inconsistent with the analysis of Figure 6.5, since here we are dealing with the value of housing services.

been found to relocate in a "new" slum, since they can afford only low-quality housing. In short, urban renewal has not seemed to help solve the housing problems of lower-income persons. Why not?

To answer this question let us look at the program in more detail. Urban renewal is a joint effort of Federal and local governments and private developers. Local public authorities choose blighted areas for renewal and future uses, subject to Federal approval. Once approval is given, the land is purchased, occupants are relocated, and the structures are razed. After the land is upgraded, it is sold or leased to private developers. The best estimates are that private developers pay about one-third of what it would cost them to purchase, raze, and redevelop. Since the city bears only one-third of this project cost (the Federal Government pays the rest) it is little wonder that the net benefit–cost ratios computed by local public authorities are high. Clearly, for each city by itself, urban renewal seems to be a bonanza. But the majority of projects that cities have guided have replaced blighted areas with commercial facilities and middle-income apartments. Thus the true beneficiaries of urban-renewal projects have been land developers and landlords.

Recently there has been a major effort to provide low-income families displaced by urban renewal (and other government problems) with adequate moving and other expenses. This new emphasis is no doubt better than the old practices, yet obviously the poor are worse off in their new neighborhoods, because if markets operated somewhat efficiently, they could have moved without urban renewal programs—and they did not.

V. SUMMARY

In this chapter we have made a detailed study of urban housing markets, problems, and policies. The housing market is a dual one, in that we buy (rent) housing stock in order to derive housing services. The relationship between the market for housing stock and housing services was explained by means of a competitive model. The spatial element came into our discussion through the concept of filtering. Empirical studies of urban housing markets are still in their infancy, but the evidence we have to date suggests that price and income elasticities are near unity, while the price elasticity of supply is less than unity. This information is especially useful for developing efficient housing policy.

Urban housing markets are beset by a number of problems and imperfections. One of the basic sources of imperfection is the impact of externalities or neighborhood effects on the value of housing. In addition, Federal and local governments have a number of policies that generate and perpetuate slums and segregated housing markets. Racial discrimination is still a major problem in urban housing markets, and the impact of discrimination goes far beyond the simple price differences paid by whites and nonwhites.

The goal of housing policy is to ensure that everyone has safe and sanitary housing at a reasonable cost. Unfortunately, we have little information on the percentage of the population occupying safe and sanitary housing. However, it is clear that the majority of the governmental tools that affect housing markets do so in a nonneutral way, aiding middle- and upper-income families rather than low-income families. With the exception of public housing, government housing policies to help the poor are quite meager. Thus we have found little evidence that our housing policy goals are being taken seriously.

SUGGESTED READINGS

DeSalvo, Joseph. "A Methodology of Evaluating Housing Programs." *Journal of Regional Science* 11 (1971): 173–186.

Edel, Matthew, and Rothenberg, Jerome, eds. *Readings in Urban Economics,* Part 3. New York: Macmillan, 1972.

Mills, Edwin. *Urban Economics,* Chapter 10. Glenview, Illinois: Scott, Foresman, 1972.

Muth, Richard. Cities and Housing, Chicago, Illinois: Univ. of Chicago Press, 1969.

Olson, Edgar. "A Competitive Theory of the Housing Markets." *American Economic Review* 59 (1969): 612–622.

Page, Alfred, and Seyfreid, Warren, eds. *Urban Analysis.* Glenview, Illinois: Scott, Foresman, 1970.

Reid, Margaret. *Housing and Income.* Chicago, Illinois: Univ. of Chicago Press, 1962.

Rothenberg, Jerome. *Economic Evaluation of Urban Renewal.* Washington, D.C.: Brookings Inst., 1967.

Taggart, Robert. *Low Income Housing: A Critique of Federal Aid.* Baltimore, Maryland: John Hopkins Press, 1970.

REFERENCES

1. "A Decent Home." Report of the President's Committee on Urban Housing, Washington, D.C., 1969.

2. Richard Muth, "The Demand for Non-Farm Housing," in *The Demand for Durable Goods,* A. C. Harberger, ed., pp. 29–75 (Chicago, Illinois: Univ. of Chicago Press, 1960).

3. Russell Uhler, "The Demand for Housing: An Inverse Probability Approach," *The Review of Economics and Statistics* 50 (1968): 129–134.
4. Margaret Reid, *Housing and Income* (Chicago, Illinois: Univ. of Chicago Press, 1962).
5. Allen Winger, "Housing and Income," *Western Economic Journal* (1968): 226–232.
6. T. H. Lee, "Housing and Permanent Income: Tests based on a Three-Year Reinterview Survey," *The Review of Economics and Statistics* 50 (1968): 480–490.
7. S. J. Maisel *et al.*, "The Demand for Housing: A Comment," *The Review of Economics and Statistics* 53 (1971): 410–413.
8. Frank de Leeuw, "The Demand for Housing: A Review of Cross-Section Evidence," *Review of Economics and Statistics* 53 (1971): 1–10.
9. Donald Guy and Hugh Nourse, "The Filtering Process: The Webster Groves and Kankakee Cases," *Proceeding of the American Real Estate and Urban Economics Association* 5 (1970): 33–49.
10. Frank de Leeuw and N. F. Ekanem, "The Supply of Rental Housing," *The American Economic Review* 61 (1971): 806–817.
11. Otto Davis and Andrew Whinston, "The Economics of Urban Renewal," *Law and Contemporary Problems* 26 (1961): 105–117.
12. Jerome Rothenberg, *Economic Evaluation of Urban Renewal*, Chapter 3 (Washington, D.C.: Brookings Inst., 1967).
13. Richard Muth, *Cities and Housing*, Chapter 6 (Chicago, Illinois: Univ. of Chicago Press, 1966).
14. Edwin Mills, *Urban Economics*, pp. 165–179 (Glenview, Illinois: Scott, Foresman, 1972).
15. E. Smolensky, Selwyn Becker, and Harvey Molotch, "The Prisoner's Dilemma and Ghetto Expansion," *Land Economics* 64 (1968): 419–430.
16. Benjamin Cohen, "Another Theory of Residential Segregation," *Land Economics* 47 (1971): 314–315.
17. R. Ridker and J. Henning, "The Determination of Residential Property Values with Special Reference to Air Pollution," *Review of Economics and Statistics* 49 (1967): 246–257.
18. J. Kain and J. Quigley, "Housing Market Discrimination, Homeownership, and Savings Behavior," *American Economic Review*, 63 (1972): 263–277.
19. John Kain, "Housing Segregation, Negro Employment and Metropolitan Decentralization," *Quarterly Journal of Economics* 82 (1968): 175–197.
20. Paul Offner and Daniel Saks, "A Note on John Kain's Housing Segregation, Negro Employment, and Metropolitan Decentralization," *Quarterly Journal of Economics* 85 (1971): 147–160.
21. Joseph Mooney, "Housing Segregation, Negro Employment, and Metropolitan Decentralization: An Alternative Perspective," *Quarterly Journal of Economics* 83 (1969): 299–311.
22. Dick Netzer, *Economics of the Property Tax*, p. 47 (Washington, D.C.: Brookings Inst., 1965).
23. Henry Aaron, "Income Taxes and Housing," *American Economic Review* 60 (1970): 789–806.
24. Henry Aaron and G. Von Furstenburg, "The Inefficiencies of Transfers in Kind: The Case of Housing Assistance," *Western Economic Journal* 9 (1971): 190.
25. Robert Taggart III, *Low Income Housing: A Critique of Federal Aid*, pp. 75–83 (Baltimore, Maryland: John Hopkins Press, 1970).

26. Robert Schafer, "The Effect of BMIR Housing on Property Values," *Land Economics* 48 (1972): 282–286.
27. Ira Lowry, "Reforming Rent Control in New York City," *Papers, Regional Science Association* 27 (1970): 196–227.
28. Joseph DeSalvo, "Reforming Rent Control in New York City: The Role of Research in Policy Making," *Papers, Regional Science Association* 27 (1970): 195–227.
29. Edgar Olsen, "An Econometric Analysis of Rent Control," *Journal of Political Economy* 80 (1972): 1081–1100.
30. Robert Bish, "Public Housing: The Magnitude and Distribution of Direct Benefits and Effects of Housing Consumption," *Journal of Regional Science* 9 (1969): 425–438.

7

URBAN
TRANSPORTATION

I. INTRODUCTION

In Chapter 1 we argued that the function of an urban area or concentration of population is to allow a greater level of satisfaction per person via (1) specialization in production and (2) a greater variety of goods and services in consumption. We also noted that the farther away from each other people choose to locate, the greater the chance is that the fruits of concentrating will be eaten up by transportation costs. Clearly the transportation system is basic to the development and well-being of an urban area. Indeed, without an efficient transportation system, the *raison d'etre* of a city may be effectively canceled.

The transportation system of nearly every urban area in the U.S. is composed of two general modes: private autos and public transit. The private auto, of course, is the more popular mode in most cities. By public transit, we mean any mode that offers service to the public upon payment of the proper fare (rather than ownership by the government). During the past half-century we have been unable to collect, move, and distribute masses of people efficiently in our cities by means of public transit. This problem is due in part to the dispersal (suburbanization) of jobs and people. Accordingly, the auto has become more and more popular, while public transit companies find it more difficult each year just to stay in business. By 1970, 80 percent of all passengers, revenues, and employment in the public transit sector were accounted for by 14 *publicly* owned companies.

The major problem facing the transportation system of nearly every city in the U.S., regardless of size, is congestion. This age-old problem, which has been known to man since at least the Roman era, occurs because many people prefer to travel at the same time *and* the transportation capacity is fixed. Many believe that the major source of this congestion in big cities is suburbanites commuting into the central cities by means of autos. They argue that if we only forced these people to take public transportation, congestion problems would be done away with. However, since 1960 the majority of central-city road users have originated inside the central city. Similarly, most suburbanites work in the suburbs. Central-city dwellers are the primary source of their own congestion! We are not arguing, of course, that traffic will fail to move more quickly if most auto users are diverted to public transit.

We hope to shed some light on other misconceptions throughout this chapter. For example, we have often heard the following arguments:

(1) We must have more public transit if the downtown is to be revived and the poor are to be helped.
(2) Highway users are subsidized; thus to even things out, we should subsidize public transit.
(3) We can never solve our traffic problems in cities until congestion is reduced to zero.
(4) Increases in public transit fares will inevitably lead to the bankruptcy of transit firms, since less patronage results, which leads to less service, which leads to even less demand, in a viscious circle.

Although each of these arguments has an intuitive kernel of truth in it, by the end of the chapter the reader should be able to identify the fallacies inherent in each.

As in past chapters on urban problem areas, we begin our discussion with a look at markets. On the demand side of the market, we consider why individuals choose the mode of travel they do, and what the possibilities are of diverting them from their present modal choice. This is especially important for auto users in regard to their becoming future transit users. On the supply side of the transport market, we focus on short- and long-run problems. In the short run, roadway capacity is given; thus the problem becomes one of utilizing this capacity most efficiently. In the long run, capacity may be varied, and many issues in transportation planning are covered. In the area of transportation policy, we take a detailed look at the nature of congestion and the various proposals for solving the problem. An extensive analysis of the more-transit versus more-highways debate is also given.

II. TRANSPORTATION MARKETS

Demand

We are all aware of the relative decline of public transit usage in the postwar period and the increased usage of autos. The decline in transit patronage has been hardly noticeable for (peak-hour) work trips in major cities. However, total work trips comprise around 50 percent of all trips, and relatively poor transit service during nonpeak hours means the auto is unquestionably more efficient for nonwork trips. It is of little surprise, then, that decreased patronage of public transit firms has been felt hardest during nonpeak hours. Increased economic growth and/or a redistribution of income in urban areas will no doubt add to the growth of automania in this country. This is because the average propensity to consume transport services goes from 6 percent for families having incomes of $1000–2000 per year to 12–15 percent for families having incomes of $7500–10,000 [1]. If modal preferences do not change, and incomes increase, the results are clear.

A second major demand trend in the aggregate transport market is the continuation of a very large number of people preferring to use the same roadway facilities at more or less the same time. Everyone is familiar with the peak-hour traffic problems in the U.S. today. Unfortunately, we have always had this problem, and as long as we "price" the use of road space the way we do, there is little chance the problem will be solved. The genesis of the peak problem is our 8-to-5 workday accompanied by a strong preference for rapid service during the peak hours. It is important for the student to understand that peak-hour congestion occurs not only on streets and highways but also on rail, subway, and rapid-transit lines, because of increases in cars and stops; that is, for essentially the same reasons we find congestion on roads or highways.

Finally, in the aggregate consumers may have made rather rational choices in going to the auto, regardless of what we always hear about traffic jams and daily congestion. The average commuting time during peak hours is about the same as it always was, but the average distance people commute has increased about 10 miles. Moreover, the average decongestion time downtown has been reduced by as much as 40 percent [2]. In short, people are actually getting better service from autos than they got before from our urban transport systems. This improvement has been gradual over the past few decades, which has made it unnoticeable to many.

Individual Mode Decisions

The aggregate demand relationships implied by the trends we have described are found by summing over the demands of households at given prices. Thus, to find out what determines the demand for autos or public transit, we shall consider the individual consumer unit of transport services—the individual or household.

In the short run, the spatial structure of the urban community is given. Thus for any individual, his place of employment, residence, and shopping alternatives are given. In addition, the transport network structure among these places is also given. To choose a mode (or various proportions of modes) that maximizes this satisfaction, a consumer will buy transport services right up to where the marginal utility per dollar of expenditures on transport services is equal to the marginal utility per dollar of expenditures on all other goods and services. Using traditional economic analysis, then, the demand for any given mode is a function of (1) the price of that model (2) one's income and preferences, and (3) the price of substitute modes.

The price of transport services for any given mode is not just the out-of-pocket cost to an individual. Unlike other commodities, transport services require users to provide an input—their time—in consuming the service. Thus the cost of driving or riding in a car includes not only the expenses for the car but also the opportunity cost of one's time. Similarly, when one rides in transit, the actual price paid by the consumer is the fare *plus* the value placed on one's time used up during the trip.

The failure to account for the value of one's time often results in an understatement of the true price of auto or transit services. A related source of bias in transport pricing is the failure to include waiting time and transfers. Most transit trips are not direct, and many auto trips involve more than a few steps of walking at both ends of the trip. One must include the total trip time evaluation, from origin to destination, to be able to obtain an accurate estimate of the true price.

One of the major problems in estimating time and therefore price for an individual is that he often has little control over the actual time consumed in transit. If others decide to travel when I do, my travel time increases, especially if the roadway is filled nearly to capacity. I, of course, have the same effect on others. These external effects may also change the relative price of substitute modes, which could cause a shift in my modal demand function.

Besides these somewhat technical problems, some auto commuters account for only out-of-pocket costs (gas and parking) when pricing the auto against transit. Clearly these consumers are irrational. Maintenance, repairs, and insurance rates are affected by the mileage driven; thus they must be included in the cost of commuting. In addition, if the individual must purchase a second car for the household because the first car is used for commuting, the entire cost of the second car (plus the first, of course) should be included in the commuting costs. Thus anyone who argues that he commutes by car because gas and parking fees cost about the same as transit fare, but autos are more convenient, may not necessarily be allocating his resources optimally; he may be underpricing the cost of the auto vis-à-vis public transit to the point where it would be rational for him to take public transit. To be sure, we have not included an evaluation of one's preferences for the privacy of autos, which could alter the overall evaluation.

Over the long run, the spatial structure of a city changes. Residential developments occur. Jobs shift from city to suburb. New roads and highways are built. All of these factors change the price of transit modes for households, whether their residential location remains the same or changes. Rational individuals react to these changes by varying their consumption until the ratio of marginal utility to price between transport services and all other goods is the same as before.

Empirical Demand Studies

Until recently, urban economists did not have any evidence on the price and cross-elasticities of demand for alternative modes of transportation by individuals. Most of the work had relied on aggregate data, and instead of estimating demand elasticities per se, these studies were directed mainly toward forecasting the number of trips by each mode in cities. Transport demand studies using individual or household behavioral models have been performed for a number of cities in the U.S., including Boston, San Francisco, and Chicago. A summary of the results of these studies is presented in Table 7-1. Empirical demand studies are of utmost importance, since they give us the responsiveness of demand by mode for given changes in prices. These responses or elasticities are key information when one considers, for example, how we might induce auto users to switch to public transit.

TABLE 7-1

Summary of Transport Demand Studies

Author(s)	Price elasticity	Cross elasticity	Year	Area
Domencich and Kraft	0.17 (1.10)[a]	0 (0)[a]	1968	Boston
	0.32 (0.59)[b]	0 (0)[b]		
	0.56 (2.26)[c]	0.14 (.37)[c]		
	2.53 (2.46)[d]	0 (0.10)[d]		
McGillivray	0.20 (0.248)[e]		1965	San Francisco
Lave	0.11[f]		1956	Chicago

[a] Work trips via transit.
[b] Shopping trips via transit.
[c] Work trips via auto.
[d] Shopping trips via auto.
[e] Estimate of both work and shopping trip price elasticity for buses.
[f] Estimate of work and shopping trip price elasticity via transit.

The study of Boston [3] compared auto and transit users across over 500 zones. Trip purposes included working and shopping. The demand model related the number of trips to travel time and costs, as well as other socioeconomic variables of each zone (population, income, employment). The findings were:

(1) Transit demand is highly inelastic with respect to fares; thus reductions in fares will bring very little increase in ridership. As Table 7-1 shows, the price elasticity for work and shopping trips was estimated at 0.17 and 0.32, respectively. That is, if a 1 percent reduction in transit fares occurred during work trips, the resultant increase in ridership would be only 0.17 of 1 percent. However, increases in fares will significantly raise total revenues.

(2) The cross-elasticity of demand for autos is very low; that is, if transit fares on work trips are lowered to zero, we only get a slight response (14 percent) in auto users switching to public transit. This 14 percent response may be compared to no response to zero fares on the part of potential shopping trip transit users.

(3) The elasticities in parentheses in Table 7-1 are responses to changes in travel time rather than fares. In all cases, the elasticities for travel-time changes exceed those for fare changes, which suggests that transit companies can increase ridership more effectively by reducing travel times rather than fares.

Robert McGillivray recently completed a study of modal choice between bus and autos using individuals in San Francisco [4]. His findings were similar to those of Domencich and Kraft for Boston. McGillivray found that a 30 percent increase in the price of buses relative to auto service would result in only a 5.6 percent reduction in bus patronage. Alternatively, if bus services were provided free of charge, patronage would increase by only 22.3 percent. Finally, a 30 percent increase in the travel time of buses relative to cars resulted in only a 7.5 percent decrease in bus travel. Thus San Francisco, like Boston, has quite inelastic demands for alternative modes. In other words, people seem to be more or less locked into their modal choices.

Charles Lave's findings [5] for Chicago corroborate the Boston and San Francisco results. A free fare system would increase transit ridership by only 11 percent. The same result could be obtained if buses ran 15 minutes faster per trip. Interestingly, Lave found that Chicago commuters evaluated their time at 46 percent of their wage rate, which explains the relative strength of travel time as compared to fares in bringing about variation in the quantity of services consumed by mode.

In summary, empirical demand studies show that modal choices are not very sensitive to price changes. In all of these studies, prices were fully accounted for; that is, each of the biases discussed earlier was taken out of the data. What these results mean, of course, is that unless preferences or other factors change drastically in the future, there will be little if any change in the existing trend of auto versus public transit usage. And more strikingly, these results cast a huge shadow over the efficacy of new huge public transport systems such as BART in San Francisco and METRO in Washington.

This information on demand elasticities also provides some ammunition against some the popular misconceptions stated at the outset of this chapter. For example, given existing preferences, additional public transit facilities will reduce the price of transit service, but will not bring many more people downtown; therefore, better transportation services alone will not necessarily bring about a revival of core areas. It is also rather doubtful that congestion can ever be completely eliminated unless the density of land use declines drastically, and then we make these less dense cities into a sea of roads. Finally, increases in fares per se will not bring about the bankruptcy of transit firms, for fare increases result in greater revenues.

Supply and Costs

The quantity supplied of a given mode is determined by the price of that mode and the cost of resources used to produce the service, other things being equal. The important issue to begin with is the product price and cost of resources used by autos and public transit. After considering this information, we can then turn to a discussion of how existing capacity can be utilized most efficiently in the short run, and the long-run planning decisions for urban transportation networks.

Costs of Auto and Transit Services

In 1969 the cost of operating a private auto varied between 8 and 20 cents per mile, depending on the type of car, roads traveled (toll or nontoll), and distance traveled [6]. This estimate includes fuel, maintenance, repair, depreciation, and insurance expenses. If parking fees and the value of one's time were included, this cost per mile would be much greater.

There is little doubt that fuel, repair, depreciation, insurance, and parking expenses have steadily increased over the past decade or so in urban areas. Just during the winter of 1973, for example, the price of fuel in some cities (Minneapolis, Seattle, and Louisville) has increased by more than 20 percent. Since we can travel faster by car today in urban areas, it is not clear a priori that travel-time cost estimates have increased. It is possible to give a preliminary answer to this question by comparing increases in incomes (a proxy for the value of one's time) to increases in travel speeds. If increases in travel speeds per hour exceeded increases in wages per hour, then we could agree that the time costs of urban travel have decreased. In the postwar period, a rough estimate of travel-speed changes is from 25 to 35 miles per hour, or about a 2 percent increase per year. The average wage rate, on the other hand, has increased by $3\frac{1}{2}$ percent during this period; thus the opportunity cost of travel time has probably risen.

Public Transit: Revenue–Cost Trends

Turning to the public transit modes, fares have more than kept pace with the overall consumer price index during the postwar period, yet costs have exceeded revenues. This latter phenomenon is due, of course, to decreased patronage. For example during the 1960–1969 period, median bus revenues decreased by 3 percent, while median operating expenses increased by 22 percent [7]. The profit squeeze has hit buses particularly hard. Private firms seem to have the highest cost–revenue ratio; thus, unless these bus firms can obtain subsidies (that is, go public), they will leave the industry in the long run. On the average, about 7 percent of the bus firms did not cover variable costs in 1960, while in 1969 33 percent did not cover variable costs.* During the same

* Based on a representative sample of U.S. city bus firms [7].

time period, passenger ridership decreased 32 percent, so the overall picture of bus transit is rather bleak at this time.

Rail rapid-transit (above and below ground) operations have not fared well financially in the U.S., although Canadian (Montreal and Toronto) systems have been successful thus far. Ten firms provide rail rapid transit service in the U.S. Of the eight operations that existed in 1960, the decennial statistics from 1960 to 1970 are similar to those for bus transit: (1) revenue passengers declined, although by only 7.3 percent, and (2) total revenue increased by 75 percent, but operating expenses increased so much faster that a deficit of $0.4 million in 1960 rose to an $80 million deficit by 1970. The only U.S. operations having operating cost–operating revenue ratios less than one are the 4-mile Newark subway line and the 13-mile rapid-transit line operated by the city of Shaker Heights, Ohio, a suburb of Cleveland. Commuter rail lines are also unable to meet expenses. In 1970, 16 lines were carrying passengers an average of 22 miles into our large cities. Only the Chicago Northwestern line had a positive net income figure in 1970.

What are the key differences between financially successful and unsuccessful transit operations? For buses there is little information to go on, since few, if any bus operations operate without financial losses. The data on empirical demand studies tell us, however, that if bus fares were raised considerably, few riders would be lost; thus revenues could be increased by raising prices. We have also learned that time was an important factor in bus ridership; thus the financial picture of bus operations would be brightened if quicker service were available. This could be accomplished through reducing traffic congestion, or by providing express lanes for buses—which has recently become popular in many U.S. cities.

Information on rail rapid-transit shows that the financially troubled firms have relatively low operating costs per passenger mile (with the exception of Boston) when compared to the Newark and Shaker Heights lines. One might suspect, then, that Newark and Shaker Heights remain relatively financially healthy because they price their service at more or less what the traffic will bear. That is, if New York, Chicago, Philadelphia and Cleveland are going to reduce their operating cost–revenue ratios, they will have to do so by increasing fares. Boston, on the other hand, could possibly work on cutting costs as well as increasing revenues. The reason the Chicago Northwestern rail commuter line operates in the black is quite simple—its costs per passenger mile are by far the lowest in the U.S., whereas its revenues per passenger mile are about average.

III. SHORT-RUN SUPPLY CONSIDERATIONS

Roads

In the short run the capacity of the urban transport system is given; thus our objective is to utilize this capacity most efficiently, given the preferences of society. As we noted in our discussion on demand, the capacity of our roads is often exceeded during peak rush hours of the day. This peak problem is a major obstacle in utilizing our road capacity efficiently, given the present pricing system of road use. That is, users do not pay any more out-of-pocket costs to use a downtown street at 8:30 A.M. than they do at 10:30 A.M., although during the earlier time it takes them longer to get where they are going. The real difference in the price (costs) of using road space is our time; during the rush hour we spend more time. In effect, we charge zero nominal prices for road usage, so instead of prices allocating road space, time becomes the allocator.

If everyone evaluated his time the same, then time would be (theoretically) an efficient allocator of road space. However, if A's time is worth $10 per hour, and B's time is worth $2 per hour, and we have numerous A's and B's congesting the streets, the A's could pay the B's travel at some other time and both would be better off. For example, if the A's could save one-half hour per trip, they would be willing to pay the B's up to $5 per trip to travel at another time. Obviously, any given B may be willing to travel up to $2\frac{1}{2}$ hours earlier or later than A travels, if B is an income-maximizer. As long as it is possible for any A and B to make a "trade" that would make either A or B better off (and no one else worse off), we have not reached an optimal allocation of resources.

Of course it is not likely that high-income persons or groups will try or be able to bribe lower-income persons or groups to stay off the roads, even using monetary bait. Clearly the problem of using existing transport capacity most efficiently is one in which a third party is required. The usual candidate is the government. Why is a third party needed? Because once a road nears capacity, the average speed per vehicle declines as more cars enter the road; thus additional cars cause negative externalities. As shown in Figure 7.1, negative externalities cause a divergence to occur between the private marginal costs MC_p of another car entering the crowded road and that car's social marginal cost MC_s. Each driver, acting as a rational consumer (and the sum of all drivers), will enter the road until the price equals the MC_p. Here

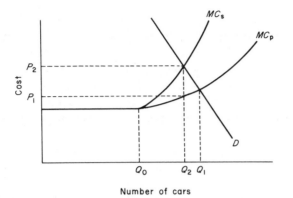

Figure 7.1 *Efficient pricing of existing road space.*

the price represents the value of another car entering the road, while the MC_p represents the cost of the next-best alternative route. However, once Q_0 cars are on the road, additional cars slow others down; thus $MC_s > MC_p$. Thus the point where society attains the optimal number of cars is where price $= MC_s$ or amount Q_2. But under our present system, "rational" consumers will enter the road until Q_1 cars are on the road. If society is to attain the optimal use of road space during peak hours, a charge similar to p_1p_2 will have to be levied against users. This charge or toll would be exactly equal to the difference between the MC_s and MC_p of the Q_2th car.

Many persons argue that it would be difficult if not impossible to set proper charges and collect them economically. These policy issues will be considered later in this chapter, when we consider the problem of congestion in more detail. However, there are other mechanisms available for ensuring a more efficient use of urban highway capacity in the short run.

One approach would be to change the level and structure of parking fees downtown. Curb parking spaces, municipal and department-store lots, and institutions often involve heavily subsidized fees; users pay only a fraction of the real cost of the space. In addition, rates are set such that all-day users pay lower fees per hour. Since all-day users are the ones most likely to be driving during the peak periods, we could certainly help reduce congestion if parking fees were not subsidized and if persons entering or leaving parking facilities during peak hours paid higher rates.

Roads could also be used more efficiently if work hours were staggered. This practice has been instituted on a limited scale by the Federal Government in Washington, D.C. This policy has a drawback if carried very far, however, in that access in the form of face-to-face contact is one of the primary benefits of having heavy concentrations of people. Thus, if the majority of people in the downtown areas did not work at more or less the same time, one of the primary functions of the city would not be served. Car pools are another alternative to the congestion problem. It may be rational for the government to subsidize those cars with two or more riders entering a city during peak congestion hours.

Transit

Besides our highways, urban transport capacity also includes all of the capital stock of transit companies. Given the preferences as expressed by the demand curve for transit services, transit firms use the same rule as any other firm else in delivering an optimal allocation of services; that is, they provide services up to where $P = MC_p$. As we noted earlier, however, demand for transit services has been decreasing, and costs increasing to the point where many firms require a subsidy even to continue operations in the short run. If we are to keep this transit capacity available, we must subsidize these firms. The question arises, how much is the optimal subsidy? By optimal subsidy, we mean that level of subsidy consistent with an efficient allocation of resources.

To derive the optimal subsidy level for transit firms [8], we first recognize that we are faced with a decreasing cost industry. Because of the peak-period nature of the demand for transit services, transit firms do not operate at full capacity or the minimum point on the long-run average-cost (LAC) curve. Accordingly, in Figure 7.2 we draw the long-run

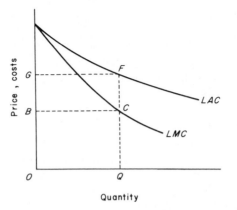

Figure 7.2 *The optimal subsidy level for transit firms.*

marginal-cost (*LMC*) curve below *LAC*. If demand cuts *LMC* at point *C*, then the optimal output is *OQ*, where *P = LMC*. Of course we could also draw a short-run marginal-cost curve through *C* and make our analysis applicable to the short run. The important point to note, however, is that if *OQ* is produced, *LAC* exceeds price *CQ* by *FC*; thus the subsidy required to keep the transit firm in business *and* offering an optimal level of output is *BGFC*.

IV. LONG-RUN SUPPLY CONSIDERATIONS

In the long run the capacity of the urban transport system may be varied. The goal is to provide that level of capacity for all modes which maximizes the satisfaction of society. This is a very difficult goal to meet, for many reasons. First, it is difficult to forecast the preferences of society. Building new highways or transit lines requires years of planning, *and* the capacity has a very long expected life; if we invest in something society does not desire, we may be wasting our resources. Second, and perhaps most important, is that most transport planning and investment is done by the public sector. Private development of land is generally in response to the market mechanism; however, at best, the public sector usually responds to market stimulae with a lag. For example, if it is profitable, developers will build new skyscrapers downtown, but we seldom see increased capacity (if needed) being built into our transport system simultaneously.

A Benefit–Cost Approach to Transport Planning

The most popular method used by economists to determine the desirability of alternative investments in the public sector is benefit–cost analysis. This approach involves forecasting the benefits and costs over the expected life of the transport project, discounting these benefits and costs to their present value, and choosing that project which maximizes net benefits to society. Obviously it is difficult to delineate all of the expected benefits of a project, and a greater problem is to put a dollar value on these benefits. Nevertheless, this approach has been quite useful, and it will be instructive to see how it applies to transport projects.

Benefit Measurement

Assume that we are on a planning board considering the construction of a new freeway through the city, which supposedly will help solve the existing downtown congestion problem. In order to measure the expected benefits from this freeway, we first have to know what traffic patterns and volumes will be in the future, given the existing road capacity and structure. This will involve forecasting both freight traffic via truck and private and public modal choices of personal travel. An inherent problem in this forecast of future traffic "demand" is that not only are transport patterns and volumes determined by the location of firms and people, but once changes in the transport system occur (such as our new freeway), they cause shifts in the location of firms and people. In a sense, supply creates its own demand. Clearly such a response could be a major factor in whether or not the new expressway will help relieve congestion. Thus forecasting the future travel patterns and volumes is not a simple task.

Given the expected traffic flows and pattern, one is ready to estimate the benefits of the expressway. The benefits may be categorized as direct and indirect. Direct benefits include the time and operating-cost savings to users of the expressway (cars, trucks, and buses). For nonusers, indirect benefits may occur in the form of less congestion in city streets. It is quite possible that the new expressway will involve changes in the income distribution (such as net increases in the price of land), and it is important to include these benefits in the evaluation. The particular weight given to changes in the income distribution depends on the objectives of the planning board.

Cost Measurement

The cost of our planned expressway may also be broken down into direct and indirect categories. On the direct side, there are fixed costs and operating costs. Fixed costs include not only the costs of constructing the expressway but also interest on the funds used to pay for the construction. In addition, the cost of land taken by the expressway is a fixed cost, which is valued at what the land could have rented for in its next-best alternative use. Operating costs are well known—gas, oil, depreciation, and so forth—along with the imputed value of one's time in using the espressway. Indirect costs include (1) congestion that may occur at ramps to the expressway (or even on the expressway), (2) increased pollution from auto, truck, and bus emissions, and (3) tax costs, which may be proxied by the probable tax liabilities of a private firm using the land [9].

Choice of the Discount Rate

Once the benefits and costs are estimated, they must be discounted to the present so that a common time base can be used to compute net benefits. A major issue (unresolved among economists) is: What is the proper discount rate to use? If transportation services and capacity were produced and consumed in private markets only, and capital markets were perfectly competitive, then persons would buy and sell assets (including roads, buses, and so on) until the yield or rate of return on all assets (including money) was the same. In such a highly simplified world, the market rate of interest would properly reflect the terms on which consumers would be willing to give up present for future consumption, that is, the market rate of interest would be the appropriate discount rate.

Of course, the workings of perfectly competitive capital markets are based on the assumption that individuals attempt to maximize their income, thus since governments may have alternative objectives in building expressways besides income maximization, it is not clear that the market rate of interest can serve as the proper discount rate for public investment projects. Even if governments did have the income maximization objective, capital markets are certainly not perfect in the real world, so the market rate of interest is no doubt a biased proxy for the discount rate.

If the market rate of interest is improper, what can be used as a substitute? Alternatively, how might we modify market rates to obtain an estimate of the social discount rate. Clearly market interest rates in competitive capital markets may fail to reflect useful important external and social effects. Thus market rates are probably higher than social rates, so if we use market interest rates for public projects, we may underinvest. Although the final choice for the social discount rate is no doubt some rate of interest below the market rate, how much below is difficult to say.

Impact of Changing Capacity on the Income Distribution

When one chooses among alternative transportation projects—say our new expressway versus adding a new line to an existing rail rapid-transport facility—the use of benefit–cost analysis implies that efficiency criteria are major in the decision. That is, we are choosing that project which yields the highest net income level to society. The question that many urban economists are asking today, however, is: What effect do new freeways and transit facilities have on the distribution of income? As we stated above in the discussion of benefits, the construction of new freeways will no doubt have an impact on the net price of land, especially at interchanges. Landowners would benefit at the expense of the rest of society, depending on how the new freeway is financed. Relocation of families and firms often involves excess burdens that are not fully compensated for, causing a change in the income distribution; affected families and firms are essentially subsidizing the new freeway users.

For a transport project to have a neutral impact on the distribution of income, the change in total benefits (marginal benefits) of the project must equal the change in total costs (marginal costs) for each income class in the urban area. This condition will seldom, if ever, hold. One of the more basic reasons is because people with higher incomes have higher imputed costs on their time, and vice versa. Thus, unless higher-income people are charged a proportionately higher price to use the new freeway, the marginal benefits for higher-income persons will exceed their marginal costs. Alternatively, lower-income people will be paying a disproportionate share of the freeway costs. Most freeways built into central cities from suburbs have involved a redistribution of income toward the higher groups, since the latter are the primary users of these roads. Reverse-commuting facilities for lower-income central-city residents could shift the process in the opposite direction.

In summary, benefit–cost analysis can be a very useful tool for helping make an efficient transportation planning decision, such as our hypothetical case of the consideration of a new freeway through a city. Benefit–cost analysis is difficult to apply, however, as we have repeatedly pointed out. Benefits are often unmeasurable, and true social discount rates are not easy to identify. In addition, benefit–cost analysis may yield an efficient but inequitable solution to a planning problem.

V. TRANSPORT PROBLEMS AND POLICIES

As we have noted many times before, the role of government policy is to assist the market mechanism in allocating resources more efficiently and achieving a more equitable distribution of income. Probably in no other urban markets has government failed more than it has in urban transportation markets. The basic cause is the way we price our transport facilities. Congestion, which is still a major problem in our cities, could not be completely done away with if we used an alternative pricing system, but we could obtain a noticeably more efficient allocation of resources at rush-hour time. In this section we shall take a detailed look at the nature and causes of congestion, along with traditional and experimental solutions to the problem. In addition, we shall consider the public-transit versus highways issue. Finally, an assessment of the efficiency and equity aspects of two new urban public-transit systems— BART of San Francisco and METRO of Washington, D.C.—is made.

Congestion

We saw in Section II that when roads reach a certain percentage of capacity, the addition of another car will cause a divergence in the social and private marginal cost of that car entering the road. This is due to congestion; the additional car slows down many other cars, causing the marginal cost of travel for these drivers to increase. Since drivers consider only private costs, too many cars will enter the road. This economic analysis of the congestion problem is conceptually useful, but if does not give much in terms of specifics for policy decisions unless the demand and marginal cost curves can be determined empirically. Just what is congestion, and how does it arise?

Types of Congestion

William Vickrey [10], and eminent urban transportation economist, has classified congestion into six types:

(1) *simple interaction*—Occurs when two motor vehicles approach each other closely enough so that one (or both) is slowed. This is an important source of congestion during off-peak hours. The total delay varies with the square of the volume of cars and trucks; that is, if I am delayed by 5 minutes, I inflict roughly 5 minutes of *additional* delay on all others I interact with.

(2) *multiple interaction*—Occurs at high levels of traffic density, where traffic is just short of absolute road capacity; movement still occurs, but the ramifications of the simple-interaction model become greater when many cars are involved. Average speed is determined by the flow of traffic, so if delays are inversely related to speed (and this relationship is constant), delays may be determined by the flow of traffic. Vickery estimates that in heavy traffic, for every minute one is delayed, he adds up to 3–5 minutes of delay to the rest of traffic.

(3) *pure bottleneck*—Bottlenecks develop where some part of a road has a given capacity that is decisively smaller than preceding or succeeding segments of the road. For example, if a four-lane highway becomes a two-lane highway, the potential for pure bottlenecks exists. Delays occur when the traffic flows near capacity levels. Delays are minimized by means of queues or diversions to alternative routes.

(4) *triggernecks*—When traffic is backed up from a pure bottleneck so that it interferes with vehicles not planning to use the road with the pure bottleneck, a triggerneck occurs. Thus, for example, cars waiting to use a crowded exit ramp may block through traffic on a highway. It is not difficult to conceive of traffic coming to a complete halt at a multiroad intersection during rush-hour traffic.

(5) *network and control congestion*—Occurs when controls (lights, traffic, police, regulations) are needed during peak-hour usage. Because budgets

are fixed, congested areas that do not have special controls but need them result in major time losses on the part of many drivers when the whole city is considered.

(6) *general density*—In the long run the level of congestion is a function of the overall density of traffic flows in the city for all transport modes of combined. General density congestion occurs at or near central business districts, such as the Loop in Chicago or Manhattan in New York City.

By categorizing congestion it is possible to identify potential solutions to the problem, other than by reducing the number of vehicles on the road. For example, simple interaction effects can be reduced by having wider roads, clearer road markers and signals, and generally stricter enforcement of traffic laws. Multiple interaction is the classic case of congestion found during peak periods, and the only method of solving this problem with existing capacity levels is to reduce the number of cars on the road. Pure bottlenecks may be cured in a similar fashion or by expanding the capacity of the roads at points where bottlenecks occur. Triggernecks may also be rectified by reducing traffic flow; however, diversions of existing flow may be just as effective. Finally, the network and general density congestion may be solved by utilizing new controls and building new capacity, respectively. Both solutions probably involve a greater expenditure than society will reap in benefits.

Traditional Solutions to Congestion

Standard policies to minimize congestion in our cities have included a variety of cursory responses in the short run and the construction of expressways and other limited-access roads in the long run. Traffic lights are often synchronized to allow the steady movement of traffic. Similarly, one-way streets are designed to increase the velocity of traffic. At potential triggernecks traffic patrolmen are usually on duty during peak hours. In addition, specific regulations on the use of lanes and bridges are set up to handle peak loads of inbound and outbound traffic. It is also traditional to add more buses and streetcars during rush hours in major cities. We are familiar with all of these policies, and we know they are useful. Yet they have not been sufficient to handle efficiently the massive increase in traffic in the postwar period.

The standard long-run policy used to solve congestion problems in our cities during the past two decades has been the construction of limited-access expressways. As we noted earlier in this chapter, however, after new highway capacity is built, congestion is often not appreciably reduced, because people who did not drive before find it convenient to use the new expressway; thus an increase in demand for highway services may exceed the increase in capacity. Also as new expressways were built into our cities, municipal parking facilities were often expanded. The latter, of course, only induced more people to drive. And as more people drive, we seem to find a need for more roads, more parking facilities, and onward we go in a viscious circle. Recent decisions by San Francisco and Boston, however, not to build any additional expressways into their central cities (or even finish existing roads under construction) is evidence that this viscious circle of more and more roads can be broken.

Alternate Solutions to Congestion

User Charges. Unfortunately, present policy in this country is based on the notion that "prices" (taxes) are used to finance highways, but not to decide who uses the highways and when. Two of the major reasons often cited for not putting user charges of roads during rush hours to obtain a more efficient resource allocation are: (1) collection costs are too high, and (2) the income distribution would be perversely effected. Vickrey has developed a fairly elaborate scheme that would equip vehicles with electronic identifiers at a modest cost [11]. At appropriate points on roads, scanning devices would identify the vehicle, note the time of day and volume of flow, and send this informaton to a central computer, which would calculate the charges and bill the drivers once a month. During the peak commuting hours, roadside signals would list the present charge of major roads, allowing drivers to use less expensive routes if they prefer. Thus the old method of collection booths and long queues does not have to be a part of user charge policies.

There is little doubt that user charges would have an adverse effect on lower-income persons. However, the goal of the user charge is to obtain a more efficient allocation of resources, rather than a more equitable distribution of income. Clearly there are many alternatives for subsidizing lower-income persons to bring their real income levels up to what they would be without the user charges.

At present there is very little empirical evidence on user charges, except that toll roads and bridges are known to carry lighter loads during rush hours than nontoll roads and bridges. This suggests that user charges, if put into effect, would have their expected impact. A. A. Walters has estimated that a more efficient use of urban highways would result if gasoline taxes were increased by at least 65 percent, which would be a substitute for user charges per se [12]. Walters also found that toll roads and tunnels in New York City were heavily underpriced during rush hours. Certainly an area for more research is determining the cost of vehicle transport at alternative times of the day in our cities, since we already have reasonable information on demand. When such information is available, there will be few, if any, economic efficiency arguments that can stand in the way of instituting higher prices for the use of highways during the peak periods. Traffic regulatory commissions could be instituted, and frequently traveled commuter routes would be probable candidates for initial charges. This approach would minimize the negative impact on the income distribution, since many commuters are from higher-income groups. There is plenty of experience with peak pricing in regulated industries (long-distance phone calls are cheaper on weekends, some airline flights are cheaper at night), so the institution of peak pricing is not a drastic or revolutionary change in policy tools.

Express Bus Lanes. If urban transport planners and decision-makers fail to establish a user charge system to minimize the congestion problem, they will have to seek other alternatives to use existing facilities more efficiently. One such alternative is the use of express bus lanes, which we shall refer to as bus rapid transit. It has been shown that bus rapid-transit systems have a commanding cost advantage over rail rapid-transit systems in U.S. cities [13]. Since bus rapid transit involves nothing more than slight modifications of existing urban freeways, it is surprising that most metropolitan areas have not converted their facilities to this cheaper, congestion-reducing form of transport.

Bus rapid transit is cheaper than rail transit for at least two reasons [14]: (1) it is faster because the relatively small size of the buses reduces the number of stops they have to make to pick up and deliver passengers, and (2) capital costs are drastically lower with buses because rights of way need not be purchased. In the long run, unlike rail transit systems, express bus systems can easily be tailored to suit the needs of the urban area as changes occur in the location of persons and firms.

To be sure, we found that empirical demand studies showed that few commuters would shift to buses from auto, but it was noted that reductions in travel time were important. Express buses reduce travel time, and do it more cheaply than any other means of public transit in this country today. Even if local authorities instituted a system of user charges, express buses would still be a wise investment, since they would lower the overall costs (direct and indirect) of travel.

Free Transit. Urbanologists have been arguing for years that the only feasible way to reduce congestion and not hurt poor families is to change to zero fares for public transit. A further objective of free transit is to revitalize downtown business. Opponents of this policy argue that it would be too costly, and that downtowns have been dying for years; thus one cannot change a long-run trend by saving people a few dollars in transportation costs. Also, if we want to help poor people, there are more efficient ways of doing it than by providing free transit services.

Domencich and Kraft recently completed a major study of the potential costs and impact of free transit in the U.S. and in Boston [3]. As of 1969, nationwide costs of free transit were estimated to be $2 billion per year, assuming that more or less the same level of service would be maintained. One-eighth of the $2 billion figure is the cost of the additional capacity needed to handle increased patronage resulting from the free fare. In the city of Boston, the elimination of fares would induce up to a 32 percent increase in ridership, and the subsidy required to bring about free fares would be about $30 per person.

To see whether free fares would do what they are supposed to do (reduce congestion, help the poor, and revitalize downtown) Domencich and Kraft compared a free-fare system in Boston with a system improved by upgrading service. They found that auto work trips under a free-fare system would be reduced by only 14 percent; thus when one accounts for the auto as a share of overall trips, the reduction of rush-hour traffic is only 6–9 percent. On the other hand, if transit service were upgraded through more efficient collection and distribution of passengers, auto rush-hour traffic could be reduced by 4–6 percent at one-sixth the cost of the free-fare program per year! The reduction of auto traffic would have only negligible effects on secondary or indirect costs. For example, air pollution from vehicle emissions would be reduced by around 3–4.5 percent during rush hours, and some parking space would be freed. The latter, of course, might induce more people to drive in the long run.

Free transit was not found to be a particularly efficient way of providing access to job centers for ghetto residents of Boston, because good service is available from ghettos only to downtown areas, whereas job centers are scattered all over the metropolitan area. Domencich and Kraft found that by providing very good direct service from ghetto areas to low-skilled job centers at zero fares, the cost would be 6 percent of what the total free transit program would cost yearly for the whole Boston area. Clearly this type of program is superior from an income-redistribution standpoint, assuming the redistribution program is financed by a nonregressive tax; that is, a tax whose burden does not fall disproportionately on low-income persons.

Finally, free transit may not be the panacea retailers have hoped for. In Boston, downtown shopping trips would increase by one-third; however, this increase was not found to be at the expense of a reduction in trips to suburban shopping centers. Thus it is difficult to argue that downtown sales would be significantly affected.

In short, free transit may not be an efficient policy tool for solving congestion and other problems, although more evidence is needed. The

U.S. Department of Transportation has pilot programs using free transit in California and Washington, D.C., which may provide the needed information. One final point before leaving free transit. Clearly not everyone has to be allowed to ride free; we could charge low or even regular prices, and issue free tickets to the poor and aged. This would minimize the redistributional aspects of the free (for all) transit program.

More Transit or More Highways?

The recent debate in regard to the urban transportation problem is whether cities should invest in more highways *or* public transit. Seldom do the participants in this debate offer the alternative that investing in both public transit and highways may be a more rational procedure to follow. In this section we shall cover some of the arguments of both sides, and also take a look at two of the new public rapid transit systems presently being constructed in the U.S.

Proponents of Public Transit

The standard arguments for cutting off further highway construction and originating or expanding public rapid-transit facilities include (1) the slowdown or decentralization of metropolitan areas, (2) the maintenance of or increase in property values downtown or along new transit lines, and (3) the minimization of noise and air pollution. Since these reasons for more transit have been discussed earlier, we shall not pursue them further here. Proponents of public transit use two additional arguments that deserve more consideration:

(1) The present system of pricing and financing transport capacity is biased in favor of highways.
(2) The costs of building new urban highways are disproportionately shared by the poor and the elderly.

Highway Bias. Part of the price of using highways or roads is what we pay in fuel and other taxes; yet we are not charged any additional cost for *whenever* we want to use the road. In other words, we are essentially charged a zero marginal price for using road space. On the other hand, transit users must pay a positive (marginal) price to use the facilities, even though in many cases these prices are reduced by subsidies. Thus we have a bias in pricing against transit users.

The method of financing highways is also biased [6, pp. 366–369]. Roads are financed with public funds, while most transit facilities have been paid for with private funds. In the past decade or so, cities and states have had up to 90 percent of limited-access highways financed via federal funds, resulting in the unfortunate decision-making process of local authorities comparing marginal benefits to one-tenth of the marginal costs of these projects. Using this criterion, it is not surprising that most major cities opted to build expressways into and around their central business districts and outer limits when possible.

Traditionally, federal and state aid to local roads and highways was based on two grounds: (1) local tax sources were not sufficient to meet the high costs, and (2) local roads do not just serve local needs. Clearly, the same justification could be made for public transit facilities since fares do not meet costs and a public service is being produced.

One of the major stumbling blocks to changing the financing of highways is that state and Federal governments have a fund for maintaining existing highways and constructing new ones that exceeds $10 billion per year—the Highway Trust Fund. This fund is collected from fuel taxes and motor vehicle taxes. Recently, Congress voted to divert a small portion of these funds into transit facilities. However, major diversions of funds will have to be made if new or additional transit facilities are to be generated. If this could be accomplished—that is, if public transit and highways were financed from the same source—voters would have a clear choice on this overall issue. The building of more transit lines then would mean the building of fewer miles of highways.

*Losses Imposed on Urban Households due to Highway Construction.**
When new highways or urban renewal projects displace residential or urban commercial areas, the law provides that the parties affected should be duly compensated for any and all losses. Theoretically, households should be paid enough compensation so that they are as well off in their new location as they were before. Sometimes, however, this is next to impossible. For example, how does one compensate for the disruption of established social and economic relationships? What is the cost of losing the privilege of buying food and other necessities at the corner store on credit, especially if one is elderly? And how can groups be compensated if highways are of no direct value to them, but instead have a negative impact on their welfare, as is the case with many of the urban poor?

Major losses have been imposed on poor families in our urban areas by highway construction, and some of the losses have become gains to higher-income families in the same cities. Many highways are built through low-income areas for obvious (cost) reasons. Homes are purchased by the state through eminent domain. Since low-income persons are poor financial risks, they often pay premiums to own their homes.

* For greater detail on this issue, see Anthony Downs [15].

On the other hand, public authorities pay the fair market value of the home, which may very well be below the price actually paid by the owner (since the latter price includes the risk premium). Clearly the owner comes out the loser. In fact, if the present occupant has not made enough payments to be the legal owner of the home, and the fair market value paid to the legal owner is less than the premium price he charged the occupant, the ejected occupant can be legally held liable for the difference in many states. Newspapers have been full of such unjust situations in the past decade.

The whole concept of the fair market value for existing homes as a compensatory principle leaves much to be desired for poor families, since if a large number of low-quality dwelling units are removed from the stock of housing, similar dwellings nearby in the city will have a higher price. Fair market values do not pay for replacement facilities or relocation expenses, which results in a loss for affected individuals. This problem has been especially acute for renters, who comprise the majority of low-income households affected by highway construction. The empirical studies done on rents before and after relocation show that the rental payments for given apartments increase yet renters are compensated only for moving expenses.

Finally, dislocated families often pay higher nonhousing operating costs in their new locations. For example, a U.S. Census Bureau Survey of relocated families in 1964 showed that 37 percent paid higher commuting expenses, 13 percent had lower commuting costs, and 50 percent reported no significant change [16].

Opponents of More Public Transit

Let me emphasize at the outset of this discussion that many of the opponents of more public transit are not necessarily proponents of more highways. The major points made in this chapter thus far, at both the theoretical and practical levels, unanimously point to the fact that we are not using our existing transport capacity efficiently; therefore, it is questionable that we need new capacity, whether this new capacity would take the form of transit facilities or highways.

One of the major arguments against building new transit systems is that costs are prohibitively high, while the benefits in terms of reducing congestion are questionable at best. To make rail transit feasible, it takes at least 25,000 passengers per hour per corridor during peak hours [13, p. 44]. Only New York City and Chicago have such traffic levels, and they already have large rail transit systems. Relatively small volumes per corridor can be expected to continue as the population spreads farther into suburbia. In short, collection and distribution costs of rail transit may be a barrier too strong to overcome. Also, the land costs for new transit lines may be prohibitively high, unless existing public rights of way can be used.

If additions to existing rail transit capacity are contemplated, one has to face the continual decentralization of population and thus greater collection and distribution costs. Decentralization of the population in metropolitan areas is not likely to be halted because 50 or 100 new miles of transit now connect suburbia to downtown. Firms move away from downtowns, with their high-rises and centrality, to outer areas for many reasons, such as the following:

(1) Technology has changed such that one-floor layouts are more efficient than vertically integrating the production process over many stories.
(2) Freight facilities (rail and truck) are becoming more accessible in the outlying regions of metropolitan areas.
(3) With suburbanization of the population, central locations are no longer needed to have an ample supply of workers.

The benefits of new or additional public transit facilities would be founded on the savings of a cheaper form of travel; that is, travel time, operating costs, and accidents would be lower per passenger mile. Indirectly, benefits would result from the decreased level of air pollution if auto-users were diverted to public transit. Opponents of more public transit, however, ask whether demand studies show that any significant changes will occur in subway ridership. As we saw earlier in this chapter, the best evidence we can bring to bear on this issue suggests that no significant changes in transit ridership would occur if additional facilities were built unless travel times were considerably reduced. Whether brand new rail transit facilities built in cities that presently have only bus transit facilities would divert many riders from alternative modes is difficult to test empirically. We shall probably have to wait and see whether the new San Francisco and Washington subway and rail transit projects are successful at diverting a significant number of auto users from the highways.

An Arbitrator's View

The traditional arguments for more public transit (that is, to restore downtown areas, help the poor, and reduce congestion and pollution) generally involve changes in the income distribution. Whether or not these traditional goals are desirable is a value judgment. Whether they will be met by means of more public transit facilities is questionable. Better service by public transit would no doubt be a great help in solving congestion problems, at least in some cities. The strongest argument made by the protransit side is actually an antihighway one: the true costs of urban highways are not borne equitably, and the method of highway financing does not help much in making efficient long-run decisions with regard to altering transport capacity.

On the other side, opponents of public transit have a solid argument in stating that existing transit and highway facilities are not being utilized efficiently. If policies can be enacted to use existing facilities efficiently, we may find that new facilities will not be needed in many cities, at least for the next decade or so. Express buses seem to be an excellent substitute for the wholesale construction of new transit lines. Both are really experiments, with the former carrying a price tag of a few million dollars while the latter would cost a few *billion* dollars. On both efficiency and equity grounds (assuming new public transit facilities and/or operations will be financed from local regressive taxes), the cheaper experiment is the one to try first.

A Look at New Public Transit Facilities

In September of 1972 the San Francisco Bay Area Rapid Transit (BART) system opened its first segment for business. Simultaneously, Washington, D.C.'s downtown was being temporarily disrupted by subway construction of the new 98-mile METRO system. These two rail transit facilities are the first of their kind to be constructed in this country in over 50 years. What do they plan to offer, and what are their chances of success?

The BART System. Three counties in the San Francisco area—San Francisco, Contra Costa, and Alameda—voted in 1962 to authorize a $792 million bond issue for the construction of a modern and efficient electric rail system of transportation. Running above and below ground, BART essentially connects cities east of San Francisco Bay with downtown San Francisco. The cars are scheduled to average 40–50 miles per hour, whereas the average rail transit trip in the U.S. is at about 20 miles per hour. Besides speed, comfort and convenience are being emphasized. All riders are supposed to have seats in the BART plan, but to date this has not worked out. In addition to speed and comfort, BART will have express service with a maximum wait at all stations during nonrush hours of 15–20 minutes, while during peak hours, service will be available every few minutes.

The BART system is being paid for by everyone living in the three counties, and the final price tag will be close to $1.5 billion. However, according to many, the benefits of the system are not being distributed equally, whether one is considering direct or indirect benefits [17,18]. This is primarily because the lines run from wealthy suburbs to downtown San Francisco, without passing through any low-income areas in Oakland or San Francisco. In essence, BART is more a suburban commuter line than a facility to ease downtown congestion. The major beneficiaries will be landowners and those who live in suburbs but work downtown. The poor, on the other hand, will not only be left out of direct service, but they will pay higher rents. Property taxes will increase to pay for BART, and the increased taxes will be easily passed on to the consumer.

Whether our assessment of the BART system from an efficiency standpoint will be borne out is of course an empirical question. It is hoped that congestion will be less than it would have been if the funds spent on BART had been spent on their next-best congestion-reducing alternative. I am not betting on this to happen. Rather, assuming that current spatial income patterns prevail over time, BART seems to be a clear case of income redistribution from the poor to the rich, sold to the public by businessmen as more or less a crusade against the automobile.

The METRO System. The resemblances of METRO to BART are quite striking. METRO is a 98-mile rail transit system that will connect the Maryland and Virginia suburbs to downtown Washington. Unlike BART, the system will pass through many low-income areas, basically because, except for its northwest sector, Washington is dominated by low-income families. The cost estimate of METRO is around $2.5 billion; if the system runs into construction problems similar to those that BART did, a more realistic price tag could be nearly $5 billion.

A number of studies have been done on METRO [19,20], and as in the case of BART the impact of the benefits will fall disproportionately on higher-income persons, while lower-income Washingtonians will pay a disproportionate share of the costs. According to W. W. Brittain, suburbanites will receive 80 percent of the benefits but will pay only 60 percent of the costs. This is especially alarming, if it is borne out as METRO continues construction and commences operation, since four of the Maryland and Virginia suburban counties of Washington now rank in the top ten counties in the country on the basis of median family income. The District of Columbia, on the other hand, with the exception of the exclusive all-white section west of Rock Creek (where median family incomes exceeded $20,000 in 1970), is primarily a poor, black area of dense poverty, with highly regressive tax systems. Clearly suburbanites could easily pay a larger share of the METRO costs.

All things considered, METRO looks like another redistribution scheme at least. Since Washington's downtown does not have the density that San Francisco has, it is not clear that congestion will be affected as much by METRO as we can expect on the part of BART. Given the present inelasticities of demand for modes, it is difficult to say whether congestion will be appreciably affected. At best, this is an empirical question.

VI. SUMMARY

The urban transportation system is so basic to urban areas that it may not pay cities to exist if an efficient transportation system is not available *and* being utilized. In this chapter we found that the major problem facing our existing transport systems was the inefficient utilization of capacity, especially during peak periods of demand. This problem is literally centuries old, and man's continual answer to the problem has been simply to increase capacity. Our postwar experience with freeways, innerbelts, and outerbelts is fairly clear evidence that building more highways does little to solve the congestion problems of cities. We discussed a number of policies for utilizing our existing transport capacity more efficiently, such as user charges, bus rapid transit, raising parking fees, staggering work hours, and encouraging car pools.

In the long run, the issue of changing capacity can be evaluated by means of benefit–cost analysis, although we found this tool to be somewhat difficult to apply. At the present time, there is a strong effort in many major cities across the country to supplement bus transit service with new rail rapid-transit service. In this chapter, we found that there are viable, less costly alternatives to new rail rapid-transit systems. In addition, existing information on the demand for urban transportation modes suggests that unless new rail rapid-transit lines significantly reduce travel times, few customers will be diverted to their use.

SUGGESTED READINGS

Domencich, T., and Kraft, G. *Free Transit*. Lexington, Massachusetts: Heath, 1970.

Downs, Anthony. *Urban Problems and Prospects*. Chicago: Markham, 1970.

Edel, Matthew and Rothenberg, Jerome, eds. *Readings in Urban Economics*. New York: Macmillan, 1972.

Hirsch, Werner. *Urban Economic Analysis*. New York: McGraw-Hill, 1973.

Hoover, Edgar. *An Introduction to Regional Economics*. New York: Knopf, 1971.

Institute for Defense Analysis. *Economic Characteristics of the Urban Public Transportation Industry*, 1972.

Meyer, J., Kain, J., and Wohl, M. *The Urban Transportation Problem*. Cambridge, Massachusetts: Harvard Univ. Press, 1965.

Meyer, John. "Knocking Down the Straw Men," *City and Suburb*, edited by B. Chinitz, pp. 85–93. Englewood Cliffs, New Jersey: Prentice-Hall, 1964.

Mills, Edwin. *Urban Economics*, Chapter 11. Glenview, Illinois: Scott, Foresman, 1972.
Netzer, Dick. *Economics and Urban Problems*. New York: Basic Books, 1970.
Wilson, J. Q., ed. *The Metropolitan Enigma*. Cambridge, Massachusetts: Harvard Univ. Press, 1968.

REFERENCES

1. Wilfred Owen, "Transport: Key to the Future of Cities," *The Quality of the Urban Environment*, Harvey Perloff, ed., p. 211 (Baltimore, Maryland: John Hopkins Press, for Resources for the Future, Inc. 1969).
2. J. R. Meyer, "Urban Transportation," in *The Metropolitan Enigma*, J. Q. Wilson, ed., pp. 41–69 (Cambridge, Massachusetts: Harvard Univ. Press, 1968).
3. Tom Domencich and Gerald Kraft, *Free Transit* (Lexington, Massachusetts: Heath, 1970).
4. Robert McGillivray, "Demand and Choice Models of Modal Spilt," *Journal of Transport and Economic Policy* 4 (1970): 192–207.
5. Charles Lave, "The Demand for Urban Mass Transportation," *Review of Economics and Statistics* 52 (1970): 320–323.
6. Edgar M. Hoover, *An Introduction to Regional Economics*, p. 364 (New York, Knopf, 1971).
7. Institute for Defense Analysis, "Economic Characteristics of the Urban Public Transportation Industry." Prepared for the U.S. Department of Transportation, 1972.
8. H. Mohring, "Optimization and Scale Economics in Urban Bus Transportation," *American Economic Review* 62 (1972): 591–604.
9. Werner Hirsch, *Urban Economic Analysis*, p. 120 (New York: McGraw-Hill, 1973).
10. William Vickrey, "Congestion Theory and Transport Investment," *American Economic Review, Papers, and Proceedings* 59 (1969): 251–260.
11. William Vickrey, "Pricing in Urban and Suburban Transport," *American Economic Review, Papers, and Proceedings*, 53 (1963): 452–465.
12. A. A. Walters, "The Theory and Measurement of Private and Social Cost of Highway Congestion," *Econometrica* 39 (1961): 676–699.
13. J. Meyer, J. Kain, and M. Wohl, *The Urban Transportation Problem* (Cambridge, Massachusetts: Harvard Univ. Press, 1965).
14. John Kain, "A Reappraisal of Metropolitan Transport Planning," reprinted in *Economics of Urban Problems*, Schreiber *et al.*, eds., pp. 163–166 (Boston, Massachusetts: Houghton Mifflin, 1971).
15. Anthony Downs, "Uncompensated Nonconstruction Costs which Urban Highways and Urban Renewal Impose Upon Residential Households," in *The Analysis of Public Output*, J. Margolis, ed., National Bureau of Economic Research Conference Series No. 23, pp. 69–106 (New York: Columbia Univ. Press, 1967).
16. James Q. Wilson, ed., "The Housing of Re-located Families: Summary of a Census Bureau Survey," in *Urban Renewal: The Record and the Controversy*, pp. 336–352 (Cambridge, Massachusetts: MIT Press, 1966).
17. D. Beagle *et al.*, "Rapid Transit: The Case of BART," in *Problems in Political Economy: An Urban Perspective*, D. M. Gordon, ed., pp. 437–439 (Lexington, Massachusetts: Heath, 1971).

18. Leonard Merewitz, "Public Transportation: Wish Fulfillment and Reality in the San Francisco Bay Area," *American Economic Review, Papers, and Proceedings* 62 (1972): 78–86.
19. Developments Research Associates, "Benefits to the Washington Area from the Adopted Regional METRO System." Washington, D.C., 1968.
20. W. W. Brittain, "METRO: Rapid Transit for Suburban Washington," in *Problems in Political Economy: An Urban Perspective*, D. M. Gordon, ed., pp. 439–443 (Lexington, Massachusetts: Heath, 1971).

8

THE URBAN
PUBLIC SECTOR

I. INTRODUCTION

Up to now we have referred to the public sector as a *single* institution that attempts to bring about a more efficient allocation of resources and a more equitable distribution of income. Even if there were only one governmental institution per urban area, the public sector would still have difficulty in using its tools (taxes and expenditures) properly to accomplish these ends, because many services produced in the public sector are not priced; therefore, it is difficult to know what the demand for these services is. Recalling that an efficient allocation of resources occurs when price (demand) equals marginal cost, we can see that the production of nonpriced services at the efficient level would only occur by chance.

In a typical urban area, however, there is not *one* governmental institution. The norm is to have many institutions, most of which overlap in their jurisdictions. Thus, even if people were charged "market prices" for the public services they consume, urban government would still be faced with a basic problem of knowing how much of any given service to produce, because there are spillovers from one jurisdiction to the next. The spillovers are externalities, which means that unless they can be measured and properly considered in the decision-making process, inefficient resource allocation will result. For example, if city A decides to spray mosquitos and some of the spray helps reduce the mosquito population in city B (located next to A), there is a divergence between the total benefits produced by A and those benefits accruing to its residents. If A does not account for this, it may underallocate resources toward the use of mosquito spray. We are assuming, of course, that A began with enough spray for its own residents only. On the other hand, B has received a positive externality, and if it does not enter this information into its decision-making process it may overallocate resources to mosquito control. Thus the chance of misallocating resources when jurisdictions are contiguous (or overlapping) is not minimal. And of course if part of A's expected benefits are consumed by B, we have a redistribution of income from citizens in A to those in B.

In earlier chapters we learned that when people concentrate in space, many externalities result. If these externalities are negative, a third party must step in and restore an efficient allocation of resources. Thus a primary reason for having a public sector in cities is the pervasiveness of externalities. But we have just seen that the very problem urban governments are supposed to solve (externality problems) also faces them in their delivery of public goods and services. Clearly the government has an awesome task to perform in urban areas.

What, How, and for Whom?

Like any other institution, governments have to decide *what* to produce, *how* to produce it, and *for whom* to produce. What to produce is relatively simple for firms, because people can express their preferences by accepting or refusing products at alternative prices. But some institutions (churches, labor unions, governments) do not sell products directly in the market place, so they cannot use traditional demand analysis to determine whether they are producing the right types and amounts of goods and services. Governments must find a substitute for traditional demand analysis in order to know what to produce.

Given that the public sector will directly produce a service, how it does so depends primarily on the various techniques available and the budget constraint. Obviously we could reduce certain crimes if the police force in every city were doubled; however, the same reduction in crime might be obtained by the employment of, say, 25 percent more capital equipment (squad cars, radios, and so on). If this is true and the cost of the additional capital is less than the cost of doubling the police (labor) force, it makes sense to use the capital. In other words, in deciding how to produce government services, standard production theory can be useful. The major problem in using traditional production theory is determining the marginal products of alternative factors of production. The basis of this problem lies in determining the output of a factor; for example, what is the output of a public school teacher, or a movie projector?

Once the decision has been made on what to produce and how to produce it, the issue of for whom may be more or less settled. If, for example, library services are to be produced at a single centralized location in a metropolitan area (so that scale economies can be realized), lower-income persons not residing near the library may be left out unless they have fairly strong preferences for library services. If public-school services in a metropolitan area are to be produced by each municipality, higher-income towns can purchase more resources for their schools, other things being equal, than lower-income towns; thus children in lower-income towns may receive relatively inferior training. In general, where the public service is not directly priced, (1) the nature of the production recipe, (2) the method of financing, and (3) the spatial location of the service can all determine who consumes the public service. Alternatively, when public services are priced (garbage collection, water and sewers, public transit), consumption is determined by traditional demand factors—tastes, income, and the price of substitute goods.

Tools of the Urban Public Sector

Thus far we have discussed the role of the urban public sector as a producer of public services. Although this is probably the most basic function of the public sector, revenue collection is also a major activity. The primary form of revenue generation by urban governments is still taxation, although federal and state transfers are becoming more significant every year. For example, of the $89 billion of total revenues generated by local governments in 1969–1970, $59.5 billion came from their own sources, and $29.5 billion came from federal and state transfers. Over one-fifth of the own-source revenue came from user charges (hospitals, education, parking); that is, prices paid for services.

In addition to the decision on what, how, and for whom, urban governments must decide on the most efficient and equitable way of financing their services. As with the production and delivery of services, methods of finance have varying effects on the allocation of resources and the distribution of income. In recent years, however, urban governments have become increasingly concerned with their lack of revenues vis-à-vis the mounting problems they face. This financial crisis at the local level is caused primarily by growth-related expenditures (education, highways, police, fire, water, sewerage) being more elastic than revenue generation. In other words, as cities grow, the percentage increase in public services required to sustain that growth is not matched by a commensurate percentage increase in tax receipts or other local revenues. In our large cities this problem has been caused by the suburbanization of firms and of the middle and upper income classes. Inflation and new service demands exacerbate this fiscal problem, so that a crisis exists in many cities. This crisis can obviously have significant repercussions on resource allocation and income distribution, the actual extent being a function of how governments decide to meet the crisis.

Besides producing services and financing them, a final tool or role of the urban public sector is regulation. For obvious reasons, society demands minimum standards in such areas as hospital services, building codes, highway speeds, and so forth. Clearly without minimum standards the marginal social costs of many services might exceed the marginal social benefits. Regulation, then, is based on the goal of attaining a more efficient allocation of resources.

The Rest of This Chapter

In the remainder of this chapter, we shall take a more detailed look at the rationale for the public sector, which leads us into a discussion of the demand for and supply of urban public services. In addition, we shall briefly consider the nature of government tools—taxes, expenditures, and regulations—as well as analyze their impact on resource allocation and the distribution of income. Finally, two selected problems of the urban public sector are covered: (1) the optimal size of urban governments and (2) the revenue crisis.

II. THE RATIONALE FOR AND MARKET OF THE LOCAL PUBLIC SECTOR

We have argued that the urban public sector exists to ensure a more optimal allocation of resources. A misallocation of resources exists in urban areas basically because of externalities; with densely settled residents and firms, divergences between private and social costs (and benefits) will be pervasive. Without a third party to step in and correct these private conflicts, society will not be as well-off as it could be. Another facet of the resource-allocation criterion that deserves more emphasis is that any change in the allocation of resources also alters the distribution of income. For example, if through taxation local governments cause less booze to be consumed, and people opt to spend more on recreation, the price of resources in recreational services will rise relative to resource prices in alcohol production. Income has been redistributed out of liquor markets into recreation markets. Thus government's role is both allocational and distributional, since efficiency and equity are affected simultaneously. Although this fact can hardly be overemphasized, for purposes of clarity we shall continue to separate efficiency and equity in our discussions.

Why Have a Public Sector?

Although positive and negative externalities are quite basic in explaining why a public sector is needed, there are certainly other issues involved. Some of the goods and services produced by governments have a rather peculiar characteristic: they can be consumed by one individual without reducing the consumption of the same good or service by any other individual. For example, I do not reduce anyone else's consumption of television programs if I consume more of this good. Economists call goods having this characteristic public goods. National defense, lighthouses, and the airwaves are cases of *pure* public goods. Most public goods are not pure (highways, bridges, beaches) because under certain conditions (congestion or excess demand) my consumption of another unit will affect another individual's consumption.

Public goods should be produced by the public sector because they will not be produced in optimal quantities otherwise. Clearly the social marginal cost of another car crossing a bridge (during a nonrush hour) is zero, once bridges are produced. Since the private sector could not find it possible to charge a zero price for any good, and a zero price is needed here to obtain an optimal allocation of resources, we argue that a third party should step in and produce the good.

Another characteristic of public goods is that exclusion is very costly, if not impossible. When one considers a pure public good such as national defense, it would be literally impossible to exclude people from consuming the good as long as they remained in this country. Traditionally, highways have been produced almost solely by the public sector because of the (expected) heavy collection costs at toll booths that would prevail if the private sector owned and operated roads. Clearly the technique of production has a lot to do with the significance of the exclusion principle. If a positive demand exists for certain nonpackagable goods and services (that is, goods and services that the private sector finds impractical to produce because a significant number of nonpaying persons cannot be prevented from consuming them), there is a basic argument for having a public sector if society desires to have an efficient allocation of resources.

Although very few cases of pure public goods exist at the local level, there are many near-public goods. To the extent that police cruisers deter crime by their presence on patrol, my consumption of this police service has little effect on others' consumption of it. However, if I require direct consumption of the time of any policeman who otherwise would have been in the cruiser, this consumption may lessen that policeman's input to the deterrent effect. Thus police services have mixed characteristics: some attributes are like public goods, while others are similar to private goods. Fire protection, building regulations, highways, and recreational areas are other examples of near-public goods produced by the urban public sector.

In addition to near-public goods, the public sector produces (or subsidizes the consumption of) merit goods; that is, goods which if not produced would be underproduced, such as education. Clearly there are social as well as private benefits to education; thus, if the private sector were left to operate on its own, not enough resources would be allocated toward education. Education has merit, so the public sector steps in to ensure that resources are allocated efficiently.

The rationale of the merit good involves not only resource allocation but also the interdependence of utility. That is, the public sector decides for the public what in fact has merit, and through its taxing and/or expenditure decisions, overproduces merit goods and services, or distributes them in kind. For example, local welfare agencies would prefer to give milk directly to children of poor families, rather than give the family a monetary subsidy that they can spend as they wish; milk is deemed beneficial for children, but beer (and less milk) has little merit. Supposedly, the public sector's objective is to maximize the welfare of all individuals, and in giving goods in kind (milk) rather than income subsidies, the decision of how to attain this joint welfare maximization efficiently is taken out of the individual's hands. Traditional economic theory, however, tells us that income subsidies can make individuals better off than any other type of subsidy or price reduction.

In addition to the principles of public goods and merit goods, the local public sector has a further reason for stepping into the resource-allocation picture in urban areas. Many of the public services that are justifiably produced by the public sector on efficiency grounds (such as sewerage, water, and public transit) are characterized by decreasing costs per unit of output. Thus long-run marginal costs fall short of long-run average costs, so if price is set equal to long-run marginal costs a loss results. If an efficient allocation of resources is desired, the public sector must subsidize these decreasing cost sectors.

The Demand for Local Public Goods

Now that we have a better undertanding of why governments exist, our next step is to determine how government decides what services to produce and in what amounts. In general, local governments produce public goods and merit goods, or services for which decreasing costs prevail. These goods and services may be categorized as follows [1]:

(1) protection
    a. police
    b. fire

(2) human resource development
    a. education
    b. health
    c. welfare
    d. recreation

(3) utilities
    a. sewerage
    b. water
    c. refuse collection

(4) general services
    a. transportation
    b. libraries
    c. administration

Most of these goods and services have either public-good or merit-good characteristics, and as such are not priced in the market as private goods are. Some, however, are priced as private goods are (utilities, for example); thus it may be realistic to use traditional economic analysis to decide how much of a given utility should be produced. Let us see how this analysis is used.

Consider a case of two individuals in the market for a public good, whose demands are described by D_1 and D_2 in Figure 8.1. The price of the public good is constant, assuming constant costs. That is, if costs are constant, then the supply curve will be perfectly elastic. If D_1 and D_2 each acted on his own, only X_1 amount of the public good would be produced. However, at X_1 the joint utility of 1 and 2 is not maximized. Assuming decision-making costs are *zero,* our two individuals could jointly demand $D_1 + D_2$ and receive X_2 of the public good. At X_2, our two-person society has attained an optimal level of this public good

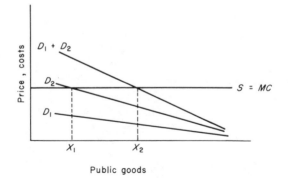

Figure 8.1   *The demand for public goods.*

Note that the aggregation of individual demands for public goods is vertical, whereas you may recall that for private goods, demand curves are aggregated horizontally (that is, at a given price, we sum over the quantities, because each individual's consumption of a private good does affect others' consumption of the same good).

The size of society is so small in Figure 8.1 that one may wonder about the relevance of this simple model. Clearly as the size of society increases, the cost of making collective decisions increases. In addition to this problem, individual incentives in the collective decision-making process are often impaired as the size of the group increases. What impact will a single individual have on the supply of clean air if he keeps his car well tuned and employs special pollution-control devices? How can he induce others to participate in these public-spirited activities? Figure 8.1 would depict such a situation if the sum of D_1 and D_2 did not reach MC at any point. Indeed, individuals gain (given that a public sector exists) by understating their true preferences for any public good. To guard against such understatement, tax prices charged for many public goods are constant, regardless of the level consumed. How, then, are demands for public goods derived?

Essentially, individuals express preferences for public goods indirectly through the voting process. For example, if we desire a harder line against criminal activity, we vote for a law-and-order candidate. However, what recourse do we have if the law-and-order candidate shifts his priorities once he is elected? Economists argue that in metropolitan areas people can "vote with their feet"; that is, they can choose to live where preferences for public goods are close to their own.* If, in fact, people do reside where tastes for public goods are similar, a more effi-

* For the original explanation of this hypothesis see Charles M. Tiebout [2].

cient use of resources will result. For example, if a given city has three groups that prefer a large, moderate, and small amount of resources to deter crime, respectively, a likely result is the production of a moderate amount of the service. The result, of course, is that two of the three groups are made worse off than they would be if the three groups each comprised their own city. Clearly, homogeneous preferences reduce decision-making costs and also allow for a more efficient allocation of resources, since we know pretty much what demand is.

Empirical Studies of the Demand for Public Services

Although it is difficult to identify conceptually the demand for public goods and services, economists have nevertheless pressed forward in attempting to estimate empirically the demand for public services. The knowledge of demand would be very useful in deciding the proper types and amounts of public services, and also the tax price that could be charged for these services.

The demand for some services can be tested by means of standard economic theory. Police, for example, are factor inputs, whose product may be proxied by a reduction in crime rates. Thus as crimes increase, other things being equal, we would expect an increase in the demand for police. The price of police is their wage rate, and as the wage rate decreases, we would expect more police to be hired, other things being equal. In a recent study of the police forces of 77 cities in California, Jeffery Chapman found these a priori hypotheses to be borne out [3]. Chapman found that as the number of burglaries and robberies increased, the demand for police increased. Wages had the expected inverse relationship with police; that is, the demand curve was downward sloping.

Where neither price nor output data are available, economists have improvised to help forecast the demand for public services. In the area of fire protection, Chaiken and Rolph have forecasted the demand for New York City by predicting the incidence of real (rather than false) fire alarms [4]. The authors found that (1) location (2) time of day, week, and year, (3) method of reporting, and (4) weather conditions were significantly related to the incidence of fire alarms.

Recently, some rather ingenious studies of the demand for state and local services have appeared. Ohls and Wales, for example, have taken state and local expenditure (price times quantity) data, and by making a few simplifying assumptions have found that a testable traditional demand model exists [5]. Using expenditure data on highways, education, and local services, the authors found all of these services to be income-elastic; that is, as income increases, demand for education, highways, and local services increases by more than a proportionate amount. Price elasticities for local services and education were estimated to be close to zero, whereas for highways the price elasticity was about 0.5. In other words, the demand for these services is price-inelastic, indicating that few, if any, substitutes exist.

Another interesting study of the demand for state and local services, done by Borcherding and Deacon, tests some of the arguments made above on the collective decision-making process and its relationship to the identification of the aggregate demand for public services [6]. Assuming that (1) governments are elected by majority rule, (2) the median voter's preferences win out in elections, (3) all services are produced at the least possible cost per unit, and (4) constant returns to scale exist in the production of all services, the authors derive a testable demand model that can show not only income and price elasticities but also the degree of publicness of each service produced. Using 1962 data aggregated to the state level, Borcherding and Deacon estimated demand functions for the following local services: higher education, highways, health–hospitals, police, fire, sewers–sanitation, and parks–recreation. Unlike the Ohls and Wales findings, the Borcherding and Deacon income elasticities were generally less than one. Only parks, sewers, and local education had income elasticities greater than or equal to unity. Local education and health–hospitals were the only services that had price-elastic demands, the former being at odds with the Ohls–Wales findings. The services that exhibited the strongest degree of publicness were higher education and highways.

The sometimes conflicting findings on demand elasticities reported here are undoubtedly a result of differences in the nature and form of demand models being tested, as well as data differences. These problems are indicative of the difficulty of testing for empirical results when we have not yet found a satisfactory explanation of the demand for urban public goods at the conceptual level. Nevertheless, governments exist and make decisions. To make more effective decisions, they need signals from the public on whether or not the types and amounts of public goods and services produced are proper. Demand estimates help in providing these signals.

The Supply, Costs, and Distribution of Local Public Goods

The supply of urban public services is determined by many factors. Economically, once the size of the budget and preferences of the people are more or less known, supply decisions boil down to understanding production technologies and the relative cost of producing each public good or service. In the introduction of this chapter we discussed the use of standard production theory in determining how much of a public good to produce. We noted that a major impediment in using standard theory is that output is difficult to define, so that we do not really know the marginal products of resources. Besides our inability to derive production functions for many public services, the nature of a supply curve for public services is ambiguous. In competitive markets under profit-maximization, we know that the portion of the marginal cost curve above the average variable cost curve is the supply curve for a firm. But can we assume that governments are profit-maximizers? Probably not. Moreover, traditional supply analysis is of little relevance if we do not know the supply price of alternative levels of output of a good.

Because of the problems just stated, the supply decisions of ideal governments have to be made on the basis of cost information under more or less existing techniques and tax structures. Whereas private firms can easily experiment on the efficacy of new production techniques or pricing structures, the public sector does not have as much discretion. Although methods of production may be varied, their real impact is difficult to assess because the outputs are often unknown. And the converse of pricing is the tax structure, which, with the exception of user charges, is at best an indication of the price people pay for a bundle of public services.

One of the major supply issues facing local governments is whether or not they should produce a service themselves or buy it from another institution. This decision can be simplified by asking which institution can produce the good more cheaply. Government may find, for reasons of scale, proximity, or the uniqueness of the local private sector, that they can have the private sector produce public services more cheaply than the public sector could. For example, if the city of Boston would like to find out the costs and benefits of alternative solutions to its traffic problems, it could turn to its own small staff of economists and engineers, or alternatively it could call on the vast array of urban specialists at the Harvard–MIT complex.

Given that a governmental institution decides to produce a service on its own, even if the people reveal their preferences and the supply schedule is known, it is not certain that an optimal allocation of resources will result. Consider Figure 8.2, where we again have two individuals whose preferences are represented by D_1 and D_2. Earlier, in Figure 8.1, we had constant costs, so that the optimal supply of public goods resulted where price was equal to marginal cost. Now assume that we have an increasing-cost service; that is, the supply curve is positively sloped as usual, but the marginal cost of producing another unit of

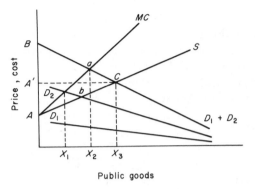

Figure 8.2 *The optimal supply of public goods under increasing costs.*

the service will exceed the supply price of that service. If this occurs, we can see that with each individual acting alone, only D_2 consumes some of the good (amount X_1). If there were zero bargaining costs, the individuals could jointly demand $D_1 + D_2$, making the equilibrium output equal X_2. But note that at X_2 joint demand exceeds supply. The optimal output of X_3 cannot be obtained. X_3 is optimal because the total consumer and producer surplus (area ABC)* is maximized at X_3. So if X_2 is produced (which we expect if governments have more or less full information except for costs), an underallocation of resources results, and welfare is lessened by abC.

In addition to the optimal amount of a public good to supply, local government must decide *which* governments will supply which services. Assuming away any institutional rigidities for the moment, we know that certain services yield scale economies; thus larger jurisdictions would be required to take advantage of this fact. Air pollution, sewage, water, health, and public transportation services would be included here. Other services, such as police, fire, parks, and libraries require access; thus large jurisdictions per se are not required to deliver these services efficiently. The tradeoff between scale economies and access discussed in Chapter 4 in the section on public-facility location (pp. 94–5) is a relevant issue in deciding the proper size of a governmental jurisdiction. Besides scale economies and access, the nature of public goods or services is important in determining the proper size of the producer of the service. If the good involves many externalities (as does mosquito

* Consumer and producer surplus are highly technical terms, but put simply, they represent (1) what consumers would be willing to pay for a good compared to what they do in fact pay and (2) what producers would have to charge to supply a good versus what they do charge. In Figure 8.2, if X_3 is produced, consumer surplus is $A'BC$, and producer surplus is $AA'C$.

spraying), one would desire to have a larger unit so that the externalities may be internalized. Pollution control is an obvious candidate for a metropolitan-scale jurisdiction.

One final issue we should consider is the distribution of local public services. Distribution is of major importance at any level of government, if for no other reason than that many public services are delivered with no user charges. Given this fact, if the services are not consumed more or less equally by all income groups, the government is serving as a redistributer of income. This may be regarded as good or bad, depending on the direction of redistribution and one's value judgments. We may assume, as we have throughout this text, that a goal of the urban public sector is to bring about a more equitable distribution of income, although it may be more realistic to assume that urban governments desire to be neutral in regard to the income distribution.

To deliver an equal distribution of services or real income to. society, the public sector can follow either of two rules [1, Chapter 9]. First, it can follow the input-equality criterion, which says that resource inputs per recipient per service should be equalized in all areas of the city. For example, in each neighborhood of equal size we might have the same size school and the same number of teachers. A second criterion is the output-equality rule, which states that service outputs per recipient in each area of the city should be equal. This rule ensures equality, but the first criterion will result in equality only if all resources are (1) of equal quality and (2) utilized in the same way. Clearly the output criterion is superior, but the student can undoubtedly cite many cases in which the input rule is used.

Pure equality in the distribution of public services is not purchased at a zero cost. In many cases, what comprises an equitable distribution of services will be inconsistent with efficiency. Consider the case of police services in a city having essentially two crime areas—high and low. If the marginal product of a policeman is greater in the higher-crime area, the equalization of output would mean that we would allocate a relatively large number of police resources to the low-crime area! Efficiency would be obtained when, given the existing level of police resources, crimes were minimized. This would require shifting resources between the two areas until their marginal products were the same in each area. In police services, it should come as no surprise that efficiency results in an unequal distribution of services.

Whether equity or efficiency should win out in delivering public services is a value judgment. Compromises no doubt are the rule in most cases. We have found in our discussions thus far that efficiency by itself is a very difficult goal to reach in the public sector, basically because

people cannot reveal their preferences, and outputs are difficult to identify. Since equity considerations bring in a whole new dimension to
this imperfect decision-making process at the local level, many well-
known economists of the public sector (for example, Richard Musgrave
and Dick Netzer) have argued that the Federal Government should
take the primary responsibility in bringing about a more equitable distribution of income.

Empirical Studies of Supply, Costs, and Distribution

As we found with demand models, traditional supply relationships
are difficult to estimate empirically because of data problems. However,
Ohls and Wales used their approach (described earlier [5]) to estimate
a supply relationship for all local services taken together, for education,
and for highways. Wages were found to be significantly related to the
supply of all local services and education, whereas capital was most
important in explaining levels of all local services and highways. These
findings are what we would expect from standard theory.

In the area of cost functions, economists have done a massive amount
of work. Cost functions relate total costs to total output, making it possible to derive average cost information from the cost functions. Average
costs are useful for showing whether or not scale economies exist in
the production of any public service. Werner Hirsch, a pioneer in this
area, has summarized a number of cost studies in two of his recent
books [1, Chapter 8; 7]. In general, the services that have been found
to exhibit U-shaped or downward-sloping average-cost curves are (1)
fire protection, (2) hospitals, (3) utilities, (4) high schools, and (5)
school administration. The lowest portion of the unit-cost curve for fire
services is reached at a population somewhere between 100,000 and
300,000. For high schools, minimum average costs occur at about 1700
pupils. For school administration services, the optimal number of students is around 44,000. For all utilities, cost curves are continuously
downward sloping.

Horizontal average-cost curves have been found uniformly for primary
and secondary education, refuse collection, and police protection. The
key to this finding is that these sectors are labor-intensive; thus other
(cheaper) inputs cannot be substituted for labor as more output is produced. It is interesting to note that many primary and secondary schools
continue to consolidate in small urban areas, even though empirical
studies show that few if any scale economies are made available through
consolidation.

In regard to who obtains public services and what types and amounts
they get, empirical research is still in its infancy. Education has received

the most attention. In general, the results show that in culturally and economically deficient areas of cities, per-pupil expenditures are as great as or higher than in economically advantaged areas. On the other hand, higher-income areas seem to get the most qualified instructors. Thus it is not clear that any real difference in service-area inputs exists for public education. In the area of police protection, more resources are allocated to higher-crime areas, but it is obvious that enough police resources have not been allocated there to equalize crime rates in all areas of the city.

III. THE FUNCTIONAL ROLES OF LOCAL GOVERNMENTS

The three tools used by the public sector are taxes, expenditures, and regulation. Up to now we have focused mainly on the economic rationale for and bases of the production and delivery of public services. Assuming that there is a proportional relationship between expenditures and services, it is clear that most of our discussion so far has covered the expenditure side of the public sector. In this section we shall take a look at how local governments raise their revenues, and the economic effects of these revenue-raising mechanisms. In addition, we shall briefly cover expenditure and regulatory trends in urban areas.

In assessing the overall activity of the public sector it is important to keep in mind the interdependence of revenues and expenditures. As revenues increase, expenditures can increase, and vice versa. If we assume a proportional relationship between expenditures and services, an increase in public services, *ceteris paribus*, could help increase economic growth in a city, which would undoubtedly increase the tax base. And of course as the tax base increases, tax revenues will also rise, all other things being equal; thus the process starts over. This simple illustration of the interdependence of expenditures and revenues points up one of the reasons why local governments like to receive intergovernmental transfers; that is, exogenous injections of revenues.

Revenue Sources and Collection

Table 8-1 shows the sources of revenues for all local governments (municipalities, counties, townships, and special districts) in the U.S. for the fiscal year 1969–1970. The state and Federal governments provide about one-third of local funds, while local governments raise the remaining two-thirds through taxes, user charges, and other sources. Contrary to popular opinion, taxes account for only about 44 percent of local

TABLE 8-1

Local Government Revenue Sources, 1969–1970[a]

	$ (millions)
Total	89,082
Intergovernmental	29,525
Revenue from own sources	59,557
General Revenue from own sources	51,392
Taxes	38,833
Property	32,963
Income	1,630
Sales	3,068
Other	1,173
Charges + Miscellaneous General Revenues	12,558
Utility Revenue	6,608
All other Revenue	1,557

[a] U.S. Department of Commerce, Bureau of Census, *Governmental Finances in 1969–1970*, p. 20 (Washington, D.C.: GPO, 1971).

revenues. Nevertheless, taxes continue to be a source of irritation for many suburbanites. We hope to explain why this is so in the next few pages.

Taxes are a financial obligation to the government. When we pay our taxes this obligation is met, but we do not necessarily receive any services. Unlike most payments (where we get goods or services directly), people at best see only indirectly the results of their tax payment. Thus there is always the lingering question whether or not the payment is worth it from the individual's standpoint. This problem could be easily solved if local governments put user charges on all of their services, but we have already seen that this is nearly impossible for some services (public administration, pollution control, police protection) and inefficient for others (nonpeak uses of roads, bridges, beaches).

How do we choose a tax? In general, economists have argued that two principles exist: the benefits principle and the ability-to-pay principle. The former proposes that individuals be taxed according to the benefits received. This principle is very difficult to apply in urban areas because many of the beneficiaries of services are in other jurisdictions; town A cannot tax the residents of town B if some of A's mosquito spraying reduces the number of insects in town B. Spillovers and public goods defy the efficient use of the benefits principle in urban areas, especially where many jurisdictions are geographically concentrated. The ability-to-pay principle is not without its ambiguities, although its major problems are not directly inherent to urban jurisdictions. The issue of defining ability to pay has always been a problem. Property, other forms of wealth, and income are candidates. But possibly a more important consideration is the relationship of ability to pay to the tax burden. That is, if property is our measure of ability, as I increase my property holdings, do my taxes increase by more than, less than, or in proportion to the increase in the value of my holdings? This question is clearly important if equity is to be considered.

Two related issues in choosing a tax are the possibilities of tax-shifting and incidence. Shifting of course is the (partial or total) avoidance of a tax. For example, a firm can completely shift a sales tax forward to the consumer if the latter has a perfectly inelastic demand for the firm's product. Similarly, if the firm's supply curve is completely elastic, the sales tax can be completely shifted forward to the consumer. So the greater the degree of inelasticity of supply, other things being equal, the less the chance of avoiding a tax. For this reason (and others) urban areas have greatly relied on property taxes. Specialized resources, which are depicted by inelastic supply curves, obviously earn rents; that is, payments above what they could make in their next-best alternative use. Taxing away most of these rents will not cause the resources to be withdrawn from use at their present site. In other words, the incidence of the tax rests solely on the specialized resource.

The principles of taxation and the final burden of taxes are important considerations in choosing a tax. In addition, policy-makers are interested in the productivity of taxes; that is, how much revenue will the tax generate? Tax choices are also important because they affect the allocation of resources and the distribution of income. With the exception of lump-sum taxes, all taxes affect resource allocation. And if tax burdens are not proportional across income classes, then a redistribution of income will occur unless benefits of services are distributed in the same (disproportionate) manner as the taxes. Let us take a look at the major tax sources in local governments and consider their effects on efficiency and equity.

Property Tax

As shown in Table 8-1, the property tax brings in about 85 percent of the tax revenues in local jurisdictions. The base of the tax is the assessed market value (or some fraction thereof, depending on the locale) of real property, where real property is usually defined as land and any structure on the land. Personal property is also included in the tax base of some locales. Financial assets (stocks, bonds) are not included in the base. As we noted above, property taxes are popular because they represent a tax on a resource that is more or less immobile. In addition, as cities grow, the value of property usually increases, so the tax has a high level of productivity.

In the past few years, property-tax rates have varied from 0.5 to about 4.5 percent of assessed real property in U.S. cities, the median rate being slightly below 2 percent. In general, core cities have significantly higher rates than suburbs. Some states grant partial exemption to selected groups such as veterans, and in many of our major cities major portions of property are exempted from taxation outright. In the city of Boston, which is not an atypical eastern city, over 50 percent of the land is held by institutions (religious, charitable, nonprofit, and government) that are exempted from paying property taxes. Thus the tax base in the core cities is biased downward when compared to suburban bases, since most of these exempted institutions seek and find central locations for accessibility reasons.

One final characteristic of the property tax is its stability as a source of revenue. Because reassessments are often irregular at best, if a temporary downturn in property values should occur, revenues will not necessarily decrease; taxes can be based on previous (higher) property values. However, this practice would be used at a cost, since in the long run, property taxes have a negative effect on improvements. People or firms can choose alternative jurisdictions in which to improve or maintain their real properties.

Now that we have an idea about the nature of local property taxes, let us consider their economic effects.* First, property taxes amount to consumption taxes on housing; thus they lead to an underallocation of resources into housing markets. This effect is not severe (if in fact important) in suburbs, since suburban communities receive services more or less commensurate with the taxes they pay. However, suburban areas have disproportionate shares of higher-income families. And as we learned in the chapter on housing, federal income-tax provisions effectively exempt higher-income families from large shares of their property-tax burdens. In the low-income areas of cities, on the other hand, the effect of property taxes on consumption of housing services and investment in housing stock is severe. The poor obviously consume less housing, and the incentive to maintain or repair housing stock is dampened.

Besides affecting housing markets, property taxes may alter the location decisions of firms. Since lower property-tax rates are found in the suburbs, other things being equal, we would expect a greater decen-

---

* This section relies heavily on Dick Netzer [8].

tralization of firms than would occur without the tax differentials. This decentralization effect of property taxes also operates through rate differences in transport modes. Railroads, which traditionally were a centralizing force in most cities in regard to firm-location decisions, own their own rights of ways; thus they are taxed more heavily than other transport modes, if for no other reason than because they have larger bases. For example, in 1957 railroads paid property taxes of 4.9 percent of their output, while airlines only paid 0.04 percent of their share in property taxes. To the extent that railroads could still be a centralizing force in this day and age, property taxes are even stronger in their tendency to cause a more decentralized urban area. In summary, then, property taxes cause cities to spread out more than they would otherwise. If people in fact prefer this, then the taxes may be welfare-enhancing. But as we saw in the preceding chapter, a more decentralized urban society is far costlier to transport, and other scale effects associated with accessibility are lost. For example, one usually does not find the best French restaurants in the suburbs.

Turning to the impact of property taxes on the distribution of income, in the aggregate U.S. the tax is proportional for all income classes except the lowest, where it is strongly regressive. In urban areas, the nonresidential part of the tax is regressive for families up to the $10,000 level. Residential property effects are difficult to ascertain, but the best evidence we have is that in most large central cities they are strongly regressive. This is especially disheartening, since most expenditures in large central cities are income redistributions in kind (health, welfare, parks); however, there is in *fact* no redistribution of income occurring! We are taxing the poor disproportionately to provide the poor with public services.

Clearly the property tax has some rather perverse effects on the allocation of resources and distribution of income in cities. These effects are especially significant when one considers the major problems facing the poor in our large cities. Hopefully, alternative sources of revenues will be found in the future that have less adverse economic effects.

Sales Taxes

Sales taxes may be general or specific. General sales taxes are a percentage amount on retail sales to final consumers. The primary purpose of general sales taxes, of course, is to raise revenues. Taxes on the sale of specific goods are often called excise taxes. Excise taxes are collected for regulatory reasons (alcohol, tobacco) and generally because the government feels the individuals have the ability to pay (luxuries). In general, sales tax rates range from 2 to 7 percent. The taxes are levied primarily by the states, although nearly 20 states allow urban areas to levy sales taxes. In fact, in some of the largest cities of the country, sales and income taxes bring in more revenue than property taxes.

The effects of sales taxes on resource allocation are well known. Less of the affected good is produced, and its price rises. In metropolitan areas where jurisdictions have differential sales tax rates, retailers will not be able to shift much of the sales tax forward to the consumer without a loss of patronage. For example, New York City had a 4 percent sales tax prior to 1965, while New Jersey and surrounding suburban areas did not have a sales tax. If New York City retailers did not shift the tax forward, we would expect no diversion of shopping patterns. However, evidence shows [9] that as much as 25 percent of retail sales in house furnishings and apparel was diverted to suburban and New Jersey stores. Of course if sales taxes are not shifted forward, the burden falls on the producer; thus factors of production will no doubt receive lower wages, which may affect the spatial distribution of mobile (labor) factors,

Sales taxes are strongly regressive; that is, the poor pay a disproportionately large share of their income in sales taxes. Even where food and other necessities are exempt, the tax is regressive for lower-income groups. Selective sales taxes and excise taxes are also quite regressive. So on distributional grounds, the sales tax does not differ much from the property tax. From an efficiency standpoint, though, it does not seem that sales taxes alter the allocation of resources nearly as much as property taxes do in urban areas.

Income Taxes

Income taxes are becoming a popular source of revenue for many local governments. The types of plans presently utilized vary from a simple payroll tax to complicated facsimiles of the federal income tax. Most cities, however, use a simple tax on gross income with few deductions or exemptions. Clearly if cities were to use a detailed plan similar to the federal plan, collection costs could be quite high. To solve this problem, states have used a tax rate of a given percentage of one's federal income tax liability.

Although income taxes do not affect any particular commodity, they still alter the allocation of resources because they alter the work–leisure relationship of individuals. Income taxes reduce one's disposable income. To reach a new after-tax equilibrium between work and leisure, the value of goods I buy with the last dollar of my income must equal the value of a dollar's worth of leisure. So the number of hours I opt to work with the tax would not likely be the same as without the tax, given that my preferences between work and leisure remain constant. In addition to altering the work–leisure ratio, income taxes on interest earned from savings bias the choice between present and future consumption. Thus people may end up investing in things they would not have without the income tax.

Income taxes may also affect the distribution of income. Where graduated rates are allowed (as in New York City), the tax is mildly progressive. But most local areas use flat rates without exemptions. These simple plans are proportional for low- and middle-income classes, but regressive for high-income groups because the latter have relatively large amounts of untaxable property income.

Nontax Revenue Sources

Table 8-1 shows that about one-third of local revenues comes from other governments (state and federal) while about 27 percent comes from user charges, utilities, and miscellaneous sources. The major share of the intergovernmental transfer comes from the states. Most of the state aid is spent on educational services, although welfare and highways receive generous help in many cities. In the past, federal aid has been in the form of conditional grants; that is, specific programs (such as water, sewerage, housing, parks, and freeways) are delineated, and restrictions are established on how money can be spent. In December of 1972, however, the Federal Government practically doubled its transfers to local government with the institution of revenue sharing. Unlike conditional grants, revenue sharing has minimal strings attached to its use.

The rationale for intergovernmental grants from states to local areas is that externalities or spillovers from one local jurisdiction to another should be internalized. For example, if the benefits from educational spending in town A are lost because its graduates move to other towns in the state, A will be likely to underspend in education because private costs at the margin exceed private benefits for A. However, the state argues that the marginal *social* benefits of education in A exceed the marginal social costs, and to ensure that A reaches this greater level of educational-service production the state subsidizes A's educational system.

A second reason that states offer transfers to local governments is to help equalize per capita budgets among cities. It is no secret that vast differences in income levels exist among cities, especially between central cities and suburbs. Since state governments often have the final say on the types of taxes (and rate limits) that local governments may use, states act as a limiting force on potential tax revenues for cities.

To equalize any resultant differences in revenue per capita, states provide grants for specific services.

The logic behind traditional federal transfers is essentially the same as the second reason for state transfers cited in the preceding paragraph. Essentially, the Federal Government is redistributing income. Previously we pointed up the fact that eminent economists in the public sector argue that it is the role of the Federal Government (and not local government) to redistribute income. Of course, income may be redistributed through both taxing and spending policies. Leaving taxes aside for the moment, the meager amount of federal transfers shown in Table 8-1 is fairly strong evidence that on the expenditure side, the Federal Government is not doing the job it could do. In fact, recalling our discussion on urban renewal, freeways, and mass transit, it is likely that a substantial portion of the federal transfers is being used for projects that benefit higher-income persons more than lower-income persons.

The remaining significant source of revenue to local government is user charges. User charges are direct payments for a good or service such as hospitals, higher education, parking, and utilities. Essentially, user charges are prices; if local governments could allow the market mechanism to decide the prices of these services (barring externalities), an efficient allocation of resources would probably result. Unfortunately, local governments apparently have more faith in their own price-setting ability than the market. Prices are often set to cover costs per unit, which in most cases will result in an underallocation of resources toward the production of the service.

Figure 8.3 shows a case in which prices are set according to average costs; thus P_1 is charged and X_1 is produced. The optimal level of output is where $P = MC$, which occurs at X_2. To be sure, at X_2 society would be paying a slight subsidy per unit of the service, but many utilities are already subsidized to ensure that they cover costs per unit. We

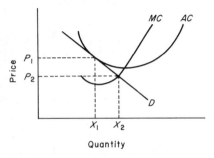

Figure 8.3 *Price regulation and optimal supply.*

noted in the preceding chapter that municipal parking lots do not recognize that the demand for their services is much greater (and inelastic) for peak-hour drivers who park all day. To achieve an optimal allocation of resources toward parking facilities, these users should be charged higher prices, but instead they are given bargain rates.

Local Government Expenditures

Now that we have surveyed the nature and economic effects of revenue sources, let us turn to a consideration of expenditure patterns and the role of regulation. Table 8-2 shows the level and percentage breakdown of direct expenditures by all local governments in the U.S. for

TABLE 8-2

Direct Expenditures of Local Governments in U.S., 1963 and 1969–1970ᵃ

	\$ (millions)		Percent 1963	Percent 1969–1970
	1963	1969–70		
Total	\$42,324	\$82,582		
Education	19,058	38,938	45.0	47.2
Highways	3,710	5,383	8.8	6.5
Welfare	2,769	6,477	6.5	7.8
Health and hospitals	2,351	4,880	5.5	5.9
Police	1,985	3,806	4.7	4.6
Fire	1,186	2,024	2.8	2.5
Sewerage	1,464	2,167	3.5	2.6
Sanitation	723	1,246	1.7	1.5
Recreation and parks	978	1,888	2.3	2.3
Natural resources	491	574	1.2	0.7
Housing and urban renewal	1,235	2,115	2.9	2.6
Air transportation	330	791	0.8	0.9
Water transportation	231	271	0.5	0.3
Corrections	282	575	0.7	0.7
Libraries	377	646	0.9	0.8
Interest on debt	1,478	2,875	3.5	3.5
Administration, general control, and all other	3,678	7,926	8.7	9.6

ᵃ 1963 data is from U.S. Bureau of Census *Government Finance in 1963* (Washington: GPO, 1963); 1969–1970 data from same source as Table 8-1.

1963 and 1969–1970. The most striking piece of information in this table is the constancy of the shares of each class of expenditure: for many of those areas where the percentage of total direct expenditures decreased (highways, sewerage, sanitation, natural resources), indirect expenditures (by state and federal governments) increased. Thus, other things being equal, service levels to local consumers did not fall in any category.

Although the constancy of shares among expenditure categories is not a necessary or sufficient condition to argue that inefficient budgetary decisions are being made at the local level, this phenomenon does cast doubt on the flexibility of local decision-making. In our discussion on the demand for and supply of local services, we emphasized the efficiency principle; that is, expenditures should be allocated across areas until the marginal products are equalized. To be sure, we noted that demand is difficult to identify. We also emphasized the difficulty in identifying outputs, and thus marginal products of services; however, we noted many indirect ways to proxy output. However, unless demand patterns and production techniques are constant, there is no reason from an efficiency (resource-allocation) standpoint to expect the level of real expenditures to remain constant across service categories. That the pattern is constant suggests that either (1) noneconomic factors enter strongly into budget-making decisions, or (2) knowledge of community preferences and the efficacy of alternative production techniques is minimal. In the former area, we have all heard that once a program begins in government it is difficult if not impossible to kill it. In regard to the second point, there is little doubt that information on demand and production is scarce.

On the other hand, although the pattern of expenditures remained constant in the aggregate, it is reasonable to argue that shifts in some cities could still occur. We should also point out that Table 8-2 shows that expenditures for administration and general control and welfare have risen at a higher than average rate. These changes are exceptions to the constant-share argument.

Finally, the choice of expenditure levels cannot rest on efficiency criteria alone. Equity must also be considered. If the expenditure shares of each service are constant over time, the equity implication is that unless local public services are consumed equally, there is little that local governments have done to rectify existing inequities. Since most of our information in this and previous chapters tends to negate the equal-consumption hypothesis, it is probably safe to conclude that, in general, local governments do not have an equalizing effect on the distribution of income through expenditure policies.

Regulation and Control

The regulatory and control powers of local governments have their primary economic effects in land use and transportation markets. Land use, zoning, and other regulatory constraints (maximum building height in commercial zones, minimum lot size in residential zones) are no doubt major factors in determining general location decisions of firms and residents in urban areas. Roads, highways, and the transmission lines of utilities also affect location patterns. There is little doubt that land-use and transportation regulations not only affect location and development but also are affected by development. In other words, an interaction effect occurs over time and makes it very difficult to identify the true role played by regulation in land use and transportation markets.

Land-use zoning and other regulatory controls should be set so that they help the market operate efficiently *and* enhance the growth of the area. Often this dual goal is difficult to meet, since once a given area is zoned, land prices for that area may rise, causing developers to seek the next-cheaper site elsewhere. This rigidity of zoning, which on the one hand is required to ensure similarity of users (and thus minimization of externalities), may on the other hand lead to a relatively haphazard land-use pattern on the periphery of urban areas. This haphazard pattern of land use has been referred to as urban sprawl. Urban sprawl is also perpetuated by low taxes on unused land, which prompts land holders to wait for capital gains, and forces developers to leapfrog farther outward to find cheaper land.

Given the purpose of regulation and control, what are the regulatory tools the government has to work with? One regulatory tool is outright government ownership. Most cities own their roads, sewerage and water facilities, traffic equipment, and transit systems. Second, laws provide a means for regulating the use of public and private land and also set performance criteria for public-service contracts. Land is often set aside for parks and recreation purposes by law. Zoning of course regulates the broad private uses of land. And when the public sector has the private sector perform work, the latter's performance is often constrained by laws. For example, if a lawyer were to go to New York City to consult on a housing-project study, he would be forbidden by law to spend the city's money on wine, women, and song. A third set of tools consists of indirect or informal controls such as taxes or subsidies. These mechanisms provide a means of altering the price and/or output of certain activities.

Regulatory tools are often used to affect the output–price decisions in land and transportation markets. For example, on the output side, regulatory boards usually decide how many buses will be used in a city and how often they will travel on each route per day. The same board will also decide the pricing policy of the bus line. The economists' rules in deciding the proper prices and outputs are of course efficiency and equity; but as we noted in the preceding chapter, there is little evidence that efficient prices are in fact being charged. Clearly during rush hours higher prices are required for efficiency, but uniform bus and transit prices (during the day) are the rule in U.S. cities.

The price and output of some services are indirectly regulated by restricting entry into the industry. This makes sense when we have a decreasing-cost sector, such as transit or utilities. However, where decreasing costs are not apparent, as in taxicab services, for example, the restriction of entry may result in an inefficient allocation of resources. In many of our major cities local governments allow only a fixed number of cabs to be licensed, and the result is often an excess demand for licenses. Since the legal price of licenses is fixed, black markets appear, and people often pay as much as $50,000 for a license to operate a cab. If the number of cabs were decided by the market mechanism alone, more cabs would be available for consumers at lower prices. In this case, regulation has not been used properly.

Although the economic effects of zoning are difficult to determine empirically, it is interesting to note that one large city in this country— Houston, Texas—has never had zoning regulations, but has not had any of the problems one might expect [10]. The land-use pattern in Houston is similar to that in other cities of comparable size and industrial structure. Few if any cases of dirty plants moving into attractive neighborhoods exist. Although the Houston case does not provide a test of what would happen if cities having zoning laws should drop them, it does lead one to believe that land markets may in fact operate more efficiently than we believe. That is, externalities may be capitalized into the value of the land, so that only a minimal effort of control is needed to ensure that land use is socially optimal.

IV. PROBLEMS OF URBAN GOVERNMENTS

In this chapter we have raised a number of basic problems facing urban governments. How do we determine the demand for public goods and services? What are efficient and equitable service levels, given the preferences of urban society? Can local governments find alternative taxes that are as productive as, but less regressive than property and sales taxes? We could easily add many more issues to this list. Two of the more popular issues facing urban governments, however, are the questions of (1) the proper size of government in metropolitan areas and (2) the financial crisis gripping central cities and many small towns outside metropolitan areas. We know that in cities that have contiguous and overlapping jurisdictions, spillovers (both positive and negative) occur that are a basic source of inefficient decision-making. To minimize this and related problems, people have argued that governments should be consolidated. We shall consider this problem and alternative solutions in detail. A second major issue facing many local governments is that service demand increases are outstripping their revenue increases. One of the major proposals to solve this problem is revenue sharing. We shall consider the pros and cons of revenue sharing and its alternatives for solving the financial crisis of local governments.

The Optimal Size of Metropolitan Governments

The typical metropolitan area in the U.S. consists of numerous municipalities, counties, school districts, townships, and other jurisdictions. In 1967, the U.S. had 81,253 local jurisdictions, although the number of jurisdictions has been declining rapidly since the 1940's. The major explanation for the decline has been the drastic reduction in school districts through consolidation. On the other hand, special districts, which now comprise over one-fourth of the total local government units, have more than doubled since 1942. Since special districts (watersheds, air-pollution control, transit lines) are often found in metropolitan areas, there is little evidence that the existence of (and possible growth in) political fragmentation in metropolitan areas will subside.

Overlapping and contiguous political jurisdictions of course lead to inefficient resource allocation, especially in service areas where externalities are involved, such as education, roads, parks, libraries, and water- and air-pollution control. In contemporary metropolitan America, many of our political jurisdictions are delineated on the basis of income. The higher-income groups are located in suburbia, while the core of low-income families are in the central city. This leads to an inequitable distribution of services, because the tax bases differ (being larger in suburbs) and broader governments do not provide central cities with equalizing grants. Not only does political fragmentation lead to inefficiency and inequitable service flows, but fragmentation is also associated with small sized governmental units. Depending on how small these units are, they may not be able to attain scale economies on some of the services they provide.

One proposal for solving the problems of political fragmentation is to consolidate each metropolitan areas into a single governmental unit—a super "Metro," if you will. Obviously there are costs and benefits in having one single government, but before going into these we might ask ourselves what the optimal level of government is in theory. This discussion will be useful in analyzing the pros and cons of Metro.

Optimal Size of Local Government*

Assume that we have a city having only a private sector. Problems such as nonpackagability of certain goods and services, externalities, and decreasing costs would lead people to argue for a government to handle these problems. If a group were organized to decide the optimal size or level of government, what criteria would they use?

First, the government must be responsive to the preferences of the people. Second, it is important for the government to minimize resource costs of any service it decides to produce itself. Third, the government should be of the proper level to ensure that all of its decisions that would otherwise produce externalities could be internalized. And finally, the government must be able to meet all of its redistribution goals.

Let us take a look at the implications of each of these principles. The first principle logically implies that the most efficient governments would be single-person jurisdictions. In practical terms, the ability to identify and respond to preferences implies small jurisdictions to most people, and this is more or less exactly what we have in the U.S. today. If governments decide to produce their own goods or services, cost-minimization is obviously important, and to the extent that scale economies exist this factor determines the optimal size of government for that service. Where scale economies exist in the real world, they are associated with larger rather than smaller jurisdictions. The last two principles both lead to larger units. To internalize externalities, jurisdictions must encompass the emitter and recipient of the externalities. And to provide for the optimal design on redistribution goals, government must be centralized with subareas that can and do express their heterogenous preferences. If the latter condition did not hold, there would be no basis for redistribution.

These four principles are not directly applicable in learning the optimal size of local governments unless we know the relative weights of each. Any choice of weights or relative importance would be purely

* This section was aided by Jerome Rothenberg [11].

speculative and a value judgment. However, it is probably safe to say that the weights would vary across metros and over time. Interestingly, three of the four principles call for large rather than small jurisdictions.

The Pros and Cons of Metro

Now that we have an idea of the basis for an optimal level of local government, let us analyze the basic arguments often cited for the metro type of government. One of the earlier arguments for Metro was similar to the rationale for allowing utilities (electricity, telephones, public transit) to be monopolies. That is, most public services were said to be characterized as decreasing-cost sectors. Even for those services not operating under decreasing costs, more than one unit producing services surely results in uncoordinated, duplicative, and generally inefficient decision-making. As we argued previously in this chapter, however, many public services are produced under constant-cost conditions. Moreover, the monopoly parallel assumes that products are standardized, which is clearly untenable for almost all public services except utilities. Anti-Metro forces agree that uncoordinated local-government behavior may be more costly than a Metro government. However, they claim that the existing jurisdictional structure in our cities is a useful way of pro-viding a variety of local services for which people can shop in alternative locales. They argue that any additional costs borne in allowing variety may be worth it in terms of utility maximization.

The anti-Metro forces seem to have a strong argument when it comes to the issues of attaining scale economies and meeting the preferences of the people. But this may not be. In general, the relationship between service variety and scale economies is a tradeoff that varies for each public service. In other words, the argument goes that as government size increases, the variety of alternative service levels and qualities will decline. On logical grounds such an argument is completely false. Certainly larger governments could offer a bundle of types and amounts of services (education, police protection) in a given area such that all preferences could be met. And on empirical grounds, it is in the large cities where we find the variety of recreational and cultural activities, or the highly specialized police, health, and welfare services; thus larger jurisdictions do in fact offer many bundles of given services. Moreover, larger jurisdictions can gather decision-making information (that is, the preferences of people through elections) more cheaply than small juris-dictions. In conclusion, the choice of having smaller jurisdictions on grounds of meeting preferences at minimal costs is strongly suspect.

The internalization-of-externalities argument is a very strong case for Metro, although it is difficult to get the affected parties to see the benefits of joining together. In a sense, this is an example of the breakdown in our economic–political system. That is, when two private parties are at odds, we have the government step in and arbitrate matters. But when two local governments are fighting, there is no third party to step in. The states might be logical candidates, but many practical and technical reasons preclude their entrance into this role. Clearly a regional jurisdiction is called for.

One of the implicit assumptions of Metro is that all of the costs and benefits of its activities are internalized. Certainly dirty water flows downstream and dirty air blows on to other areas. One important fact about Metro is that it internalizes only the externalities within the metropolitan area. Obviously, not all spillovers are metropolitan in scale. For example, we saw in Chapter 6 that adverse neighborhood effects in slums affect housing formation and maintenance in low-income areas of our central cities. Suburbanites, of course, would not vote to aid low-income housing under a Metro plan, because suburbanites would not benefit directly from such a program. Thus a real cost of Metro would be inefficient decision-making unless services and the inherent problems they solve are more or less metropolitan in scale. This illustration of the difference in problems is one of the major reasons why suburban areas refuse to join central cities in consolidating urban government.

In summary, Metro would provide an easy solution to internalizing some spillovers, but it would create other problems in the process. In the limit, the optimal solution to the internalization problem would involve a series of "problem shed" jurisdictions; that is, the geographical scope of every government activity would be delineated, and each person living in the area or shed for a given service would become a "voter" in the production of that service. Problem sheds for every service would mean that given persons might be in a large number of sheds; thus collective decision-making could be a very costly procedure. Imagine going to the polls 25 different times throughout the year! The case for Metro in providing a more efficient means of redistribution is not clear-cut. As we noted earlier, eminent public finance economists have argued that redistribution should be left to the federal income tax, since its progressive characteristics cannot offset regressive taxes at the local level. But what about the unequal distribution of local services? It seems intuitively clear that Metro could do a more efficient job of ensuring that redistribution occurs in services, because metro would have the existing mechanisms to vary production levels or bundles. Whether the Metro-wide populace would continually vote for such a program is of course another matter.

The Outlook for Metro

Only three metropolitan areas in North America have embarked on the experiment of Metro: Toronto, Canada; Dade County, Florida; and Indianapolis. Tampa voters have rejected Metro three times in the past six years. It is not likely that many urban areas will turn to Metro in the near future, unless on a selected-service basis. The reasons for this guess are speculative, but one seems to be that only downtown businesses and nearby residents are pushing strongly for Metro. Those firms and residents outside the core city see the Metro-seekers as desirous of relieving their heavy tax burdens at the expense of the suburbanites. The latter, of course, reject this scheme for obvious reasons. With a growing suburban population, central-city interests do not have bright future prospects either. One power group that could potentially help the pro-Metro side is ghetto residents. However, in the past five years, many leaders of low-income and ghetto areas have argued for the political power to control their own destiny; thus they are arguing for further political fragmentation rather than consolidation.

Whatever the future of Metro, recent court decisions have stated that everyone in a metropolitan area has the right to receive equal basic services such as education, regardless of how these services are financed. Such decisions could lead to a centralization of the delivery of certain services in the long run.

The Financial Crisis and Revenue Sharing

During the middle 1960's the aggregate economy was close to full employment without any serious inflation, and surpluses in the federal budget began to appear. Economists were concerned that these surpluses might act as a drag on the aggregate economic activity. The basis for this fiscal drag is our progressive Federal income tax, which can increase government revenues at a greater rate than increases in national product. Unless existing government programs are designed to spend this surplus (or a serious problem of inflation does the same thing), the surplus will slow down the economy. Economists argue that to solve the problem Federal taxes should be cut or expenditures increased (or both). But at the state and local levels, expenditure demands seemed to outstrip increases in revenues; thus state and local representatives argued for a tool called revenue sharing, whereby the Federal government would give its surplus to state and local governments to help them out of their financial difficulties.

The Heller–Pechman Plan

The most popular revenue-sharing plan was developed by Walter Heller and Joseph Pechman.* Essentially, the Heller–Peckman plan argued for a permanent allocation of funds from the growth-elastic Federal treasury to state and local areas, since state and local revenue increases barely kept up with national income increases. Given the continual huge increases in demand for state and local services, local revenue sources would not keep up with demand. It is important to note that the Heller–Pechman plan was argued as a supplement to, rather than a substitute for conditional grants to state and local governments. Conditional grants, which carry stipulations on how the money is to be spent, are used primarily to finance services that are characterized by spillovers; thus, to ensure efficiency, the grants are earmarked for these service areas. Revenue-sharing funds would be categorized as unconditional grants, and they are not given for resource-allocation reasons per se. Instead, unconditional grants are given when states and/or local areas have unequal fiscal capacities to finance services. The basis of revenue sharing as Heller and Pechman saw it was equity.

The basic feature of the Heller–Pechman plan was that a regular share of the federal income taxes was to be distributed to state and local areas each year, without strings attached on the areas of expenditures. The allocation was to be made on the basis of population. Some of the more specific details were that:

(1) The distribution each year would be automatic, which could be facilitated by putting up monies in a trust fund.
(2) Since highways already have their own trust fund, this area would be excluded from the use of the grants.
(3) The population basis for allocating the monies would be adjusted by tax effort,† and a small share of the funds would be directly allocated to the poorest states.
(4) No specific mechanism was included to ensure that states distributed part of the funds to local governments.

Since the Heller–Pechman plan was proposed, many alternative revenue sharing plans have come forth. They are basically the same, except that they vary in terms of the allocation criteria, and most have a "pass-through" clause that ensures that urban areas in each state will receive a reasonable share of the funds granted to that state.

* The Heller–Pechman plan is described and criticized in H. Perloff and R. Nathan, *Revenue Sharing and the City* [12]. A more recent analysis and critique of this and other plans is *Financing State and Local Governments* [13].

† Tax effort refers to the amount of taxes collected per dollar of income in a given jurisdiction.

The New Revenue-Sharing Plan

After years of bickering, Congress finally passed a revenue-sharing bill in 1972. The plan calls for allocating $30 billion to state and local governments between 1972 and 1976. The law allows for funds to be used for any ordinary expenditure, although the funds cannot be used to get matching grants from the Federal Government in other federal programs. The funds are automatically allocated out of a trust fund, as Heller and Pechman proposed. While states will receive a little more than half of the total fund, all local governments will get something. The criteria for allocating funds to a local jurisdiction include (1) population, (2) tax effort, and (3) the relative income factor (relative per-capita income). Thus larger cities that have heavily taxed themselves and have relatively low per-capita incomes are favored under the distribution formula.

One further provision in the new law is that states have the power to pass their own laws on allocating funds among local units, although they are constrained in their choices. States may simply use population and the relative-income factor, or some combination of both. In addition, whatever formula they choose must be applied uniformly throughout the state. Thus, whereas the Federal Government gave equal weight to population, tax effort, and relative income, states may decide their own weights. Certainly it is possible for cities to lose a great deal of revenue through this clause in the long run.

In assessing the value and impact of the new revenue-sharing law, we must first ask ourselves whether the conditions of a federal surplus and state and local financial crisis still exist. On both counts the answer is no. Vietnam, inflation, and the expansion of other programs have meant an average deficit of over $25 billion per year during the first Nixon administration. Moreover, many state and suburban jurisdictions have shown healthy surpluses in the recent past. Thus the historical rationale (and some logical reasons also) no longer exists for revenue sharing as we have used the term.

The situation we now face is to allocate scarce federal funds efficiently *and* attempt to meet the needs of urban areas that do not have adequate fiscal capacities. Such urban areas are located in low-income states and, in some cases, the central cities and small towns of high-income states Will the new law solve these cities' fiscal problems? Obviously the meager amounts are not large enough, but they can surely help. However, the existing formulas place only a one-third weighting factor on relative per-capita income; thus poor towns in poor states will not be helped any more than, say, wealthy big towns in high-income states, other things being equal. Clearly the basic purpose of unconditional grants—namely, equalizing the revenues of governmental units—will not be met by the new revenue-sharing program.

In regard to the financial plight of central cities in high-income states, the outlook for the current program is also pessimistic. Since about one-half of the metropolitan population now lives in the suburbs, central cities do not have an advantage on population grounds. And of course the many exemptions on property taxes within the central city depress its tax effort. In short, revenue sharing, as is currently structured, does not seem to be the answer to the financial ills of our cities.

What are the alternatives to revenue sharing? Certainly consolidation is one answer, but for reasons cited earlier, this approach is not likely to occur in the near future, at least on a grand scale. One proposal [14] is to have the Federal Government take over the financial responsibilities for welfare programs immediately, and if federal surpluses should arise, this responsibility would be extended to include minimum services in primary and secondary schools.

In conclusion, the financial problems of our large cities, which are merely reflections of unsolved problems of poverty, crime, and under-utilized human resources, will not be solved by the new revenue-sharing plan. What our lawmakers did with revenue sharing was "give everyone a piece of the action." But everyone does not have the same need for a piece of the action, and the assumption of equal need is the basic fallacy of the new revenue-sharing plan. Inefficient politically fragmented jurisdictions will be perpetuated by revenue sharing, and fiscally responsible but relatively poor units will not be made any better off in relation to higher-income areas.

V. SUMMARY

In this chapter we have found that the public sector of our urban areas is faced with many formidable tasks. First, it has to produce many (public) goods and services that the private sector is unwilling to produce, but which society is thought to desire. However, to meet this goal, local governments have to determine the preferences of the community, which is a difficult task. Even if these preferences were known, the problem of producing and distributing these services efficiently and equitably is major. Second, the public sector must also raise revenues in such a way as to minimize the nonneutral effects on the allocation of resources and distribution of income. Given the alternatives available to urban governments by law, this is also a difficult task. In addition to the problems inherent in meeting these two major tasks, urban governments have the undesirable characteristic of having many jurisdictions that are either contiguous or overlapping. This situation often leads to a misallocation of resources. One solution proposed to solve this problem is consolidation, but at present it is not a popular solution. One seemingly age-old problem in the area of generating revenues is the issue of obtaining enough funds to meet demands. We found that the new revenue-sharing plan passed by Congress in 1972 will do little to solve the financial crisis facing many of our major core cities. These cities will have to seek alternative revenue sources, and major candidates at this time are more user charges (for example, commuter taxes) and further reliance on income taxes.

SUGGESTED READINGS

Bish, Robert. *The Public Economy of Metropolitan Areas.* Chicago: Markham, 1971.

Bish, R., and O'Donoghue, P. "A Neglected Issue in Public Goods Theory." *Journal of Political Economy* 78 (1970): 1367–71.

Edel, Matthew, and Rothenberg, Jerome, eds. *Readings in Urban Economics.* New York: Macmillan, 1972.

Federal Reserve Bank of Boston. "Financing State and Local Governments, 1970."

Groves, Harold. "Imbalance in the Fiscal System," (ed.) *Critical Issues in Public Finance in an Underdeveloped Region,* edited by W. J. Smith, pp. 16–25. Office of Research and Development, West Virginia Univ., 1971.

Hirsch, Werner. *The Economics of State and Local Government.* New York: McGraw-Hill, 1970.

Hirsch, Werner. *Urban Economic Analysis.* New York: McGraw-Hill, 1973.

Mills, Edwin. *Urban Economics,* Chapter 12. Glenview, Illinois: Scott, Foresman, 1972.

Mitchell, W., and Walter, I., eds. *State and Local Finance.* New York: Ronald Press, 1970.

Netzer, Dick. *Economics and Urban Problems.* New York: Basic Books, 1970.

Netzer, Dick. *Economics of the Property Tax.* Washington D.C.: Brookings Inst., 1966.

Perloff, H., and Wingo, L., eds. *Issues in Urban Economics,* Part 3. Baltimore, Maryland: Johns Hopkins Press (for Resources for the Future, Inc.), 1968.

REFERENCES

1. Werner Z. Hirsch, *The Economics of State and Local Government* (New York: McGraw-Hill, 1970).
2. Charles M. Tiebout, "A Pure Theory of Local Expenditures," *Journal of Political Economy* 64 (1956): 416–424.
3. Jeffery Chapman, "A Model of Crime and Police Output," unpublished Ph.D. dissertation. Univ. of California at Berkeley, 1971.

4. Jan Chaiken and John Rolph, "Predicting the Demand for Fire Service," P-4625. Santa Monica, California: Rand, 1971.
5. James Ohls and Terence Wales, "Supply and Demand for State and Local Services," *Review of Economics and Statistics* 54 (1972): 424–430.
6. Thomas Borcherding and Robert Deacon, "The Demand for the Services of Non-Federal Governments," *American Economic Review* 62 (1972): 891–901.
7. Werner Z. Hirsch, *Urban Economic Analysis,* Chapter 12 (New York: McGraw-Hill, 1973).
8. Dick Netzer, "Impact of the Property Tax: Its Economic Implications for Urban Problems." Joint Economic Committee, 90th Congress, 1968.
9. Henry M. Levin, "An Analysis of the Economic Effects of the New York City Sales Tax," in *Financing Government in New York City,* pp. 635–692 (New York: New York Univ. School of Public Administration, 1966).
10. Bernard H. Siegan, *Land Use Without Zoning* (Lexington, Massachusetts: Heath, 1972).
11. Jerome Rothenberg, "Local Decentralization and the Theory of Optimal Output," in *The Analysis of Public Output,* J. Margolis, ed., National Bureau of Economic Research, pp. 31–64 (New York: Columbia Univ. Press, 1970).
12. H. Perloff and R. Nathan, *Revenue Sharing and the City* (Baltimore, Maryland: John Hopkins Press, 1968).
13. *Financing State and Local Governments* (Boston, Massachusetts: Federal Reserve Bank of Boston, 1970).
14. R. A. Musgrave and A. M. Polinsky, "Revenue Sharing—A Critical View," in *Financing State and Local Governments,* pp. 17–51 (Boston, Massachusetts: Federal Reserve Bank of Boston, 1970).

9

URBAN POVERTY: PROBLEMS AND POLICIES

Although we found a number of drastic downturns in living standards during the development of U.S. cities in Chapter 2, since the depression of the 1930's most Americans have thought that (except for a few slum pockets in most of our major cities) poverty is a rural problem. By 1968, however, over half of the people officially designated as poverty stricken by our Federal Government were in metropolitan areas. And by 1970, the incidence of poverty in metropolitan areas had climbed to 53.2 percent of the total persons stricken with poverty throughout the country. Clearly if poverty is a major problem nationally, it will have to be fought in urban areas.

In this chapter we shall take a detailed look at the nature and consequences of poverty. We shall focus on economic poverty concepts, although we do not mean to imply that poverty is just an economic problem. There are many possible definitions of poverty. The definition of poverty is a very serious matter, because given the resources available to fight poverty, the definition will determine how the battle is fought. So we shall take a detailed look at alternative definitions of poverty and their implications. Regardless of one's definition, the consequences of poverty are the same—persons and families are forced to exist under very poor living conditions.

As a prelude to discussing alternative policies for solving the urban poverty problem, we shall take a rather close look at the factors that cause poverty. It is important to keep in mind the feedback effects when discussing the causes of poverty. For example, we hear people say that low levels of education and various forms of discrimination cause poverty, and this is no doubt true. But also, once a family is poverty stricken, the children (and adults) are apt to get less education and also to be discriminated against because of their socioeconomic standing in the community. In other words, over time poverty causes low levels of education and discrimination as well as vice versa. Poverty is a viscious circle in the long run for many families. In our discussion of the causes of poverty we shall more or less assume away this feedback effect, but we shall not forget this problem when we consider policies for solving urban poverty.

I. MEASURES OF URBAN POVERTY

The Concept of Poverty*

The usual definition given for poverty is that poor people do not have the economic (or other) means to obtain an acceptable standard of living, where the latter is decided somehow by society. This definition is of course filled with subjective criteria, which we shall not quarrel with at the moment. Instead, let us attempt to consider some of the basic components of an economic definition of poverty. Our inquiry is guided by the understanding that the type of definition finally chosen will more or less dictate the policies needed to solve the problem efficiently.

A family consumes goods and services according to some rationale, which previously in this book we have said is utility-maximization. If two categories of consumer goods are available for purchase—necessities and luxuries—the family will consume both until the marginal utility per dollar of expenditure is the same for both goods. This level of consumption of each good, denoted by Y_1 and X_1 in Figure 9.1, is the

* Many of the points discussed in this section rely on Harold Watts [1].

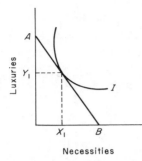

Figure 9.1 *Constrained utility maximization for a single family.*

utility-maximizing level, given the family's tastes expressed by indifference curve *I*, product prices, and current income. Although poverty is usually described as not consuming an a priori specified amount of necessities (usually all necessities), it may be more useful to view poverty as an income constraint. In this way, we focus on an objective property of a family's situation, rather than its behavior. Although the latter no doubt has its place in the social–psychological study of poverty, we desire to focus on the economic side.

Poverty, then, may be viewed as a restriction upon the set of consumption choices facing families. More specifically, we are speaking of income as the restriction. This approach has the characteristic of not imposing our tastes on families. That is, we do not say families must consume given amounts of food, clothing, shelter, medical care, and so forth. We assume that people can choose rationally for themselves. Moreover, we need not worry about the level of satisfaction particular families obtain from a given budget. We merely identify the poverty budget and let the individual choose, whereas the tradition has been to say that certain "necessities" must be consumed for a family to be above the poverty income level. A rather fundamental issue, of course, is: What is the proper income constraint level? The answer is that society, through elected officials or whatever, decides. Let us take a look at some of the issues involved in choosing the income constraint.

Poverty Income

Current income, which is illustrated in Figure 9.1, is only a first approximation of one's real budget constraint. A more relevant income concept would be permanent income, which boils down to current income plus or minus transitory components. The latter are factors related to time that would cause our consumption to be higher or lower than we would expect from simply considering current income. For example, the permanent income of a medical-school student is much higher than the scholarship or other funds he receives; therefore we would not expect him to be eating hot dogs every night. Instead, he could easily borrow to have an average or above-average living standard today.

The permanent-income approach to poverty measurement obviously expands the time horizon under consideration. This allows for variations in one's human and nonhuman accumulation of earnings or wealth. In deriving a permanent-income poverty level, we would adjust current income for any expected and possibly implicit earnings families may get from assets such as stocks, bonds, land, and housing. Whether or not these earnings are tangible, they still should be included in the permanent-income constraint. For example, capital gains or losses must be considered, as well as the implicit (rental) value of owning one's home.

In addition to the returns on nonhuman wealth, one must also consider the (expected) earning capacity of families themselves. By stretching the time horizon, we do not count the medical student as being poverty stricken. Moreover, we do not count the unemployed dishwasher the same as an unemployed electrician. Clearly the unemployed dishwasher is poorer, because the electrician has a much higher expected income. In addition to expected earnings, the permanent-income concept of human wealth includes the value of homemade goods and services, as well as transfer payments among households.

Given the notion of a permanent-income measure of poverty, how do we go about obtaining a workable poverty index? Clearly we must derive an index that is comparable over time and space for families of various sizes. The simplest approach would be to use a current-income figure, based on more or less equal levels of deprivation. This is the way the Federal Government derives its poverty figures. By adjusting this current-income figure for human and nonhuman wealth factors, we would have a permanent-income poverty line.

But surely the spirit of the consumer-utility analysis discussed earlier implies that poverty is not merely a line. If the line is $5000 and my permanent income is $3000, I am worse off than someone who has a permanent income of $4900. In other words, the income constraint becomes stronger as one's permanent income declines. To account for this factor, a simple approach would be to use as an index the ratio of permanent income to the poverty-line income. This index has more reasonable implications for counting up the poor than a simple poverty line. The latter, of course, involves merely a head count, whereas the ratio approach implies that heads should be weighted by how far away people are from the poverty line.

To be sure, the ratio approach involves a value judgment concerning the degree of poverty as one's permanent income falls below the poverty line. Specifically, we are assuming that successive decreases in one's permanent income below the line bring increasing marginal disutility. If this assumption is true, we have a very useful basis for policy. Now we can compare the amount of poverty reduced per dollar spent across families at varying degrees below the poverty line.

To summarize, we have defined poverty as a permanent-income constraint on family consumption behavior. Since families have various preference structures, this income constraint represents a wide variety of combinations of necessities and luxuries. To derive an aggregate measure of the level of poverty, instead of using a head count of those below the poverty line, we argued that the ratio of permanent income to the poverty line might be used. The implicit assumption behind this approach was that poorer and poorer families get increasing disutility from lower income, and vice versa. When we add up those below the poverty line using this assumption, we can derive an aggregate index of poverty that is useful for showing the productivity of antipoverty policy expenditures.

Present Measures of Poverty

The Federal Government does not calculate poverty by means of the ratio approach described above. Essentially the government uses a poverty-line income figure based on the amount of purchasing power needed to sustain an average low-income family on a temporary or emergency diet. The historical development of this official poverty line is both instructive and interesting.

In the 1964 *Economic Report of the President,* the Council of Economic Advisors adopted a figure of $3000 as the poverty line for a nonfarm family of four. This figure was derived only after some fighting and bickering among government officials. The Social Security Administration was called upon to develop the poverty line. They chose to estimate the poverty line by figuring out what poor families would need to meet dietary costs, and then, given that low-income families spent about one-third of their income on food, the dietary cost would be multiplied by 3 to determine the poverty-line income. Dietary cost estimates were obtained from the Department of Agriculture. One estimate provided for a low-cost budget and permitted a minimum diet consistent with (1) the food preferences of low-income families, and (2) the basic nutritional requirements needed to avoid health problems. This low-cost budget amounted to 28 cents per person per meal, or $3.36 per family per day. Multiplying $3.36 by the number of days in a year, and then by the factor of 3 gives a poverty line of $3955.

However, welfare agencies were not allowing amounts even close to $3955 for families of four on public assistance. So the agriculturalists were called upon to produce another food budget. This one was referred to as an economy budget, and as stated earlier, was based on a diet for temporary or emergency use only. This diet cost 23 cents per person per meal, which resulted in a poverty line of $3165. This was the basis for the Council's $3000 figure, and the basic method for computation has not changed as yet. According to the $3000 line, 20 percent of the people in the U.S. were in poverty in 1962.

Obviously the $3000 figure was criticized, and most of the criticism came from officials who believed the line was too high! To be sure, they raised some reasonable points, most of which were discussed in the preceding section on current versus permanent income. That is, farm families have income in kind, and smaller families need less than $3000. Also real income is received by homeowners in the form of imputed rents and possibly home-grown vegetables. And some families could live off savings or even borrow. Interestingly, the Social Security Administration accounted for most of the criticisms (exceptions were income in kind, savings, and possible borrowings), and the same percentage (20 percent) of the nation's population was still designated as poverty stricken. Only the composition of poverty changed from making the adjustments.

There is a rather strong case for arguing that the Social Security Administration and Council grossly understated the true poverty line in this country. First, the dietary costs assumed that food was purchased and prepared in a most efficient and skillful way, which is realistically too much to ask of poor families. Second, many poverty families remain poverty stricken for more than a temporary period, so that emergency diets would lead to severe health problems. Given our first point, this only strengthens the argument that the economy budget of 23 cents per person per meal is an absurdity. At the very least, the low-cost budget should have been allowed, which would place the poverty line at close to $4000. Third, the multiplier of 3 was derived from a 1955 study, whereas a 1961 study showed that low-income families spent only one-fourth of their income on food. Thus, to allow a purchase of nonfood items consistent with the consumption patterns of low-income families, the poverty line should really be about $\frac{4}{3}(3955) = \$5272$. This figure might be reduced to account for income in kind and savings, so that a reasonable estimate of the poverty line would probably be around $5000 for 1962.

II. THE NATURE OF URBAN POVERTY

Poverty Trends in the U.S.

Notwithstanding our criticisms of the official poverty-line calculation and the implicit criticisms one could make from the first section of this chapter, it will be useful to see how well the country has fared in its war on official poverty. Table 9-1 shows information for selected years on the official poverty line, the number below the line, and the racial composition of those in poverty. The poverty-line data are adjusted upward every year for increases in overall consumer prices. The data show that the war was being won from 1959 through 1969, but afterward a turnaround occurred. To be sure, we do not know how far below the poverty line these families are. Every indication is that through the end of 1972 the new trend of increasing numbers in poverty has continued. Table 9-1 also makes it rather clear that nationwide, blacks have a disproportionate share of their population in poverty.

When one considers metropolitan areas (see Table 9-2), the picture is about the same as far as the 1969 reversal goes. As in the nation, only 9.5 percent of the total metropolitan population was poverty stricken in 1969. But by 1970, 10.2 percent of the metropolitan population fell below the poverty line, while only 9.9 percent of the national population was in poverty (see Table 9-1). Clearly metropolitan areas have borne a disproportionate share of the increased poverty since 1969. As

TABLE 9–1

Poverty Trends in the U.S., 1959–1970[a]

	1959	1964	1968	1969	1970
Poverty line (dollars)	2,973	3,169	3,553	3,743	3,968
Number of persons below line (thousands)	39,490	36,055	25,389	24,289	25,522
Percent of population	22.4	19.0	12.8	12.2	12.6
Number of whites below line	28,484	24,957	17,395	16,668	17,484
Percent of white population	18.1	14.2	10.0	9.5	9.9
Number of blacks below line	10,475	11,098[b]	7,617	7,214	7,644
Percent of black population	55.1	49.6[b]	34.7	32.3	33.6

[a] U.S. Bureau of Census, Current Population Reports, *Characteristics of Low Income Population*, Series P-60, No. 81, November, 1971.

[b] Includes all nonwhites.

TABLE 9–2

Poverty in Metropolitan Areas, 1969 and 1970[a]

	1969	%	1970	%
Total below poverty line (thousands)	12,320	9.5	13,378	10.2
White	8,200	7.3	9,017	8.0
Black	3,855	24.4	4,129	25.9
Total in central cities	7,760	13.4	8,165	14.3
White	4,527	10.2	4,770	10.8
Black	3,068	24.7	3,228	26.2
Total outside central cities	4,560	6.3	5,213	7.1
White	3,674	6.4	4,247	6.1
Black	786	23.2	901	25.0

[a] U.S. Bureau of Census, Current Population Reports, *Characteristics of Low Income Population*, Series P-60, No. 81, November, 1971.

might be expected, the incidence of poverty is far greater in central cities than it is in the suburbs for all persons. But this finding does not hold for blacks. Whether blacks live in the central city or the suburbs, about the same share (25 percent) are in poverty. Other things being equal, this means that the suburbanization of blacks may have little effect on their income. This finding is quite surprising and will receive more detailed analysis later in this chapter.

Before going on to discuss the characteristics of the "official" urban poor, it may be interesting to stop and consider the nature of the problem if alternative estimates of the poverty line were used. The 1970 estimates of the official poverty line shown in Tables 9-1 and 9-2 are based on a somewhat revised formulation. The major revisions are the accounting for changes in overall consumer prices by means of the consumer price index (CPI), and a readjustment of the farm poverty line in relation to the nonfarm line. These revisions caused a slight increase in the number of persons in poverty. One more point of information about the revised poverty-line income data is that they *include* dividends, interest, social security payments, public assistance, welfare payments, unemployment compensation, public and private pensions, and other income. On the other hand, the revised income data exclude income paid in kind and the net rental value of owner-occupied homes, which jointly account for about 4 percent of personal income. In addition, the revised poverty line excludes the borrowing capacity of individuals. Overall, then, the revised data are undoubtedly superior to the old data.

But as we argued earlier, the official poverty line calculation grossly understates the true poverty line because low-income persons cannot be expected to live on temporary diets indefinitely. As an alternative estimate of the incidence of poverty, we have set our $5000 calculation described earlier as the adjusted official poverty line for 1963, and computed the other years by adjusting the $5000 base for changes in the CPI. These results are shown in Table 9-3. This adjusted poverty line, based on a minimal but nutritionally adequate diet and consistent with the nonfood purchasing habits of low-income families, shows that the incidence of poverty is about twice what the government purports it to be. In 1970, the data show that over one-quarter of the families were in poverty, based on their current incomes. How can this share of the population survive on such meager levels of current income? By borrowing. Clearly those persons near the "true" poverty line of $6340 could command a much greater level of current consumption than $6340. However, as we move downward, lower-income families have difficulty borrowing; thus the real poor are relatively very poor. This borrowing hypothesis, if in fact true, in a sense says that the adjusted poverty line in Table 9-3 overstates the actual poverty line. From a policy standpoint, it also tells us that if private credit tightens up for long periods, the incidence of poverty may drastically increase.

One other measure of poverty shown in Table 9-3 is a simple but useful definition based on the income distribution. Since poverty is possibly as much a problem of being at the lower end of a broad income

TABLE 9-3

Alternative Poverty Line Estimates for the U.S. (1970 dollars)

Year	(1) Official poverty line	(2) Percent of families below	(3) Adjusted official poverty line	(4) Percent of families below	(5) Median family income	(6) Percent of families below one-half median
1959	2,973	20.8	4,755	41.9	6,808[b]	19.9
1964	3,169	17.4	5,065	35.2	7,758[b]	18.8
1968	3,553	11.3	5,680	27.3	9,102[b]	18.3
1969	3,743	10.5	5,985	24.8	9,433[b]	18.5
1970	3,968	12.6	6,340	26.1	9,867	18.9

[a] U.S. Bureau of Census, Current Population Surveys, 1968–1970.
[b] 1969 dollars.

distribution as it is an inability to have command over various bundles of goods and services, it would seem reasonable to define poverty as some fraction of the median family income. Victor Fuchs [2] has argued that a reasonable estimate of the extent of poverty would be all those families below one-half the median. Although Fuchs makes no special claims that the fraction one-half is the proper one, his measure is inviting for many reasons.

First, the median family income level rises over time, just as standards of living rise. Moreover, as standards of living increase, consumption patterns change, and the Fuchs measure accounts for these changes each year automatically. Our official index, on the other hand, is restricted to food expenditures as its base, and to a multiplier of 3 or 4 (unless we determine that the food share of low-income family budgets has changed). Second, the Fuchs measure emphasizes the distributional aspects of poverty, which we argued were very important in our discussion on the concept of poverty. If people's incomes are within striking distance of the average they may not feel poor, other things being equal. But anyone whose income is only a small fraction of the average will have a heavy burden to carry, and the chances are that this burden will increase as the fraction becomes smaller. Finally, the Fuchs approach provides a realistic basis for measuring the success or failure of our antipoverty programs. Interestingly, the data in Table 9-3 show that with the Fuchs measure of poverty as a guide, we have not made any appreciable gains in solving the poverty problem. Poverty programs are potentially most productive if they deal with those families at the lowest end of the income scale. Barring statistical anomalies, the data in columns (4) and (6) of Table 9-3 are rather strong evidence that our antipoverty programs have been too small and weak. The student should note that it is entirely possible to have zero percent of the population below half the median, so we have not discussed an unattainable goal with the Fuchs approach.

Characteristics of the Urban Poor

Now that we have an idea of the incidence of poverty both nationally and in metropolitan areas, it may be useful to learn about the characteristics of the urban poor. Some of these points will no doubt be informative, since they do not square with the general opinions usually attributed to society.

First, in addition to the numerical incidence of poverty being greater among blacks, the extent of poverty as measured by income per family member is also greater among blacks. As Table 9-4 shows, in both the

TABLE 9–4

Income per Family Member and Size of Families below the Poverty Line, 1969[a]

	All races		Black		White	
	Persons per family	Income per family member ($)	Persons per family	Income per family member ($)	Persons per family	Income per family member ($)
U.S.	3.9	548	4.8	505	3.6	568
Metropolitan areas[b]	3.9	573	4.6	548	3.6	588
Central cities	4.0	584	4.5	552	3.6	613
Outside central cities	3.8	555	5.1	533	3.5	560
Outside metropolitan areas	4.0	523	5.0	458	3.6	551

[a] Bureau of Census, "The Social and Economic Status of Negroes in the United States," p. 40, 1970.

[b] As defined in 1960 census.

central city and suburb, poverty-stricken blacks had lower incomes per family member than whites in 1969. Part of this problem may be attributed to blacks having larger families than whites, other things being equal. But other things may not be equal. For example, if blacks had smaller families, they might not participate in the labor force as much or work as many hours; thus their incomes could fall by more than the assumed decrease in family size.

Second, unemployment rates in urban poverty areas are higher than the surrounding nonpoverty areas as well as the nation. Using data from a survey of the poorest one-fifth of the nation's 100 largest metropolitan areas in 1967, Ryscavage and Willacy [3] reported that the unemployment rate in these poverty areas was 6.8 percent, while the national rate was 3.8 percent, and the rate in the surrounding urban area was 3.4 percent. This result is not unexpected. The breakdown of unemployment between blacks and whites showed that within urban poverty areas, whites had an unemployment rate of 5.3 percent, while the black rate was 8.9 percent. Outside these poverty areas, however, the black unemployment rate was almost double that of whites (6.1 versus 3.2 percent), while nationally the black rate (7.4 percent) was more than twice that of whites (3.4 percent). The heaviest burden of the incidence of unemployment fell on young workers. In fact, both men and women between the ages of 16 and 24 were the only age groups to have an unemployment rate above the average of the urban poverty area. Teen-agers had an average jobless rate of 23.5 percent.

A third characteristic of the urban poor is that, contrary to popular opinion, nearly all of those capable of seeking work do so. The Ryscav-age and Willacy data show that the labor-force participation rate, de-fined as the percentage of the civilian population either working or seeking work (that is, in the labor force), was 57.3 percent in urban poverty neighborhoods and 60.4 percent in the nonpoverty urban neigh-borhoods. The 3.1 percent differential is almost entirely accounted for by the greater incidence of disabilities in the poverty areas. Nonwhite men and women had higher labor-force participation rates than white men and women respectively in urban poverty neighborhoods. Interest-ingly, nonwhite labor-force participation rates were also higher than white rates in the nonpoverty neighborhoods of urban areas for both sexes.

When we turn to those persons in urban poverty areas who are not in the labor force, we find that a disproportionately large share of these people would like to work when compared to the preferences of those outside the labor force who do not live in urban poverty areas. In a study of six major cities during 1968–1969, nonparticipants living in pov-erty areas cited health as a major factor for not being in the labor force [4]. Family responsibilities were not a significant deterrent from entering the labor force. Neither of these reasons was important in a nationwide sample of nonparticipants. This study also found that 28 percent of the nonparticipants expressed a desire to work, while less than 10 percent nationwide expressed a desire to work. Of the 72 percent in the poverty areas who did not desire to work, their reasons (health, disability, in school or training program, family responsibilities) in gen-eral precluded their entrance into labor markets. As we might guess from the evidence on labor-force participation rates cited above, more black nonparticipants (in terms of percentage) desired to work than whites.

A fourth characteristic of the urban poor is that the *majority* of poverty families and unrelated individuals do not receive public assistance. Not only are poverty-stricken families alleged to be lazy, but it is often cited that too many are on welfare rolls. The evidence does not bear this out. In 1969, only 45 percent of black poverty families and 21 percent of white poverty families received public assistance [5]. The percentages are lower for unrelated individuals. In general then, the urban poor are not people who refuse to work so they can collect welfare checks. Instead, they participate where possible, at par with the nonpoor. A major difference between the poor and nonpoor shown by the evidence presented thus far is that the urban poor do not fare as well in the labor force; that is, they have higher unemployment rates.

A fifth characteristic of the urban poor is the relatively low-paying jobs held when compared to nonpoverty urban areas. Ryscavage and Willacy found that 57 percent of the urban poor were employed in semiskilled, unskilled, and service occupations during 1967; only 30 percent held white-collar jobs. In nonpoverty areas, over half held white-collar jobs and less than one-third were in semiskilled, unskilled, and service jobs. Thus, not only is poverty associated with relatively high unemployment rates, but those who do find work are employed mainly in low-paying, undesirable occupations.

A sixth characteristic of the urban poor is that the households are increasingly being headed by females. This is significant because females not only have family responsibilities but also earn lower wages than males. The decreasing absolute number of persons under the poverty line through 1969 reported in Table 9-2 was primarily made up of male-headed households. In 1970, persons in female-headed households represented 7046 of the 13,378 persons under the poverty line in our metropolitan areas. Nearly one-third of all white female-headed households in metropolitan areas were under the poverty line, while for blacks the figure stood at 52.7 percent. Male-headed households, on the other hand, had an incidence of poverty of only 5.7 percent. Given the higher incidence of poverty among the aged and disabled, these data on female-headed houses reflect a situation in which it may be very difficult for any but a small share of the poverty families to work their way out of poverty.

A seventh characteristic of the urban poor is the high incidence of poverty among children. In 1968, over 42 percent of the official urban poor were children under 18 years of age. Nearly two-thirds of these children lived in central cities. And at least one-half of these poor children lived in households that are not likely to become economically self-sustaining. The long-range implications of these data are clear and, unfortunately, not pleasant.

Consequences of Urban Poverty

Thus far we have discussed the concept and incidence of poverty, and the characteristics of the poor. The adverse labor-market experiences encountered by many of the poor result in low absolute and relative income and lead to many problems in both the short and the long run. Many of these problems are inherent in having low income, but others are not. Our purpose here is to point out some of the problems faced by the urban poor because they are poor.

The residential location of the urban poor is more or less fixed, especially if they are black. We have already seen in the chapters on housing and transportation that it is difficult for those living in ghetto areas to obtain housing in nonghetto areas. Given that one is poor and black, the chances of successfully owning one's own home are slim. Poor people are bad credit risks, and the private sector will not readily loan money for home purchases. The upshot of this situation is that poor people cannot avail themselves of (among other things) the tax breaks that go to homeowners in our present federal tax structure. Thus poor people pay relatively high prices for housing to the extent that they would prefer to own their own homes but cannot.

Even in rental markets, poor families get lower-quality housing than higher-income families for equivalent rents. In a government survey of the Houston area during the early 1960's, almost 80 percent of the $40–60 per month rentals occupied by low-income families were very run down, while only 21 percent of the apartments in the same price range occupied by families with incomes from $3000–6000 were run down [6]. The findings were similar in Atlanta.

The entrapment of poor families in slum areas in the short run means not only that they pay higher real housing costs but that their food bills are higher than those of persons living in nonslum areas. In a 1966 survey of food prices in six major metropolitan areas, the Federal Government found that prices were associated with store size, rather than geographical area per se [6]. But since small stores charge higher prices and are more prevalent in poor areas, poverty-stricken families end up paying higher food prices. Moreover, produce was found to be relatively stale in poor areas, and stores were generally less clean. Some argue that since poor people buy their foodstuffs in small quantities, this pattern is what they prefer, and therefore there really is no price discrimination against the poor. But because people are poor and may not know when their next dollar is coming in, they are more or less forced to buy in small quantities and live on a day-to-day basis. I am sure most of the poor would prefer to be able to buy larger quantities and plan ahead—if they had the financial means to do so.

A further consequence of being locked into living in a low-income area is that one's children consume a lower-quality education. Poor families cannot "vote with their feet"; that is, they cannot shop around and live in that school district which is consistent with their tastes.

Thus they are denied the freedom of choice that adversaries of the Metro form of government emphasize so strongly. Moreover, the traditional method of financing public education (property taxes plus state grants) almost ensures a higher-quality education for children from higher-income families. Because people are poor, they receive a relatively poor education.

Finally, another short-run consequence of being poor is the difficulty one has in obtaining credit for consumer durables and services. For those lucky enough to receive substantial welfare aid, of course, this problem is less severe. The tragic aspect of the credit rating system used in this country in relation to the poor is that once a person is tagged as a bad risk, it is difficult to remove this tag. Thus the poverty family trying to pull itself up by its bootstraps has taller hurdles to jump, merely because of poverty in the past.

In the long run, poverty families that remain poverty stricken accumulate all of the negative characteristics and consequences discussed thus far. Without doubt, poverty is a viscious circle. Poor labor-market experiences, low levels of education, and higher real living costs merely serve to deepen one's descent into poverty. And poverty itself feeds back on one's job experiences, education, and living costs in a negative way that strengthens the circle. From a humanitarian standpoint, this is tragic. From an economic standpoint, the viscious circle of poverty means a clear loss of potential output each year and a lifelong burden for many existing and future families.

III. THE CAUSES OF POVERTY

Poverty is caused by many factors, but in general we may categorize these factors as either personal or social. Some people are temporarily or permanently disabled, either physically or psychically (or both), and as a result are unable to compete successfully in labor markets. Others are physically and psychically able to compete, but their skills and capabilities are outmoded or more generally not needed. Technological changes in the economic system have automated many persons out of jobs and into the ranks of the poor, especially the aged. Short-term downturns in the aggregate economy are also felt severely by low-income persons. Witness the increase in poverty in the U.S. since 1969. Thus having the requisite personal characteristics to compete successfully in labor markets is a necessary but not sufficient condition to alleviate a poverty situation. Alternatively, if one does not have the personal characteristics usually associated with the successful job holder, history tells us that this does not preclude such an individual from earning a decent wage. When aggregate demand is increasing quickly in all cities, even the poor have a chance to earn a wage above the subsistence level.

Economists have identified a number of factors that cause urban poverty; among the more important of these are: (1) whether people are willing to participate in labor markets, (2) education, (3) discrimination, (4) inmigration, and (5) the aggregate demand for labor. Let us consider each of these factors briefly, and then we can go into a more detailed discussion of the determinants of each factor and its relationship to urban poverty. People cannot get a job and keep working unless they are willing to enter and stay in the labor force. So labor-force participation is a key to understanding the level of poverty. Educational attainment and achievement is considered to be a major determinant of one's occupation and thus the wage rate he earns. Given the labor-force participation rate (LFPR) and levels of education in a city, it does not follow that wages for a given type of work will be equalized, because labor-market imperfections exist. One of these imperfections—discrimination—hampers the labor-market performance of many workers among the urban poor. Of course, increased levels of inmigration on the part of low-income workers would result in lower wage rates for the poor, other things being equal. And as we noted above, overall economic activity levels are proportionately related to the demand for labor, so that aggregate fluctuations certainly affect the income of the poor.

All of these causal factors—LFPR, education, discrimination, inmigration, and the aggregate demand for labor—simultaneously affect the level of poverty in urban areas. Moreover, the incidence of poverty will affect each of these causal factors over time. For example, the accumulation of poverty in a given family may lead to such discouragement that no member seeks employment. And as we have noted in previous sections of this chapter, being from a low-income family or area can determine the type of education and thus job and wage that one gets. As Figure 9.2 illustrates, the causal factors of poverty are simultaneously the consequences of poverty over the long run. Poverty is a viscious circle that feeds upon itself. This is a useful fact to keep in mind when we consider policies to combat poverty.

Labor-Force Participation Rates

Poor people are said to be lazy, and unwilling to work or search for work. The facts, of course, are exactly the opposite. The urban poor, and especially the black poor, have LFPR's comparable to or higher

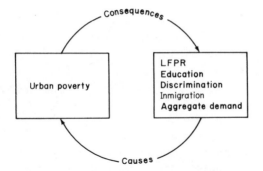

Figure 9.2 *The viscious circle of poverty.*

than those of nonpoor whites. Nevertheless, we do have many poor who do not participate in the labor force. Why is this so?

As with poverty itself, the determinants of the LFPR in urban areas may be categorized as personal factors and economy-wide factors. Many of the poor choose to stay out of the labor force for reasons of age, health, family responsibilities, or previous (negative) labor-market experiences. These personal factors explain the majority of those unwilling or unable to participate. The remainder of nonparticipants are motivated basically by economic conditions beyond their control; that is, aggregate demand.

The reaction of potential participants to changes in aggregate economic activity levels can be illustrated by relating unemployment rates in a given city to the LFPR in that city. Unemployment rates u, of course, are inversely related to economic activity levels. The relationship between LFPR and u may be either positive or negative. As u increases, people may be discouraged and drop out of the labor force. This relationship is illustrated by DW in Figure 9.3, and is called the discouraged-worker effect. On the other hand, as u increases the head of a poverty

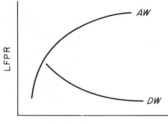

Figure 9.3 *Additional- and discouraged-worker hypotheses.*

family may be laid off or have his/her working time curtailed, thus causing additional family members to enter the labor force and seek work. A positive relationship between LFPR and u is termed the additional-worker effect (AW in Figure 9.3).

It is very important to know whether or not poor persons (families) react as discouraged or additional workers. Why? Because unless the discouraged-worker hypothesis is borne out, policy designed to lower unemployment levels (of the poor) will do little good to the extent that the poor are not participating in the labor force. That is, if the additional-worker hypothesis holds, increases in aggregate demand (lowering of u) will lead to lower LFPR's, as shown in Figure 9.3. And lower LFPR's will not help in the battle against poverty.

The additional- and discouraged-worker hypotheses reflect a more basic factor behind the decision to enter or leave the labor force—expected earnings. In many cities low-wage jobs are often readily available to the poor, but the wage rates are not attractive if they do not exceed one's price of leisure. Similarly, those already in the labor force and working must earn a wage rate greater than their price of leisure if society expects them to remain on the job and/or in the labor force. So beyond the personal reasons for the LFPR's among the poverty stricken, the economic arguments at the individual level involve explaining one's reaction to his expectations of success in labor markets. The decision is not just whether one should enter or leave the labor force, but whether he will earn more real income by not being in the labor force.

Empirical Studies of LFPR's

Most of the empirical studies of LFPR's among the urban poor are tests of the general hypotheses stated above; that is, LFPR's are generally determined by economic conditions and poverty family characteristics. The major study done on LFPR's among the urban poor was by Joseph Mooney [7]. Using a sample of poverty areas in 52 SMSA's, Mooney related unemployment to LFPR's for white and nonwhite males and females. The data were taken from the 1960 census. For males, the LFPR was not particularly sensitive to unemployment, but Mooney did find an inverse relationship, indicating that the discouraged-worker hypothesis may hold. White females' LFPR's were not significantly related to unemployment. Nonwhite females, on the other hand, reacted strongly to variations in unemployment rates, and the relationships bears out the discouraged-worker hypothesis. This finding was even stronger for nonwhite females who have a husband present. To test further the reaction of females to changes in economic conditions, Mooney added a variable that measured the demand for female labor in each SMSA to his model. He found that as the demand for female labor in the SMSA increased, nonwhite women responded (positively) but white women did not respond.

Of course there are many personal factors besides sex and color that can affect LFPR's. Age, educational level, and the age of one's children could be important. Larry Sawers [8] accounted for these factors with the Mooney sample data and found no significant change in Mooney's results.

We might conclude, then, that society has a far better chance of getting nonwhite females into the labor force through economic-activity policies than it does of getting white females or males to participate.

Education

Education enhances one's thinking ability and overall human performance; thus, other things being equal, increasing doses of education for most people will raise their wages. The increase in wages results from an increase in demand; firms will pay higher wages for more productive workers. In addition to formal education, training and experience also enhance one's productivity, and more of these two factors of course yields higher wages for an individual. Our arguments here rely on standard economic theory, which assumes away any discrimination in labor or educational markets.

Since education and training enhance one's earning ability, they help build what economists call human capital. Human capital is the knowledge and skills embodied in a person that can be used to earn income. Thus education is an investment in oneself, and as such it has a rate of return. To determine whether any given person should invest in further training or education, one must compare the discounted costs of the additional education to the discounted expected returns. If the latter exceeds the former, one should go ahead and invest. Although it may be true that through further education poverty-stricken persons could earn higher wages, this does not mean that they will invest. Why? Because most poverty families have relatively high discount rates; that is, they have a strong preference for a dollar now rather than a dollar plus interest in the future. The higher the discount rate, the lower the net return on education. One of the fundamental reasons for poor people having high discount rates is their low-income position. That is, poor people need all of their current income just to subsist. And poor people have difficulty borrowing to further their education. High discount rates and credit restrictions preclude their "rational choice" of more education and higher income levels, demonstrating again that poverty is truly a viscious circle.

Trends and Empirical Studies in Education

From an empirical standpoint there are two questions of extreme importance that must be answered in regard to the impact of education on poverty. First, are people in the poverty areas of our cities obtaining more education? And second, for those who are getting more education or training, is it paying off? If these two questions can be answered affirmatively, then from an educational standpoint, the viscious circle of poverty may have a weak link.

Table 9-5 shows data on educational attainment for persons at or below the poverty line and the average U.S. citizen. It is clear that the gap between these two groups is being closed. Recently released data [9] from ten ghettos of major metropolitan areas show that as of 1966, most whites *and* blacks are completing 12 years of school, which compares well with nonghetto areas. In some of the ghettos, blacks completed more years of schooling on the average than whites. In addition, the success rate of ghetto blacks and whites in training programs was about the same. This evidence seems to show that poor people are becoming more educated, and they are closing the educational gap. Contrary to some popular beliefs, poor blacks are more or less on par with poor whites in terms of buying education.

So the basic question now is: Does it pay for the poor to buy more education? The evidence is not favorable, especially for nonwhites. For example, using 1966 data on poverty areas in 12 major SMSA's, B. Har-

TABLE 9-5

Median Years of Educational Attainment for Poverty Persons[a]

	1970[b]		1969[c]	
	Poverty	Nonpoverty	Poverty	Nonpoverty
All persons	9.2	12.1	8.8	12.2
White	9.3	12.2	8.9	12.3
Black	8.8	10.4	8.2	9.9

[a] U.S. Bureau of Census, Current Population Reports, *Characteristics of Low Income Population*, Series P-60, No. 81, November 1970.

[b] Persons 14 years and older

[c] Family heads 25 years and older

rison found that a high-school education adds an average of $25 per week to the income of whites, but only $8.33 per week to the income of nonwhites [9]. Given a 40-year work life and a 6 percent discount rate for both whites and nonwhites, Harrison found that the discounted present value of returns from a high-school education are $19,000 for whites and $6000 for nonwhites. Since nonwhites could probably earn more than $6000 during their high-school years, their opportunity cost exceeds the direct discounted benefits of attending high school. So unless high school is a step to further education, it is not clear that completing high school is rational on purely economic grounds. These rather dismal results for ghetto nonwhites also apply to the nonwhite population in the nonghetto areas of the same SMSA's. Seemingly, the assumption of no discrimination made earlier when describing the effect of education on earnings does not hold for nonwhites in our major metropolitan areas.

Although further education for urban nonwhites may have a low payoff, it is important that further education does lead to a higher probability of obtaining a job. This hypothesis was also tested by Harrison. He found that while the risk of unemployment decreased when whites obtained another year of high-school education, this risk did not fall for nonwhites. Increases in education had no impact on the unemployment rate of nonwhites, holding age, sex, training, and other characteristics of the worker constant. So education not only fails nonwhites in terms of leading to significantly higher wages, but it does not even help much in their getting a job.

The implications of the Harrison study for policy are that education alone will not solve the urban poverty problem for black ghetto residents. This finding is corroborated for the nation as a whole by Weiss [10], who found that except for 36–45-year-old males, black educational attainment *or* achievement had no significant relationship to black earnings. Under present conditions, then, if our policy is to increase education for all, the clear result will be a greater degree of income inequality in this nation. In ghetto labor markets, policy must direct its focus to the imperfections in labor markets. The Harrison and Weiss findings are rather strong evidence that racial discrimination is the real hurdle, rather than education, in solving the urban poverty problem for nonwhites. Education does seem to help, however, if one is white.

Two remaining matters related to whether it pays to further one's education are (1) the efficacy of further education for low achievers and (2) the impact on the rest of the family of obtaining more education. If we were able to eradicate discrimination in labor markets, could low achievers be expected to take on additional schooling to solve their poverty problem? This question is especially interesting, given our discussion on the education and labor-market problems of nonwhites. Hansen and co-workers addressed this issue by testing a national sample of 2400 persons who failed the Air Force qualification test in 1963 [11]. When factors such as school achievement, training, race, and marital status were included along with years of schooling, the latter had no significant impact on one's earnings. The authors also found that the rate of return of low achievers for another year of schooling was below the rate of return for average students. Clearly, regardless of one's race, the further education of low achievers in school may make little economic sense.

Thus far we have focused on individuals, but we know most individuals are members of families. For individuals, we have found that high discount rates, racial discrimination, and achievement records are significant factors in explaining whether or not further education pays. But when one considers the total family, the further education of individual members is a burden, especially for nonwhites. For example, children aged 14–19 brought in 12.3 percent of family income in 1960 [12] nationally for all races, but for nonwhites the fraction was 20.5 percent. In the South, nonwhite children earn 26.6 percent of their family income. In such families, the burden for the rest of the family becomes larger the longer the child stays in school. No doubt some family members express this to the child, which may have an adverse effect on his school work. The educational policy for low-income areas then, given the discount rate, labor market imperfections, and achievement level of the student, cannot be a policy of providing better teachers and more educational machinery alone. Income subsidies to families may also be needed to keep youngsters in school. This is especially important for low-income families with children who are average or above average achievers.

Discrimination

Discrimination can occur in many markets (labor, education, housing) and on many grounds (race, sex, religion, ethnic origin). Discrimination is said to occur in any of these markets when race, sex, and so on are significant factors in explaining the opportunities open to any individual in these markets. Keep in mind that discrimination is not a one-shot affair. The ramifications of discrimination today against an individual may be felt throughout that person's lifetime. This is important, because if we could wave a magic wand and do away with discrimination in all forms, those discriminated against in the past would still bear relative burdens for the remainder of their lives. Payment of reparations to blacks, for example, is not an illogical demand of black activists, but in fact from an equity standpoint does have a sound economic basis.* Since our focus here is on the determinants of poverty, we shall deal primarily with discrimination in labor and education markets. This is not to suggest that discrimination in housing markets has no impact on the income positions of blacks and others. To the contrary, we argued in Chapter 6 that because of race and the tax structure, the urban poor and blacks have a lower real income because they pay higher prices to own their own homes.

In labor markets, one can be discriminated against during the job search, at the time of job entry, or while on the job. Poor people have to rely on friends, relatives, or existing institutional information about job opportunities, whereas higher-income persons can buy such information from professional agencies. Thus, because of their income positions, poor people have fewer informational sources for prospective jobs. At the job portal, low-income persons, black persons, and females are often placed in secondary jobs that promise little chance for further training or advancement regardless of their educational levels [14]. Orderlies and nurses' aides in hospitals are typical examples. One's address and personal appearance can be major factors in determining where he is placed in a firm.

On the job, discrimination often occurs in the form of equally productive workers receiving different wages. For example, blacks with equal capacity on a given job may be paid lower wages than whites. Alternatively, the same result occurs if the black is more capable than the white but both are earning the same wage. Another form of wage discrimination occurs when white employers have a preference for white workers (and an aversion to nonwhite workers), and the employer hires equally capable nonwhite workers only at lower wages than he pays whites. Of course racial wage discrimination on a given job can occur even when equally capable whites and blacks earn the same wage rates, since nonwage benefits may vary among the races.

Turning to education markets, we have already presented some strong evidence in this chapter that education is not the panacea for poverty reduction that some would have us believe. In addition, educational facilities are not equally available to all in the metropolitan areas of this country. Because of the primary method of school financing (property taxes plus state funds), in many metropolitan areas children attending school in the wealthier suburbs have more educational resources

* For an interesting discussion of this issue, see Robert S. Browne [13]. "The Economic Case for Reparations to Black America," *American Economic Review, Papers and Proceedings* 62 (1972): 39–46.

available. Children of low-income families often receive inferior education because their parents are poor. This is a sad state of affairs. Although the busing of children across school districts may be significant to many parents on racial and safety grounds, from society's standpoint busing is one way of offering a more equal level of educational resources across income classes. This is not to say, however, that busing is the cheapest way to equalize the distribution of educational resources in a metropolitan area.

Evidence of Discrimination

Economists have traditionally found that discrimination occurs in skilled occupations such as construction trades. Recent information, however, suggests that low-income blacks and others have not been spared the problem of discrimination even in semiskilled or highly skilled jobs in the central city. For example, in the Harrison study, an upper limit on wages was found in all ten urban ghettos considered, regardless of one's educational level. The range of the upper limit was from $1.56 per hour in San Antonio's Chicano barrios to $2.04 per hour in the Bedford–Stuyvesant section of New York City. Interestingly, Peter Doeringer found a similar wage ceiling for the poverty area of Boston [15]. The existence of a wage ceiling in spite of increasing educational attainment is clear evidence of wage discrimination. At the very least, the people on the receiving end of this type of discrimination are being held down into secondary or dead-end positions.

One of the low-paying occupations traditionally manned by blacks is that of janitor. In a recent study of the racial wage difference between white and nonwhite janitors in the Chicago labor market, David Taylor found that white janitors earned a slightly higher wage [16]. Taylor also found that white materials handlers earned more than nonwhite materials handlers. The racial differential of materials handlers (an unskilled job) was much greater than the differential for janitors. Taylor argued that the larger differential occurred in materials handling because it is a job with advancement potential, whereas the janitor's job is a dead-end position.

Turning to a consideration of skilled jobs, until very recently construction trades (electricians, plumbers, bricklayers, carpenters, hodcarriers, and so on) could choose who they wanted to enter the lengthy apprenticeship programs required for a person to become a full fledged member of the unions. Nepotism was always a major factor in deciding the chosen few, and very few blacks were ever chosen. Recently the U.S. Department of Labor began an antidiscrimination campaign in the construction trade sector of some of our major cities. Quotas for minorities are set up for each job, and contractors are supposed to meet their quotas. Although the minority-group person must usually start as an apprentice, he now has that opportunity on a limited basis, which is better than the previous arrangement.

It is not clear, however, that the poor from minority groups would be making a rational choice to enter long apprenticeship programs [17, 18]. To date, evidence shows that minorities enter apprenticeships at an older age, and they also have lower life expectancies. When this information is coupled with their high rates of time preference, the discounted present value of expected earnings is not as great as it would be for the average white worker. Many economists have argued that apprenticeship programs are lengthened, not for training purposes, but to restrict the supply of labor and thus keep wages of the journeyman higher. If this is true, then the Department of Labor program may not be a complete success because of the relatively heavy burden the poor pay during the apprenticeship stage.

Other Causes of Urban Poverty

The two remaining causal factors of urban poverty outlined above are inmigration and the aggregate demand of the economy. We have already discussed inmigration in Chapter 3. We noted certain push and pull factors that determine migratory flows. Traditionally, poor economic conditions have pushed people from rural areas into cities, while better economic conditions in the cities simultaneously pulled people from the farms. For nonwhites, 2.1 of the 5.1 million increase in metropolitan population between 1960 and 1970 was due to net inmigration. The corresponding figure for whites was 3.2 out of 15 million. Between 1960 and 1970 two of the four major regions of the U.S. (Northeast and West) had a greater amount of nonwhite population growth due to net inmigration than to natural increase. Nonwhite inmigration data for specific cities are found in Table 9-6. The exodus of the poor from the South and abroad is still continuing. And as more nonwhites move into metropolitan areas, to the extent that they are not equipped to successfully compete in urban labor markets the problem of urban poverty will continue.

One might pause and argue that those choosing to migrate into cities are not necessarily poor. However, empirical studies show that as the level of inmigration into the core cities of our metropolitan areas increases, the level of poverty increases.*

---

* For example, see W. S. Kee [19].

TABLE 9–6

Population Change for Nonwhites in Selected Cities 1960–1970[a,b]

	1970 nonwhite population[c]	Change 1960–1970[c]	Net inmigration[c]	Percent of change
New York	1,844	703	436	62.0
Chicago	1,156	322	113	35.1
Detroit	673	185	98	53.0
Philadelphia	670	135	40	29.2
Washington	547	129	38	30.4
Los Angeles	642	225	120	53.3
Baltimore	426	98	32	32.7
Houston	328	111	56	50.4
Cleveland	293	40	−3	—
New Orleans	270	35	−11	—
Atlanta	256	70	33	42.9
St. Louis	257	41	−1	—
Memphis	244	60	23	38.3
Dallas	218	87	47	54.0
Newark	214	75	32	42.6

[a] Cities were selected that had 200,000 or more nonwhites in 1970.

[b] U.S. Bureau of Census, "The Social and Economic Status of the Black Population in the United States, 1971." Current Population Reports, Series P-23, No. 42 (1972): 125.

[c] Thousands of persons.

Turning to aggregate demand as a causal factor of poverty, the idea here is that as aggregate demand increases, unemployment will decrease, thus enhancing the chances of the less skilled to get jobs. This argument is based on the queue theory of labor markets, which argues that workers are ranked by employers according to their potential productivity and expected wage rates. The most productive are selected from the queue for hire first, and the lesser skilled and the poor wait. They continue to wait until total labor demand forces the employer to hire them, and this usually occurs when the overall economy is at or near full capacity.

It may not be efficient to rely on increasing aggregate activity levels to solve urban poverty problems. As employers go to the end of the queue, they are selecting workers who will require training and other special consideration before they become productive. For firms at the margin this special consideration may not be possible. In short, the aggregate-demand argument, like all of the other determinants of poverty, cannot stand alone to solve the urban poverty problem.

IV. URBAN POVERTY POLICY

The traditional policies used to deal with poverty in the cities have differed little from policies used elsewhere—minimum-wage laws, public-assistance programs, and education. Over the past 12 years, however, the public sector has taken a more active role in dealing with the manpower and training aspects of the poor and unskilled. In addition, new experiments have begun in the area of income maintenance. A program to help ghetto businesses has also received some support. Each of these programs, from the traditional through the new experiments, will be described and analyzed in this section.

Traditional Antipoverty Policies

One of the first policies to deal with the income problems of the poor in this country was state minimum-wage laws. Presently, over three-fourths of the states and the Federal Government have minimum-wage laws. Although there are many criteria for choosing the minimum wage level in any given state, certainly one of the factors considered would be whether an average sized family could subsist on the wage. However, even if the minimum wage *is* set at a poverty level, it does not follow that we will solve the problem of poverty. Why? Because in many cases the institution of minimum-wage laws ends up in increasing unemployment.

Consider the unskilled-labor market described in Figure 9.4a. Workers are hired on a competitive basis by a profit-maximizing firm; L_1 amount of labor is hired, and a wage rate of W_1 is paid all workers. At L_1 the additional revenue obtained from hiring another worker is exactly offset by the marginal cost (wage rate) of that worker. Now if a minimum wage is set above W_1 by law, say at W_M, the profit-maximizing

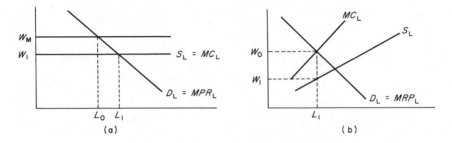

Figure 9.4 (a) *Minimum wages and the competitive firm;* (b) *minimum wages and the noncompetitive firm.*

258   9. *Urban Poverty: Problems and Policies*

employer will lay off L_0L_1 amount of workers. Increased wages through higher minimum-wage laws do not have to result in unemployment, however. In Figure 9.4b, a noncompetitive labor-market situation exists; that is, employers (called monopsonists) do not compete for labor. As a profit-maximizer, the employer hires workers until the additional revenue of the marginal worker (noted *MRP* in the diagram, for marginal revenue product) is exactly offset by the additional cost of that worker. This is at L_1 in Figure 9.4b; but note that now workers are not paid their *MRP*, as they were under competition in Figure 9.4a; workers receive W_1 instead of W_0. In addition, fewer workers are hired under a monopsony labor market. Instead of hiring workers to where $S_L = D_L$, we now find that workers are hired up to where $MC_L = D_L$. If we attach a minimum-wage law above W_1 but below W_0, the profit-maximizing response on the part of the employer would be to increase employment.

Unfortunately, most empirical studies of specific regions and industries show that minimum-wage laws do in fact displace workers; thus the more relevant theory described above is that of competitive labor markets. Thus, although minimum-wage laws have certainly helped many workers, those marginal workers who are the least productive have undoubtedly been severely hurt. Minimum-wage laws, then, are not the answer to hard-core poverty cases.

A second traditional policy designed to alleviate short- or long-term poverty problems is that of public assistance. Table 9-7 shows trends in the various categories of public assistance. Although there have been

TABLE 9–7

Public Assistance Trends in the U.S. ($ millions)[a]

	1960	1965	1968	1970
Total payments	$3,785	$5,476	$9,768	$14,467
Percent federal	51.7	54.0	52.6	51.8
Percent state	36.4	34.1	34.7	—[b]
Percent local	11.9	11.9	12.7	—[b]
Old-age assistance	$1,922	$2,046	$1,778	$ 1,866
Aid to dependent children	1,055	1,809	2,851	4,857
Blind and permanently disabled	381	651	783	1,073
Other (medical and general assistance)	427	970	4,356	6,671

[a] Bureau of Census, *Statistical Abstract of the U.S.*, 1971, p. 291.

[b] Not available.

TABLE 9–8

Monthly Payments of Public Assistance Programs in the U.S. (1970 dollars)

	1960	1965	1968	1970
Old-age assistance	77	79	78	78
Aid to dependent children	140	171	188	187
Blind	90	101	103	104
Disabled	90	86	105	112

sizeable gains in the overall disbursement levels in the past decade, it is interesting to note that the average monthly payments, when measured in constant dollars, have not increased much at all. The monthly data are presented in Table 9-8. Except for the program of aid to families with dependent children, there is very little change in real monthly payments between 1960 and 1970. These data imply that if more and more families and persons are becoming eligible, they are being meagerly assisted. Although public-assistance programs are useful, they are not supposed to be a long-term solution to the poverty problem. However, what about the blind and permanently disabled? Can they be expected to compete successfully in labor markets? Can they be expected to live on a little more than $100 per month? The answer to both of these questions is no.

Although the evidence is not available, it is probably safe to argue that few if any of the public-assistance or welfare programs close the poverty gap for more than a small minority of welfare persons. Yet there is a strong trend now in the nation to minimize these existing programs. This trend is based on the argument that people receiving welfare are lazy and ought to be working. Although this argument may be valid for the 15 percent of those who receive welfare who could enter the labor market, the present system of payments precludes their doing so on rational grounds. For example, if a person is receiving $250 per month welfare for no work, would it pay him to take a job at $2 per hour? Probably not. At $2 per hour his monthly income would be $320 for a 160-hour work month. He would lose his welfare check of course. So the increase in income for working 160 hours is only $70, which is less than 50¢ per hour. Given that most people on welfare cannot earn high wages in labor markets, one can see why some of those receiving welfare assistance are reluctant to enter the work force or hold a job.

The third traditional policy tool employed to help the poor is education. Many have no doubt been helped by the increase in real expenditures over time in this important sector. But nonwhites and the poor in general have not received equal treatment in the larger metropolitan areas. Moreover, whereas education seems to affect the wages of whites significantly, the marginal product of another year of schooling for nonwhites is relatively small and tends toward zero in many of the ghettos of our major cities. For these reasons and the ones cited earlier in this chapter, it is rather clear that education is not a sufficient condition to solve the urban poverty problem, since discrimination in labor markets can completely erode the increase in one's earning power derived from more education. Education is of course a necessary condition for reducing poverty in the long run. We should not let down in this area. To ensure that the fruits of education are consumed, however, we must have greater efforts toward minimizing discrimination in urban labor markets.

Manpower Programs

The basic philosophy of manpower training and planning is to build useful skills and work habits into all human beings, not just school-age children. As we shall see, however, many of the manpower-training programs do in fact deal with young adults who did not successfully (1) complete school or (2) compete in labor markets. Historically, manpower programs began with the inception of the Area Redevelopment Act (ARA) of 1961. This program provided for a small sum to be used for retraining workers in depressed towns to give the workers useful skills. ARA was soon replaced by the Manpower Development Training Act (MDTA) of 1962, which initially was an extension of ARA, but expanded its efforts in retraining both adults and youths. By 1964, the Economic Opportunity Act was passed, which has (through amendments) provided for the basic manpower programs we know today: Jobs Corps, Neighborhood Youths Corps (NYC), Job Opportunities in the Business Sector (JOBS), Work Incentive Program (WIN), and others. Table 9-9 gives data on the size of these programs in recent years. Let us take a look at the nature and purpose of each of these programs, and also consider how well they have fared.

One of the first of the new manpower programs instituted by the U.S. Office of Economic Opportunity was the Job Corps. The Job Corps is an around-the-clock program for disadvantaged youths 16–21 years of age. The program includes basic education, prevocational and vocational training, counseling, physical conditioning, and recreation. The basic assumption of the Jobs Corps is that its enrollees need a change

TABLE 9-9

Enrollments in Federally Assisted Manpower Programs (thousands of persons)[a]

	1968[b]	1969[b]	1970[b]	1971[b]
MDTA	60.4	56.7	53.7	62.4
NYC	189.5	149.1	137.9	144.7
Job Corps	32.5	29.8	20.7	22.1
JOBS	38.9	57.3	87.9	86.3
WIN	—	56.2	84.9	106.2
Others	34.0	84.5	70.6	86.7
Total	355.3	433.6	455.7	508.4

[a] U.S. Department of Labor, "Manpower Report of the President" (1972) p. 57.

[b] As of the end of April.

in their environment plus training to be able to compete successfully in labor markets. Obviously this program is very expensive, which explains the low enrollments shown in Table 9-9. Enrollees are allowed to stay in the program up to two years. Almost all empirical studies of the Job Corps have shown that enrollees do in fact earn higher wages after completing the program. One study used a national sample of former enrollees from urban programs and found that nonwhites were helped considerably more, the longer they were allowed to stay in the program [20]. This finding seems to imply that two years may be too short a period for some persons.

NYC is a program of work and on-the-job training for disadvantaged youths 14–19 years of age. The program is for persons in or out of school. For those out of school, the amount of formal education offered is minimal, while those in school get a chance to earn money and work. The primary goal of NYC is to develop useful work habits. The majority of evaluations of NYC have been favorable. For example, in a cost–benefit analysis of NYC in five urban areas in Indiana, it was found that (1) NYC helps the earning power of males (but not females), (2) high school dropouts (but not high school graduates) benefit greatly from NYC, and (3) the longer a person stays in NYC the greater his earnings afterward [21]. On the average, NYC pays in-school participants about $1200 per year; thus, if the Congress drops NYC, the income of over 100,000 ghetto families will be severely reduced.

By the late 1960's, the private sector entered the manpower-training picture in a major way with the JOBS program. In 1968, offices were opened in the 50 largest cities of the U.S. to persuade local employers to hire the disadvantaged. These offices were run by local business executives who were members of the National Alliance of Businessmen. The Federal Government was prepared to pay the marginal cost of hiring, training, and keeping on the job these disadvantaged workers. Within a year, over 300,000 jobs were pledged by the business sector, but only a very small fraction of these pledges actually resulted in job placements (see Table 9-9). Although most of those helped in JOBS have been black males under 22 years of age with very poor work histories, it is important to point out that the retention rate of workers in the JOBS program is not high [22]. Many businesses have not sought reimbursement from the Federal Government, possibly because they would like to "cop out" of the endeavor cleanly at their chosen time. Unlike the Job Corps and NYC, JOBS has not been an overall success.

The WIN program is for persons 16 years old or older in families that receive payments from the Aid to Families with Dependent Children (AFDC) public-assistance program. WIN enrollees not only receive their welfare payments under AFDC, but they also get training-incentive payments. Local welfare agencies refer enrollees to employment-service offices for placement, training, and other needs of the enrollee. Pay levels are no less than the minimum wage if one is placed on a job. Child day-care, medical, and other social services are provided for the enrollee and his or her family. Thus far, the WIN program has been severely constrained by limited funds for child-care services. Since the majority of AFDC families have female household heads, until the child-care issue can be resolved WIN cannot become a significant tool for reducing urban poverty in the long run.

In the past few years the government has begun new manpower-training programs and dropped old ones. This type of activity is reflective of the experimental stage that manpower programs are still in. Until we get the bugs out, such programs will help only a few of those in poverty. If we have learned anything from the manpower programs of the 1960's, it is that it takes a long time—up to two years and longer—to prepare disadvantaged persons for success in labor markets. I suspect that when we accept this fact, we will model our programs accordingly, and begin to take bigger strides in reducing poverty.

Income-Maintenance Plans

As we attempt to educate, train, or retrain poor people, they remain more or less poor as they go through this human capital-building process in the short run. Those who are untrainable will remain poor in the long run. So regardless of the success rate of our manpower and education programs, we must have some form of income maintenance if we want to reduce the poverty gap to zero.

If one believes that our present antipoverty policies reflect the preferences of society, then society to date has opted not to reduce the poverty gap to zero. However, the welfare-payment increases noted in Table 9-7 are evidence that more money is being spent for public assistance. As we argued earlier, the basic argument against increasing public assistance is that welfare is said to reduce the incentive to work. As our example of a household head getting $250 per month welfare (compared to $320 per month he could earn on a job) showed, this argument is on firm grounds. But the important point here is that our *existing* welfare programs have work disincentives. Welfare programs need not "tax" income earned at 100 percent, as our present programs do. (That is, for every dollar earned on a job, the person loses a dollar of welfare.) If the person in the example did not lose his $250, but could keep, say, two-thirds of it, then his marginal tax rate on earned income would be only 33 percent. He would bring home $320 + 0.67($250) = $490. Under this plan, then, the person would have an incentive to go to work. In general, the lower the marginal tax rate, the greater the incentive to work will be. Of course the lower the marginal tax rate, the greater the cost of welfare or income-maintenance programs.

Economists have devised a number of income-maintenance plans, most dubbed the negative income tax. Most of the plans involve three basic features. First, a minimum level of income is guaranteed for every family.* This level can be set at any amount, although if one desires to reduce the poverty gap to zero, it would have to be set at the poverty line. The second feature is the marginal tax rate on earned income, which may be set at any level less than 100 percent. Obviously one would want to choose a tax rate as far below 100 percent as is feasible. The third feature of all such plans is that a breakdown level of income exists; persons earning income above the breakeven level would no longer receive welfare payments.

These three features can be stated algebraically as follows:

$$\text{Breakeven income level} = \frac{\text{Guaranteed income level}}{\text{Marginal tax rate}}$$

Clearly if one knows two of these variables, he can determine the third. For example, if we argue that the urban poverty line is $5000 for a

* This does not mean that every family in the country will get a check for this minimum level. Only those unable (or unwilling, depending on the program) to work would receive the minimum.

family of four and we desire to eliminate the poverty gap completely, then the guaranteed income would be $5000. If the marginal tax rate is 50 percent it follows that the breakeven level of income is $10,000. In other words, welfare families would continue to receive some welfare payments until they earned over $10,000. Table 9-10 shows the earned income, welfare payments, and total income under this plan.

In the past few years the Federal Government has begun experiments with various negative-income-tax plans in Trenton, Paterson–Passaic, and Jersey City, New Jersey, and also Scranton, Pennsylvania; Seattle, Washington; and Gary, Indiana. The Trenton experiment began in 1968 and ran through 1971. Paterson–Passaic, Jersey City, and Scranton began in 1969 and were completed in 1972. To date, only preliminary evidence is in on the Trenton project [23]. Whereas static economic theory and many skeptics argued that the negative-income-tax plan would result in withdrawals from the labor force, the results are overwhelmingly against this position. Using a variety of marginal tax rates and guaranteed income levels, the income transfers had no effect whatsoever on earnings of those persons affected. The results from the Seattle experiment should be especially interesting, since unlike the other cities Seattle has had a significant jump in its unemployment rate in the recent past (due to drastic cuts in federal expenditures for aircraft). The Gary experiment will also be attractive to those interested in urban poverty because the primary focus is on black, female-headed households.

It is rather clear that our existing welfare programs have a built-in bias against inducing people to work. If we want to reduce the welfare rolls to those more or less unable to work, we must provide incentives to those who can work. The negative-income-tax plan seems to be a useful candidate for this purpose. Whether the negative income tax should replace all public-assistance plans, as some economists have ar-

TABLE 9–10

A Hypothetical Negative-Income-Tax Plan

Earned income ($)	Welfare payment ($)	Total income ($)
0	5,000	5,000
2,000	4,000	6,000
4,000	3,000	7,000
6,000	2,000	8,000
8,000	1,000	9,000
10,000	0	10,000

gued, is another issue. Unless the guaranteed minimum income is at
or near the poverty line, substituting the negative-income-tax plan would
merely continue the poverty gap for those unable to work.

Black Capitalism and Community Development

Two of the more experimental programs aimed at promoting the welfare of black ghettos are (1) black capitalism, which involves aiding
promising black entrepreneurs through subsidies, loans and other means,
and (2) community-development programs, which attempt to build the
black ghetto community into a viable economic and political unit that
can compete with the outside world.

Black capitalism is an outgrowth of the riots that plagued our cities
in the 1960's. Leaders in the black communities of our large urban areas
noted that the vast majority of businesses operating in ghettos were
owned by whites. The government and the private sector have made
a few halfhearted attempts to correct this inequity [24]. The Federal
Government's loan and other programs have only been aids to failure
on the part of inexperienced black entrepreneurs. In the few ghettos
where large corporations have built plants, huge losses have been the
rule unless the firms have guaranteed markets [22, Chapter 3]. Although
black capitalism may be a useful idea for helping a few entrepreneurs,
the efforts to date show that the impact on the overall poverty problem
in ghettos is very small. Like the manpower programs, black capitalism
will have to be tailored into a long-term general (business education)
program before it can function with success. Small loans and subsidies
to entrepreneurs with good ideas cannot go far in today's business world.
But the lessons learned can be useful; in order to see these unsuccessful
expenditures bear fruit, we will have to give support to entrepreneurs
for more than a few trials.

In addition to black-capitalism programs, many urban ghettos have
community-development agencies that perform the more general function of attempting to upgrade the economic power of the ghetto. Some
agencies are funded privately, while others receive public support. The
community-development approach is not just a broadening of black capitalism, but is a way of generating black economic and political power.
Profits, which are the guiding light of most capitalists, are secondary
under this approach. The agencies are generally involved in developing
black businesses, providing training and counseling, and establishing
an esprit de corps in the ghetto community.

From a social–psychological standpoint, community-development programs can and have aided the ghetto community greatly. If nothing

else, a new awareness of pride in one's community may lend a long-run view of life and enhance one's ability to cope with his problems. These agencies may affect the time preferences of some people, causing them to be more willing to search for work or education than they may have been otherwise. Thus, in the long run, the social–psychological effects could bring about economic changes for many in our ghettos.

However, the short-term economic rationale of the community plan, which essentially is to generate a community economy that is competitive with the outside world, is more or less doomed to failure. The reason is that the ghetto economy has so many leakages that income multipliers calculated for ghetto areas are very close to 1.0; that is, there are practically no multiplier effects. For example, in the Hough area of Cleveland, the income multiplier was computed at 1.03 [25]. This means that for every dollar spent in the Hough area, only 3 cents of additional economic activity is generated. Until the spending habits and economic structure of the ghettos change drastically, we cannot expect ghetto economies to compete in any way with the outside world. For this reason and others, many economists have argued that we should attempt to do away with ghettos and disperse the people throughout the city. But we noted in Table 9-2 that the percentage of blacks in poverty in the suburbs is the same as it is in the central city. Unless fundamental structural changes occur throughout the city in many markets, we cannot expect the urban poverty problem to be solved.

V. SUMMARY

In this chapter we have taken a detailed look at (1) the nature of poverty, (2) the causes and consequences of poverty, and (3) policies prescribed to combat poverty. Although there are many possible measures and definitions of poverty, we found it useful to distinguish between degrees of poverty for those persons below an acceptable poverty line. We also found that while some of the characteristics of the urban poor are well known, others are not. For example, the urban poor are just as willing to work as the nonpoor, and the majority of the urban poor do *not* receive public assistance. One striking piece of evidence on the urban poor is that as of 1970, over half of the urban poor lived in female-headed households.

The causes and consequences of poverty are highly interrelated. Although we noted a number of potential causes of poverty, it is important to keep in mind that for many, being poverty stricken is almost a sufficient condition for remaining poor. For example, low levels of education are often cited as a major cause of poverty. But if a person is a member of a poor family, a good education is very difficult to obtain, basically because of the family's poverty condition. Empirically, willingness to participate in labor markets and increased levels of education were found to be necessary but not sufficient conditions for alleviating poverty.

Traditional policies to combat poverty have been useful, but there is still a large percentage of our population in poverty. Although new programs may hold promise for some of the poor, it is my belief that our social and economic system has poverty as a byproduct. Basic structural changes may have to occur before we really solve the poverty problem.

SUGGESTED READINGS

Downs, Anthony. *Urban Problems and Prospects.* Chicago: Markham, 1970.

Downs, Anthony. "Who Are the Urban Poor." Committee for Economic Development Supplementary Paper No. 26, 1970.

Kain, John, ed. *Race and Poverty.* Englewood Cliffs, New Jersey: Prentice-Hall. 1969.

Kain, John, and Persky, Joseph. "The North's Stake in Southern Rural Poverty," in *Essays in Regional Economics,* edited by J. Kain and J. Meyer, pp. 243–78. Cambridge, Massachusetts: Harvard Univ. Press, 1971.

Levitan, Sar, *et al. Economic Opportunity in the Ghetto.* Baltimore, Maryland: Johns Hopkins Press: 1970.

Mills, Edwin. *Urban Economics.* Chapter 9. Glenview, Illinois: Scott, Foresman, 1972.

Piore, Michael, and Doeringer, Peter. *Internal Labor Markets and Manpower Analysis.* Lexington, Massachusetts: Health, 1971.

Tabb, William. *The Political Economy of the Black Ghetto.* New York: Norton, 1970.

Thurow, Lester. *Poverty and Discrimination.* Washington D.C.: Brookings Inst., 1969.

U.S. Department of Labor. "Manpower Report of the President," 1968–72.

Wilcox, Clair. *Toward Social Welfare.* Homewood, Illinois: Irwin, 1969.

Zeller, Frederick, and Miller, Robert., eds. *Manpower Development in Appalachia.* New York: Praeger, 1968.

REFERENCES

1. Harold Watts, "An Economic Definition of Poverty," in *On Understanding Poverty,* D. P. Moynihan, ed., pp. 316–329 (New York: Basic Books, 1968).
2. Victor Fuchs, "Redefining Poverty and Redistributing Income," *Public Interest* (1967): 88–95.
3. Paul Ryscavage and Hazel Willacy, "Employment of the Nation's Poor," *Monthly Labor Review* 91 (1968): 15–21.
4. Harvey J. Hilaski, "Unutilized Manpower in Poverty Areas of Six Major Cities," *Monthly Labor Review* 94 (1971): 45–52.

5. "The Social and Economic Status of Negroes in the United States," p. 43. U.S. Bureau of Census, 1970.
6. Phyllis Groom, "Prices in Poor Neighborhoods," *Monthly Labor Review* 89 (1966): 1085–1090.
7. Joseph Mooney, "Urban Poverty and Labor Force Participation," *American Economic Review* 57 (1967): 104–119.
8. Larry Sawers, "Urban Poverty and Labor Force Participation: Note," *American Economic Review* 62 (1972): 414–421.
9. Bennett Harrison, "Education and Underemployment in the Urban Ghetto." *American Economic Review* 62 (1972): 796–812.
10. Randall Weiss, "Effect of Education on the Earnings of Blacks and Whites," *Review of Economics and Statistics* 52 (1970): 150–157.
11. W. L. Hansen, B. A. Weisbrod, and W. J. Scanlon, "Schooling and Earnings of Low Achievers," *American Economic Review* 60 (1970): 409–418.
12. Lewis Solomon, "A Note on Equality of Educational Opportunity," *American Economic Review* 60 (1970): 768–771.
13. Robert S. Browne, "The Economic Case for Reparations to Black America," *American Economic Review, Papers, and Proceedings* 62 (1972): 39–46.
14. Peter B. Doeringer and Michael J. Piore, *Internal Labor Markets and Manpower Analysis* (Lexington, Massachusetts: Heath, 1971).
15. Peter B. Doeringer, "Ghetto Labor Markets—Problems and Programs," Program on Regional and Urban Economics, Discussion Paper No. 35, Harvard Univ., 1968.
16. David P. Taylor, "Discrimination and Occupational Wage Differences in the Market for Unskilled Labor," *Industrial and Labor Relations Review* 21 (1968): 375–390.
17. Alex Maurizi, "Minority Membership in Apprenticeship Programs in the Construction Industry," *Industrial and Labor Relations Review* 25 (1972): 200–206.
18. Alex Maurizi, "Comments and Reply," *Industrial and Labor Relations Review* 25 (1972): 696–705.
19. W. S. Kee, "The Causes of Urban Poverty," *Journal of Human Resources* 4 (1969): 93–99.
20. Stephen Engleman, "Job Corps: Some Factors Affecting Enrollee Earnings," *Industrial Relations* 11 (1972): 198–215.
21. Michael Borus *et al.*, "A Benefit–Cost Analysis of Neighborhood Youth Corps: The Out of School Program in Indiana," *Journal of Human Resources* 5 (1970): 138–159.
22. Sar Levitan *et al.*, *Economic Opportunity in the Ghetto: The Partnership of Government and Business* (Baltimore, Maryland: Johns Hopkins Press, 1970).
23. Harold Watts, "The Graduated Work Incentive Experiments: Current Progress," *American Economic Review, Papers and Proceedings* LXI (1971): 15–21.
24. William K. Tabb, "Viewing Minority Economic Development as a Problem in Political Economy," *American Economic Review, Papers and Proceedings* 62 (1972): 31–38.
25. William H. Oakland *et al.*, "Ghetto Multipliers: A Case Study of Hough, "*Journal of Regional Science* 11 (1971): 337–345.

10

THE URBAN
ENVIRONMENT

I. INTRODUCTION

The urban environment has many facets, but we wish to cover only three areas in this chapter: the physical, social, and economic aspects of the environment. Up to this chapter we have emphasized primarily the economic agents within urban areas and their economic behavior. Although we shall not deemphasize economics in this chapter, we shall take a closer view of two aspects of the physical and social environmental characteristics of urban areas, namely, the problems of environmental pollution and urban crime.

Pollution has always been a severe problem in one form or another in our cities. Because a massive constant demand is being made on environmental resources in cities, one would expect environmental crises to occur in cities. From pre-Roman times to the present, material wastes inherent in the production and consumption processes of urban man have placed a constraint on his well-being. The inability to cope with human wastes resulted in severe health and other problems during the Roman era. The automobile is causing similar problems in contemporary urban America. Man, however, is adaptable, and historically he has been able to cope with each environmental problem through shifting his preferences and/or production techniques.

Like pollution, man's incessant criminal behavior against man has also been perpetrated for centuries. Throughout our history, crime in American cities has always been a severe problem. The very nature of the city—a massive concentration of many types of people—almost ensures that some people will be included who prefer to commit offensive acts against other persons or property. The nature and economics of the urban crime problem give us one example of man's reaction to himself and his environment.

Of course neither pollution nor crime is unique to urban areas. Both exist and always have existed outside of the city. However, the incidence of such activity in a heavily populated area has far greater ramifications in the form of (negative) externalities. The infamous smog of Los Angeles, believed to be accentuated if not produced by unburned hydrocarbons from auto exhaust emissions, is a case in point. If the population of Los Angeles were 5000 or 50,000 rather than 5 million, it is likely that the problem would be less severe. Although each individual sees himself as driving only one car and therefore producing only a very minor part of the problem, the greater the number of other single individuals there are, the worse it is for all of them. In short, levels of pollution are important, and the more dense the population, the more severely one taxes the physical environment. Similarly, the urban riots of the 1960's are a perfect example of how a few in big cities can bring havoc to the lives of many in a short period of time. Although the concentration of production and consumption activities in space provides many benefits, the potential costs in the form of environmental pollution and outbreaks due to social unrest are also greater when compared to a population that is evenly distributed across space.

II. ENVIRONMENTAL POLLUTION

The General Problem

Pollution may be defined as a return to the environment of materials in a harmful state. By materials we mean minerals, fuels, gases, and organic matter. In producing goods we use many materials—food, forest products, metals, and other minerals. When these transformed materials or goods are no longer useful, we return them to the environment; that is, the air, land, or water. If these transformed materials are not recycled or returned in their natural state, they place a burden on the environment, since the air, land, or water must do the recycling.

Although land, water, and the air do in fact have tremendous capabilities for recycling, they also have limits. When these limits are reached, a pollution crisis exists; for example, water begins to smell, large populations of fish die, or air-pollution alerts are proclaimed. Clearly the environment is a great natural resource base that must be used efficiently.

The limits of the environment (at least air) are reached more quickly in urban areas, other things being equal. In general, the distribution of production activity is the key to understanding the broad incidence of pollution, although some types of production (beet sugar, pulp and paper, tanneries) pollute more than others. The distribution of production across space is more or less consistent with the distribution of people. Let us take a look at two of the major pollution problems of our cities, air and water pollution.

Air Pollution

Historically man has always polluted the air. However, even nature whips up dust storms, tornados, and volcanos that fill the air with particulate matter. If man were randomly scattered over space, this *primary* form of air pollution would not be a major problem, since the particulates sooner or later fall to the ground; where they fall is basically a function of weather systems, rather than the distribution of population. However, if huge doses of particulate matter are emitted into the air in densely populated areas, the air remains dirty unless the wind carries the particulate matter away.

To be sure, particulates such as smoke and fumes from industrial plants do obscure sunlight, dirty buildings, corrode metals, and adversely affect plant life. However, the best evidence we have on the level of emission of particulate matter is that it has drastically declined in the past few decades. Anyone who saw Pittsburgh in the early 1950's and goes back today will know what we mean. New abatement practices by the steel industry have made it possible to keep a freshly washed car in Pittsburgh clean for a day or more, rather than a few hours. One other factor that has helped reduce particulate matter is the substitution of liquid and gaseous fuels for solid fuels. This substitution was not costless, however, from an environmental standpoint.

The major sources of air pollution in urban America today are secondary pollutants such as carbon monoxide, hydrocarbons, and sulfur and

TABLE 10-1

1970 Air-Pollution Emissions in the U.S. (millions of tons)[a]

Source	Carbon monoxide	Sulfur oxides	Hydro- carbons	Nitrogen oxides	Particles
Transportation	110.9	1.0	19.5	11.7	0.8
Fuel combustion[b]	0.8	21.5	0.6	9.4	6.0
Industry	11.4	6.4	5.5	0.2	13.3
Refuse disposal	7.2	0.1	2.0	0.4	1.4
Miscellaneous	18.3	0.2	7.3	0.5	4.0
Totals	148.6	29.2	34.9	22.2	25.5

[a] U.S. Bureau of Census, "Statistical Abstract of U.S.," p. 175, 1972.
[b] Stationary sources.

nitrous oxides. See Table 10-1 for a breakdown of these emissions. Secondary pollutants are formed through a reaction of two or more primary pollutants in the air. Secondary pollutants are thought to be far more dangerous to human health than primary pollutants. The standard example of secondary pollution is smog. Many cities have severe air-pollution problems because the unburned hydrocarbons from auto emissions react with particulates in the air to form dirty gaseous pockets that extend a few hundred feet above the city.

Table 10-1 also shows the sources of pollutants in the United States. The principal source of most pollution is the auto. In terms of solving the air-pollution problem of our cities, we must either drive more efficient cars or find some other form of transportation. The issue is just about that simple. Both alternatives will mean an increase in costs to everyone, so we may as well face up to this fact if we want to reduce air pollution in our cities. Electrical utility plants and industry are the other major sources of air pollutants in this country. Since electricity can be transported rather cheaply, it is possible that we could put all of our generating plants in lightly populated areas. Mine-mouth generating plants near the portals of coal mines have become popular in the past decade, and this is a step in the right direction. Industry, however, locates in or near cities for agglomeration and other factors discussed in Chapter 3. Thus the alternative to "dirty" producers is not necessarily relocation as much as it is a shift in their production processes to a cleaner technique.

Although there has been a widespread concern for the problem of air pollution in this country for nearly two decades, we still do not have any strong evidence on the relationship between air-pollution levels and human health. In a few cities (London, New York, and Donora, Pennsylvania) it has been found that an excessive number of deaths have occurred among persons with respiratory problems during long, severe smog episodes. However, we do not as yet have any firm evidence on the impact of air pollution of various types and amounts on man's health over the long run. One study has estimated that if we reduce emissions by 50 percent in our metropolitan areas, the average life expectancy of each person in these areas will increase by at least three years [1]. In terms of decreased morbidity and mortality, this reduction would save over $2 billion per year. This is a conservative dollar estimate.

Overall, the costs of air pollution to society have been estimated at anywhere from $4 billion per year upward to $25 billion. These estimates include not only the health costs but also the loss of crops, extra cleaning and repair bills, and so forth. Since we do not know the real impact of secondary pollutants over the short or long run, it is quite likely that these aggregate estimates are biased. The direction and magnitude of the bias are difficult to assess.

Water Pollution

Water pollution occurs when materials enter bodies of water. Materials may be degradable or nondegradable. Degradable materials are those that can be broken down by bacteria in the water; however, in this process some of the dissolved oxygen in the water is consumed, which retards plant and fish life. Domestic sewage and other organic and inorganic wastes such as food, pulp and paper, and chemicals are the common degradable materials entering our waters. In urban areas, domestic sewage and industrial wastes are the chief contaminants of our water resources.

The key point to understand with water pollution is that there is a limit to how much material any given stream or body of water can degrade. The limit exists because as the degradation process increases in any body of water, the amount of dissolved oxygen decreases. If this limit is reached—that is, if all of the dissolved oxygen is used up— degradation still occurs, but it does so anaerobically. Anaerobic degradation involves bacterial action on materials. An anaerobic stream emits foul odors, and usually looks black and bubbly. No fish or plant life can survive in it. Once a stream becomes anaerobic, it often takes decades to restore it to a semblance of its once-clean state. Unfortunately, many of the streams and harbors in our large cities are at or near the anaerobic stage.

Streams and lakes do not become anaerobic overnight. As pollution builds up, plant life (which is the basic source of dissolved oxygen in waterways) and fish begin to die. This is nature's tip to us.

The degradation capacity of waterways is dependent not only upon the levels of wastes and dissolved oxygen in the water but also upon the temperature of the water. High water temperatures accelerate the degradation process, resulting in a lower amount of dissolved oxygen. Thus dirty rivers and lakes take on foul odors on hot summer days as the amount of dissolved oxygen tends toward a zero level. Besides nature, industries (especially electric power generating stations) are the basic cause of water-temperature increases. Industry uses water for cooling purposes, which raises the temperature of the water. If this warmer water is not cooled before it is returned to the waterway, the latter's ability to degrade pollutants will be reduced.

The total costs of water pollution to society are not known. Whatever the level of costs, water pollution affects nearly everyone. In our major cities, heavy expenditures on swimming pools and other recreational facilities would not have been required if our streams were clean enough for people to swim in and picnic by. People who like to swim but cannot afford to buy their own swimming pools are certainly worse off because of water pollution. Not only does dirty water reduce recreational opportunities, but it is also more expensive to cleanse for drinking and other purposes. The fishing industry of Lake Erie was a thriving activity two decades ago, but today it is dead because Lake Erie is so polluted. The use of swordfish as food has been banned by the Federal Government because the flesh contains an excessive amount of mercury.

Other forms of pollution also plague urban areas. Solid wastes have become an acute problem in many cities, and until recently the most popular method of dealing with solid wastes was incineration. This approach of course results in air pollution unless extremely costly precautions are used. Although noise is not a part of the overall materials balance in the environment, most living creatures are hurt by excessive noises. Industry and traffic are the basic sources of excessive noise in cities.

The Economic Problem

The inherent economic characteristic of any form of pollution is the misuse of a common-property resource. Common-property resources are the air, rivers, lakes, oceans, and so forth. Everyone shares in the ownership of these resources, but the form of ownership is somewhat unique. Unfortunately, there is no built-in mechanism in our economic system to ensure that common-property resources are used efficiently and equitably. The market system works quite well when materials are produced with ordinary resources; but when they are to be returned to the environment via common-property resources, there is no spokesman or allocating agency to ensure that materials are recycled. The problem, then, given that common-property resources have limits, is that we may exceed these limits. Then many suffer because of the actions of a few. For example, because a few cities and firms polluted Lake Erie for years, everyone who enjoyed eating fresh Lake Erie fish can no longer do so.

Most economists agree that our present market system is unable to control or abate pollution.* Rational firms and households will pollute if they want to maximize profits and utility respectively. Barring efficient management of our common-property resources by government or some other institution, our only chance for reducing pollution is to do one or more of the following: (1) totally redesign our production processes so that we minimize the wastes produced, (2) recycle more of our pollutants, and (3) recover a greater share of the nonrecycleable by-products from our existing production processes. All of these alternatives are costly, and therefore we find few firms or households consciously making efforts in these directions unless forced.

In addition to altering the overall production process, we could minimize pollution problems by locating our dirtiest producing units in spatial locations where the weather, topographical conditions, and other environmental factors are such that the common-property resources can work efficiently. For access reasons, however, many goods and services have to be produced in or near the city. The benefits of concentrating people and space would be seriously impaired if we distributed firms optimally from an environmental standpoint. Clearly there is a tradeoff between growth under the existing institutions in society and environmental control. Given our existing economic system, more growth will mean less environmental control. In the short run, more concern with the environment would result in less growth. Over the long run, however, man has a tremendous ability to adapt; thus I would expect the environmental constraint placed on growth to be real, but not strong enough to deter growth.

The Optimal Level of Pollution

From an economic point of view, the optimal level of pollution is *not* a zero level. From our discussion in previous chapters, we can recall that an optimal allocation of resources toward the production of any good occurs when the price of that good equals its marginal cost. If

---

* For an interesting argument against this position, see William P. Gramm [2].

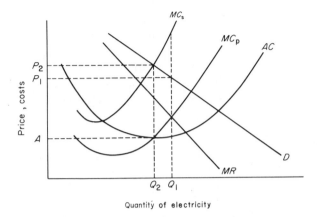

Figure 10.1 *Pollution and the monopolistic firm.*

an electric power plant is located along a stream in a city, and if the
plant does not cool the water it uses to stream temperature before re-
placing the water in the stream, then there is a divergence between
the private cost of producing a kilowatt of electricity and the social
cost of producing that kilowatt. Figure 10.1 illustrates this situation.
The social marginal cost MC_s diverges from the private marginal cost
MC_p at an increasing rate because as production increases, the temperature of the water increases. And as we noted previously, higher water
temperatures speed up the degradation process, which lowers the level
of dissolved oxygen at a faster rate.

A profit-maximizing electric plant would produce Q_1 and charge price
P_1. But at Q_1 society is not happy; the MC_s exceeds the demand price or
marginal benefits of another kilowatt. If governments were efficient
watchdogs for society, they would step in and through some means
(taxes, subsidies, and so on) induce the plant to produce only Q_2 kilo-
watts, because at Q_2, society's marginal benefits (as proxied by price)
are exactly offset by the MC_s of producing the electricity; that is, an
optimal allocation of resources is attained. Note that at Q_2, $MC_s > MC_p$,
which means that some pollution is occurring. With given tastes and
technology, there will always be some level of pollution. From an
economic standpoint, our job is to find what the optimal level is. In
Figure 10.1, of course, the optimal level is the amount of pollution associated with Q_2 level of electricity production.

Other things being equal, we might expect the level of pollution associated with an efficient allocation of resources (optimal level of pollution) to be greater in cities [3]. Indeed, if the level of pollution is
proportional to city size, we would expect the optimal amount of pollu-

tion to rise with city size. However, this expectation is not borne out. Consider the following model. I benefit from polluting with my car, since it is cheaper or more convenient for me to travel that way. If everyone else does the same, then in a given sized city the marginal benefits to the aggregate of drivers can be represented by MB_1 in Figure 10.2. If another city has twice the density of population and a proportional increase in polluting drivers, then we can draw a second MB curve (MB_2) to the right of MB_1. We draw MB_2 to the right of MB_1 because the benefits from polluting are private, and private demands are aggregated horizontally. Now the damages from increasing pollution levels rise, so we can draw the marginal costs of polluting as MC_1 and MC_2, where $MC_2 > MC_1$. Clearly the costs of pollution are borne by everyone (that is, pollution is a public "bad") so we sum the MC curves vertically as we did in Chapter 8. Obviously the price of pollution is greater in city 2.

Figure 10.2 shows that the optimal amount of pollution is *less* in city 2. Certainly if city 2's population is more dense than that of city 1, this is what we would expect. Thus, although in the real world we may find greater levels of pollutants in larger cities when compared to small towns, this is probably not an optimal situation. In fact, it is fairly clear evidence that a supoptimal situation exists.

Attaining the Optimal Level of Pollution in Practice

Now that we have an idea of what the optimal pollution level is, how can it be attained? Since we are dealing with common-property resources, it is almost a certainty that rational individuals and firms

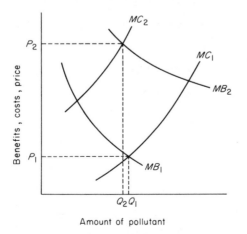

Figure 10.2   *The optimal level of pollution and city size.*

will not reach this level on their own. As in all other cases where third
parties are required, the obvious candidate for leading us to the optimum
is the government.

How might the government proceed? Recalling an example of the
electric power plant in Figure 10.1, the dollar value attached to the
pollution is the difference between MC_s and MC_p. At the optimal output
level, this amount is P_2A. Thus this plant could be charged a constant
tax per unit equal to P_2A, which would ensure that the optimal amount
of electricity, Q_2, is produced. Of course, we are assuming that the
government knows the level and shape of the MC_s curve, which is
relatively easy to estimate in this case, but exceedingly difficult to estimate with other pollutants. Pollution taxes are often referred to as
effluent fees or charges, since they are levied on the amount of effluents.

In cases where the government does not know a great deal about
the real costs or damages of pollutants, as occurs with air pollution,
an alternative to the effluent charge must be found. One thing we do
know about air pollution is that as the level of air pollution decreases,
the marginal cost of reducing pollution in the air increases. Thus we
have a downward-sloping curve for the marginal cost of abatement
(MCA) in Figure 10.3 to denote that at higher and higher pollution
levels we could abate the marginal ton more cheaply. The student should
take special care not to confuse the negatively sloping MCA curve in
Figure 10.3 with the positively sloping MC curve in Figure 10.2. It
is not unreasonable to argue that MCA could be estimated empirically
for each city or air shed in the country.

Given MCA, it remains to determine the marginal damages of the
pollutant. At first the damages would be minor, so our marginal-damages

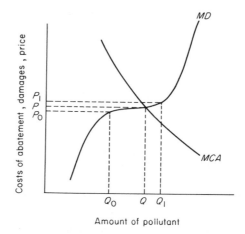

Figure 10.3 *Deriving the optimal level of pollution in practice.*

curve would not begin at the origin of Figure 10.3. Once pollutants build up, the marginal damages may increase at an increasing rate until man adapts. After the adaptation has occurred, any further dosages of the pollutant will soon result in infinite marginal damages. So the marginal-damages curve would look like a reversed S.

The optimal price and quantity in Figure 10.3 are OP and OQ, respectively. If we found that MCA was practically horizontal over the relevant range of pollutants in an air shed, and if a priori evidence suggested that MCA cut the MD curve at the latter's horizontal or flat area, then we would set the price of pollution (emission fee) at a point near OP. The quantity of pollution would then be more or less restricted to the area between OQ_0 and OQ_1. If our policy goal is to attain the optimal level of pollution in a way that minimizes error, we would choose the price as the basis for policy. Why? Because the variation around price (P_0P_1) is much less than the variation around quantity (Q_0Q_1) [4].

Alternatively, if the MCA were practically vertical over the range of pollution in our city, and the MCA cut the MD curve on either of its steep portions, we would have a fairly solid idea of the optimal *quantity* of the pollutant, but we would not know the proper *price* or emission fee to charge. Many economists have argued that in this case the government should issue a fixed quantity of "pollution certificates" that give the right to pollute to the highest bidder. These certificates would be transferable, and the sum of the pollution allowed would be exactly equal to the optimal quantity we have previously determined. Supposedly, conservationists, industrialists, and others would bid for these certificates; thus the optimal price of pollution would be determined. Over time, new knowledge of MCA or MD for given pollutants could result in expanding or contracting the supply of certificates. For example, if we found that a given pollutant was more dangerous than previously thought, the government could reduce the supply of certificates for this pollutant, which of course would drive up the price of emitting that pollutant.

When compared to the emission charge, the pollution-certificate approach to attaining the optimal level of pollution probably seems rather cumbersome. However, they both achieve the same result from an efficiency and equity standpoint. Most important, they provide an incentive for industry, households, and other institutions to find a cleaner means of doing business.

There are two additional methods government could use to attain the optimal level of any pollutant, but both are inferior to the emission or effluent charge and certificate programs. Subsidies can be granted to firms or individuals to cut back on production or on pollution generating activities until the optimal amount of pollution is obtained. This approach is efficient; that is, we obtain the optimal level. But who pays for the subsidy? The general taxpayer does, but the general taxpayer does not necessarily directly or indirectly consume the product or service produced by the polluter. Subsidies force everyone to pay for the polluter's wrongs. Moreover, subsidies provide disincentives to seeking the cleanest production process over time. In the long run, then, subsidies not only are inequitable but are also inefficient.

The final method available to attain an optimal level of a given pollutant is direct regulation or control. This is the most popular approach in the real world, probably because of its simplicity. For example, we restrict the sulfur content of fuels in almost every major city in this country. Emission standards are set on new cars, which are now required to have pollution-control equipment. Direct controls, if enforced, can result in a reduction of the controlled pollutants, but they have little other impact. There is little chance that direct controls will result in the optimal quantity of any given pollutant, since the optimal quantities will vary across cities because of different environmental conditions. If we have a given control standard, some cities will have less than the optimal quantity, while others will have too much of the pollutant. Clearly, direct controls are not efficient in either the short or long run. If direct controls are spatially inefficient, they are also spatially inequitable. If the controls force my city to have a suboptimal amount of any given pollutant, we are consuming an overshare of the burden of pollution control.

In summary, to attain an optimal level of pollution in the short run we could use taxes or charges, certificates, or subsidies. Each of these alternatives gives a reasonable chance of attaining the optimal level. Direct controls (by themselves) give very little, if any, chance, especially across cities or air sheds. In the long run, the tax and certificate approaches provide incentives to find cleaner processes or production or to relocate plants in areas where the environment is more capable of handling pollutants. Subsidies do not provide either of these incentives in the long run, while direct controls can change the production processes and also cause plant relocations, provided that we do not have national control standards.

Environmental Policy

State and local governments have had regulatory laws against air and water pollution for decades, but there was little enforcement of these laws until about 1960. At that time the Federal Government entered the pollution field in a serious way. Although the Federal Government has jurisdiction only over interstate pollution problems, it has been able to provide research and financial assistance for intrastate pollution-abatement programs. Without federal help, probably few states or cities would have done much about enforcing pollution-control laws, the primary reason being that firms threaten to relocate in other areas. The general principle of federal legislation in the pollution field is to let the states do the cleaning up, which is fine except for border problems. Differences of opinion in contiguous states could result in severe problems in some of our major metropolitan areas—New York, Chicago, Philadelphia, Washington, St. Louis, and Kansas City are just a few of the major metropolitan areas that stretch into two or more states. For example, if Chicago and Illinois were lenient in enforcing air pollution laws (in real life, exactly the opposite is true), the city of Gary, Indiana could be forced to bear a large undesirable burden in the form of dirty air.

Water-Pollution Policy

Our present water-pollution policy consists of two basic tools: (1) the construction of municipal water-treatment plants, and (2) regulation of waste discharges into waterways. Neither of these tools seems to be doing an adequate job [5]. Under the municipal waste-treatment construction program, the Federal Government pays up to 55 percent of the capital costs of each plant. The present Administration has kept this program from being successful by failing to authorize for expenditure the funds appropriated by Congress. The Administration argues that any further expenditures in this field would be inflationary because our construction sector is at full capacity. Although this may be true, if the present Administration speaks for the people, then Americans prefer more pollution to a possibly slower increase in aggregate prices. Whether or not this is a bargain is of course a value judgment.

In addition to the lag of capital expenditures at the city level, another problem with our existing policy is that we do little about operations once plants are constructed. Although capital costs are the most significant cost factor in treating wastes, changes in techniques can be made, and the Federal Government could easily diffuse and help harness new technology as it becomes available. During 1973 the Nixon Administration vetoed (and Congress failed to override the veto) a bill that would have provided funds for assisting in the operations of sewage-treatment plants in small towns.

A further problem of our present policy program is that some industrial plants can amortize their pollution-control equipment in five years This policy amounts to a subsidy to those that do the polluting. As we showed in the previous section, subsidies are both inefficient and inequitable in the long run.

The efficacy of the regulations used to control water pollution varies across cities in regions. Although the Federal Government has helped states develop standards, the states are required to enforce these standards. And under plant relocation threats, many states have been unwilling to enforce the law.

Although our water pollution control policies are stronger today than they were a decade or more ago, we still have a long way to go in terms of attaining an (economically) optimal policy. It is probably fair to say that we are presently more or less groping in the dark under some rather rigid institutional constraints. Until our institutions can begin to see the light and formulate some efficient policies *and* enforce them, we are not likely to make more than marginal gains toward cleaning up our waterways.

Air-Pollution Policy

The record with air pollution is about the same as with water pollution. The basic policy has been for the Federal Government to pass laws requiring states to set acceptable standards (emission levels) of pollutants. Many cities (for example, Los Angeles) and states have taken the initiative to formulate and enforce rigid standards on easily detectable pollutants such as sulfur dioxide. In addition, the Federal Government has moved slowly but steadily in the area of automobile production standards to minimize the emissions of carbon monoxide and hydrocarbons. Another positive factor is that the Federal Government has divided the nation into air-quality-control regions, which are air sheds that in many cases correspond to metropolitan areas. The recognition of the air shed as the basic policy unit is a step in the right direction, as long as the Federal Government can effectively referee interjurisdictional disputes that are inevitable under such a program.

Beyond standards for new cars, sulfur dioxide, and nitrous oxides, we have no further air-pollution policies. Apparently we are unwilling to modify existing inefficient policies by, say, levying emission fees on sources of pollutants. Given the institutional constraints, our major problem is enforcing existing standards. Controls are more difficult to enforce with air pollution than they are with water pollution, because the wind and other pollutants can make it next to impossible to find out where pollutants originate. Regulation, of course, is not the best tool for attaining the optimal level of pollution in urban air sheds. Until our institutions recognize this fact, our air-pollution policies will remain semieffective, but inefficient and inequitable.

Summary

Pollution involves returning materials to the environment in a non-recycled state. Although the environment has a capacity to break down certain materials, in urban areas we often come close to exceeding that capacity. The result is dead (anaerobic) streams and air pollution, which are referred to popularly as environmental crises. Although it is difficult to estimate the damage caused by pollutants, one could measure abatement costs fairly accurately. Thus it seems that economically efficient and equitable methods of dealing with pollution are possible. The key is to get out government to "price" our common-property resources. Unfortunately, government sticks to the traditional role of regulation and control, which helps only during crises.

III. URBAN CRIME

According to the 1967 President's Commission on Law Enforcement, the economic costs of crime exceed $30 billion annually in the U.S. Since urban areas have a greater proportion of crime than rural areas, there is little doubt that most of the costs of crime are being borne by urbanites. Crime itself is a negative externality, in that it lowers the utility of the affected persons or property owners. Crime is also a redistribution process, whereby the criminal is attempting to obtain increased income or satisfaction at the expense of others. In general, crime rates increase with city size; thus as cities grow and develop, increases in crime act as constraint on further growth and development. In addition, certain geographical areas of cities become pockets of crime; thus expansion of housing and shopping areas occurs elsewhere. Clearly, crime not only involves a major cost to urban society but also affects the level and spatial distribution of growth and development in our (central) cities.

In this section we shall take a look at the nature of crime, the behavior of the criminal, and policies to reduce crime. Two particular activities of crime are considered, loan-sharking and narcotics trade. The operations of both of these activities are similar. We shall find that the public's decision to act as a moral judge is the basis for having laws against loan-sharking and narcotics use. Although these laws may yield positive benefits to society if rationally enforced, it is not clear that at the margin the benefits exceed the costs. Economics, we shall find, has little if anything to do with our existing policies that deal with actual or potential criminals. This situation is unfortunate, since the application of basic economic principles to the urban crime problem yields some very useful and interesting policy conclusions.

The Nature of the Urban Crime Problem

In cities, potential criminals have a variety of accessible properties or persons that are potential victims. It is well known that crime rates per capita are much greater in the central-city areas of our major metropolitan areas than they are in small towns or rural areas. Table 10-2 provides some recent information on these trends. Violent crime (murder, rape, assault) rates in SMSA's are more than twice those in non-SMSA cities. Property crime (robbery, burglary, larceny) rates in SMSA's are almost double those of non-SMSA towns. Property crimes are committed for economic reasons, while violent crimes (unless committed during robbery, burglary, or theft) are primarily noneconomic in nature. Accordingly, our discussion will be primarily restricted to property crimes.

Data on crime rates have to be taken with a grain of salt, because they are based on reported crimes. Without doubt, many crimes go unreported for various reasons; thus the data are generally biased down-

TABLE 10-2

Urban Crime Rates[a] in the U.S., 1968–1971[b]

	1968	1969	1970	1971
In SMSA's				
Total	2,803	3,096	3,396	3,547
Violent	376	417	457	491
Property	2,427	2,679	2,939	3,056
In Other Cities				
Total	1,358	1,519	1,848	1,891
Violent	137	145	181	193
Property	1,221	1,375	1,666	1,698

[a] Reported crimes per 100,000 population.
[b] U.S. Bureau of Census, "Statistical Abstract of the U.S.," 1970–1972.

ward.* Although national pools are not always reliable, it is rather interesting to note that a late 1972 Gallup poll showed that one person in three living in central-city areas had been a victim of some crime in the past year, either against their person or property. This is a startling figure, even if it is overstated by as much as 10 or 20 percent. The incidence of criminal activity is no longer restricted to a small percentage of the population.

Except for shoplifting, vandalism, and burglary, the incidence of most urban crime is confined to the downtown and ghetto areas. Since these areas are inhabited by businesses and primarily low-income persons, it is clear who the major victims of crime are: the poor and business establishments. The poor of course are the ones who can least afford losses to criminals; most businesses can pass the costs of crime control on to their customers in higher prices.

Individual Criminal Behavior

People commit crimes to increase their satisfaction; thus it is quite reasonable to view criminal behavior with standard economic tools. The private benefits from crimes are the monetary or psychic gains derived. For example, shoplifters sell their goods for cash. Young vandals, usually merely out on a lark, get short-lived psychic satisfaction out of their crimes. Narcotics users are in the same class as vandals. In general then, the private benefits to a criminal of committing an unlawful act may be measured by the income he receives. As with standard economic goods, we would expect the marginal private benefits of criminal activity to decrease as more of the same acts are performed.

The costs of committing an unlawful act, unlike the benefits, may be consumed over one's lifetime. To be sure, one may "earn" enough money from a given criminal act to last a lifetime, but this is the exception. Most crimes yield only small sums. The major cost factors to the criminal are the probability of being arrested and convicted; if sentenced, the criminal will forgo earnings. If the probability of being caught and convicted for a crime is 0.5, and the expected sentence for the crime is 10 years, a person can expect to give up 2.5 years' worth of income for every crime of this sort he commits. To be sure, there are also costs in hiring defense lawyers, forgoing income during court proceedings, and having a criminal record if one desires to enter

---

* The downward bias may be partially offset in a year for a given crime in a specific city, since (1) the data are gathered by city police forces and (2) police budgets are based (in part) on the level of crime. Clearly it could be in the interest of police forces to overstate the level of crime.

noncriminal labor markets. However, we can hold these constant for the moment.

The rational criminal will continue to commit crimes until the marginal private benefits are exactly equal to the marginal private costs.* If the private marginal benefits are equal to the expected income gain, and the private marginal costs are proxied by the income loss, then it follows that we can forecast the criminal behavior of individuals if we know their incomes, *ceterus paribus*. If the probability of arrest and conviction and expected sentences are the same for everybody, then those having higher incomes have more to lose. Thus we would expect lower-income persons to commit more crimes on a priori grounds.

Our conclusion is strengthened if the costs of committing crime take up more than a year, and thus must be discounted to their present value. Since lower-income people usually have higher discount rates, this results in a lower expected cost, or alternatively, a *higher* probability for committing a crime. Many people argue that to deter crime we must raise the income of the poor. As we have found with other problems, however, income increases alone are not enough. We must also attempt to lower the discount (time preference) rate of actual or potential criminals. Better economic conditions in our ghettos are necessary but not sufficient conditions for controlling economically motivated crime.

The behavior of the rational criminal provides the basis for our policy decisions in the area of law enforcement. The traditional approach to deterring crime in this country is to raise the expected cost. This is done by increasing the probability of arrest and conviction, or raising sentences. In the past decade or so, policy administrators have argued that lenient courts have made their jobs more difficult. Clearly, if the probability of conviction decreases, this will lower the expected cost of committing a crime. Other things being equal, we would expect more crimes to be committed. So the police administrators are no doubt correct, if all other factors can be considered constant. However police resources have increased, and average earnings have also increased; thus lenient courts have probably done little more than slow the increase in the expected costs of committing a crime.

We are not arguing for longer or shorter prison sentences, or a higher or lower rate of convictions. There are social costs involved in criminal acts, and we do need some mechanism to minimize such acts. Social costs are involved in all criminal acts that we attempt to deter, if only in the amount of resources used up in deterrence. So there are sound

* Both the benefits and costs are discounted to their present value if they are borne for more than one year.

economic reasons for controlling crime. The real issue is: What is the optimal strategy? Before tackling this question, it may be useful to consider two specific types of crime that are prevalent in urban areas—loan-sharking and narcotics traffic. From looking at these two criminal activities, we will have a better idea of the problems involved in developing and applying an optimal strategy of urban crime control.

The Economics of Loan-Sharking and Narcotics

People in low-income areas of our cities have high probabilities of committing crimes, if for no other reason than because of the relatively low expected cost of committing a crime. As we argued above, the low expected costs are primarily due to low income levels. Low-income persons also have difficulty borrowing in legal channels; thus they are prime customers for loan sharks. Loan sharks provide a useful service for gamblers and narcotics addicts as well as law-abiding debtors. If low-income narcotics addicts cannot get needed funds from a loan shark, they will turn to crime. Clearly, poverty, loan-sharking, narcotics, and the general crime rates of our cities are inextricably related.

Loan-Sharking*

Technically speaking, loan-sharking is defined as the lending of money at interest rates higher than those prescribed by law. According to the 1967 President's Commission on Law Enforcement, loan-sharking provides the second largest source of revenue for organized crime in this country. We set legal limits on interest rates and have truth-in-lending clauses to help the poor, but from all indications, we end up hurting the poor. Let us see why.

Small consumer loans are very expensive for banks or other established institutions to handle. Small loan companies cannot lend to unknowns. To those they do know or can trust, small loan companies usually have a ceiling of $800. Thus loan sharks have a rather large potential market. And they know how to extend their market. For example, the typical loan shark setup is the "6 for 5" plan; that is, I borrow $5 this week and pay back $6 next week, a healthy 20 percent per week interest charge. If I cannot pay the full $6, the shark will allow me to pay merely the interest of one dollar. As interest and/or principal charges pile up over time, representatives of the shark (called runners) may induce me to gamble so I can hit the jackpot and pay off everything.

* This section relies heavily on L. J. Kaplan and S. Matteis [6].

Since there is little chance that the odds of this underworld gambling activity are fair, I have almost no chance to win. Yet I continue to try. And I go further in the hole.

The victims of the loan shark are usually poor people. If we really want to help poor people borrow money at reasonable interest rates, then the government should provide this service. Alternatively, we could ensure every family a guaranteed income at the poverty line. To attempt to enforce antiloan-sharking laws and not provide an adequate income base for our poor makes little sense. To be sure, loan-sharking will probably always exist among certain types of people. This is no excuse, however, for loan sharks to get rich, in part, at the expense of the urban poor who have nowhere else to turn.

Narcotics

Hardly a day goes by in New York or other large cities without another person dying from an overdose of narcotics. Heroin is the major killer, and its supply is almost completely controlled by professional criminals [7]. Marijuana and LSD markets, on the other hand, are in the hands of many, including a large share of young adults.

Heroin comes into this country basically from France. The French get opium from Turkey, and transform it into heroin. In this country, heroin is distributed clandestinely because of its illegality. Since distributors desire to minimize their expected costs, they attempt to expand their markets in many directions. For example, if Joe X distributes 1 pound of heroin in New York City and one of the final users is 80 persons removed from Joe X, the chances of Joe X being caught are minimal, because the user has probably never heard of or seen Joe X. So a pyramid effect occurs in distributing narcotics. A similar structure occurs in loan-sharking, with the runners at the bottom of the pyramid.

The price of heroin will vary over time and across space. Unless the market is controlled by a monopolist, prices will be determined by competition among pushers. Pushers can compete in many ways. Varying the quality of the product is one form of competition. Often people die of overdoses because they do not know what their pusher really sold them. Inventories play a key role with the pusher, and thus in determining price. On the one hand, inventories are evidence if one is caught. On the other hand, inventories bring large profits when the price of heroin shoots sky high. The alternative to holding huge inventories is merely to water down one's existing stock as the price increases in the streets. Users often cannot tell a priori what they are taking; thus we would expect only minimal inventories to be held by pushers.

Unfortunately, there is little if any empirical evidence on the demand for heroin. Among users, the price elasticity no doubt tends toward zero. For marijuana, however, a recent study of U.C.L.A. students showed that the price elasticity was slightly greater than one [8]. If U.C.L.A. is representative of most college campuses, then a policy of supply restriction would be efficient in terms of getting people to consume less marijuana. That is, if supplies are shut off the price will rise, and marijuana users will find substitutes.

The proper policy in heroin markets is difficult to determine. Often the social costs far exceed the private costs because addicts have to commit crimes to finance their habit. Therefore, supply restriction does not seem to be a rational (short-run) alternative, since we merely serve to drive up the price of heroin and thus crime rates. If we are going to work on the supply side, it will have to be in terms of completely removing heroin and all hard drugs from society, or legalizing them. Although legalization is an efficient policy in many areas of crime, such as gambling and prostitution, it is not necessarily the proper one here. The short-run costs of legalized heroin may be quite high. On the other hand, supply eradication is next to impossible. Probably the best society can do is minimize this problem in the long run by educating people on the problems of heroin and providing everyone with an adequate income. These two policies will raise the expected costs of consuming heroin.

Urban Crime Policy

The trends on urban crime in Table 10-2 are clear evidence that our present policies of regulation and control are not working. Just as with pollution and congestion, regulation and control policies are ill-suited to do the (economic aspects of the) jobs they set out to do. To reduce crime, economic incentives must be used, at both the individual and aggregate levels. Other things being equal, this means eradicating discrimination in urban labor markets, so that equally qualified people can get equally decent jobs. This will be a start at raising the incomes of the poor, but I believe that a greater effort of redistributing income from the haves to the have-nots is also needed.

Incentives are important not only for potential criminals but also for actual criminals. At present, practically all funds used in penal institutions are spent for nonrehabilitation or noneducational purposes. This approach is not working, and the fact that over half of all prisoners released are back behind bars within five years is solid evidence that we are not helping ourselves or the prisoners over the long run. Modern prisons have been said to be crime schools; that is, prisoners learn how to commit crimes more efficiently while they are serving time. It is not absurd to think that it may pay some criminals to get caught and convicted, so that they can go to prison and learn the latest tricks of the trade.

Incentives must also be used by law-enforcement agencies themselves. At present, we say that the output of a law-enforcement agency is commensurate with its total expenditures; thus, when budget renewals come around, the status quo is more or less conserved. This is a wasteful and dangerous policy. Law-enforcement agencies must account for their budgets on economic grounds; that is, does the marginal product of hiring another policeman (in terms of crime deterrence) equal the net marginal cost of hiring that policeman (total wages minus any revenues from fines)? Until we use such simple allocation rules, there is little chance that we will attack our crime problems rationally.

Finally, our law-enforcement system and laws are inequitable in the way they treat many parties [9]. People and firms lose forgone earnings when they fight court cases, even when they win. Why do we not pay those tried and acquitted? We pay the jurors the opportunity cost of their time, but the defendant is left to pay the bill imposed on him by the law. Similarly, only a few states and cities compensate victims for losses (personal and/or property) to criminals. If the public sector is willing to help defray the costs of natural disasters (floods, hurricanes, torandos) why can we not compensate for manmade (criminal) disasters?

SUGGESTED READINGS

Brown, Douglas. "The Economic Effects of Air Pollution Legislation: The West Virginia Case," *American Institute of Mining, Metallurgical, and Petroleum Engineers, Council of Economics Section, Proceedings* (1970). 205–220.

Herfindahl, Oris, and Kneese, Allen. *Quality of the Environment.* Baltimore, Maryland: Johns Hopkins Press (for Resources for the Future, Inc.), 1965.

Kneese, Allen *et al. Economics and the Environment.* Baltimore, Maryland: Johns Hopkins Press (for Resources for the Future, Inc.), 1970.

Mills, Edwin. *Urban Economics,* Chapter 13. Glenview, Illinois: Scott, Foresman, 1972.

Perloff, Harvey, ed. *The Quality of the Urban Environment.* Baltimore, Maryland: Johns Hopkins Press (for Resources for the Future, Inc.), 1969.

President's Commission on Law Enforcement, "The Challenge of Crime in a Free Society," 1967.

Ruff, Larry. "The Economic Common Sense of Pollution." *The Public Interest* (1970): 69–85.

Schreiber, A. *et al. Economics of Urban Problems: An Introduction.* Boston, Massachusetts: Houghton Mifflin, 1971.

REFERENCES

1. Lester Lave and Eugene Seskin, "Air Pollution and Human Health," *Science* 169 (1970): 723–733.
2. William P. Gramm, "A Theoretical Note on the Capacity of the Market System to Abate Pollution," *Land Economics* 45 (1969): 365–368.
3. Sam Peltzman and T. Nicholaus Tideman, "Local Versus National Pollution Control: Note," *American Economic Review* 62 (1972): 959–963.
4. Abba P. Lerner, "The 1971 Report of the President's Council of Economic Advisors: Priorities and Efficiency," *American Economic Review* 61 (1971): 527–530.
5. Allen V. Kneese, "Environmental Pollution: Economics and Policy," *American Economic Review, Papers, and Proceedings* 61 (1971): 154–166, plus discussion of Kneese's paper, pp. 167–177.
6. L. J. Kaplan and S. Matteis, "The Economics of Loansharking," *American Journal of Economics and Sociology* 27 (1968): 239–251.
7. Simon Rottenberg, "The Clandestine Distribution of Heroin, its Discovery and Suppression," *Journal of Political Economy* 76 (1968): 78–90.
8. C. T. Nisbet and F. Vakil, "Some Estimates of Price and Expenditure Elasticities of Demand for Marijuana Among U.C.L.A. Students," *Review of Economics and Statistics* 54 (1972): 473–475.
9. George Stigler, "The Optimum Enforcement of Laws," *Journal of Political Economy* 78 (1970): 526–536.

AUTHOR INDEX

Page numbers in italic indicate page on which a complete reference may be found.

SUBJECT INDEX

A

Accelerated depreciation, 141
Accessibility, 2, 79
Additional worker hypothesis, 247–248
AFDC, 258
Agglomeration effects, 8, 79
Ancient world cities, 13–17
Area Redevelopment Act, 260
Athens, 15
Auto travel
  costs, 172
  trends, 167–168

B

Babylon, 14
Baltimore, 23, 24, 32

BART, 190–191
Base models of growth, 48–51
Benefit–cost analysis, 177–180
Bid price curves
  of firms, 81–82
  of households, 110–111
Blockbusting, 145
Boston, 19–23, 56–57, 80, 93, 170–171, 185
Boulder, 58
Breakeven income level, 263
Building codes, 152

C

Canals, 24
Capitalized value, 99